PowerPoint® 2002 For Dummies®

The PowerPoint 2002 Window

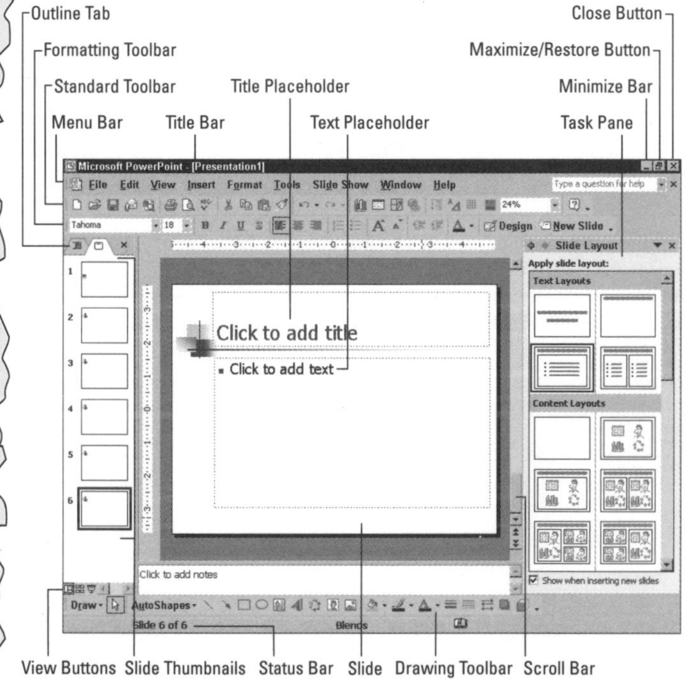

Formatting Commands

Command	Keys
Bold	Ctrl+B
Italic	Ctrl+I
Underline	Ctrl+U
Center	Ctrl+E
Left Align	Ctrl+L
Right Align	Ctrl+R
Justify	Ctrl+J
Normal	Ctrl+Spacebar

Drawing Toolbar

Draw Menu
Autoshapes Menu
Arrow
Oval
Insert Word Art
Insert Picture
Line Color
Text Color
Dash Style
3D Style
Select Objects
Line
Text Box
Fill Color
Line Style
Rectangle
Insert Clip Art
Arrow Style
Insert Diagram or Organization Chart
Shadow Style

Editing Commands

Command	Keys	Command	Keys
Undo	Ctrl+Z	Select All	Ctrl+A
Cut	Ctrl+X	Find	Ctrl+F
Copy	Ctrl+C	Replace	Ctrl+H
Paste	Ctrl+V	Duplicate	Ctrl+D

Commonly Used Commands

Command	Keys	Command	Keys
New	Ctrl+N	Print	Ctrl+P
Open	Ctrl+O	Help	F1
Save	Ctrl+S	New Slide	Ctrl+M

For Dummies: Bestselling Book Series for Beginners

PowerPoint® 2002 For Dummies®

Formatting Toolbar

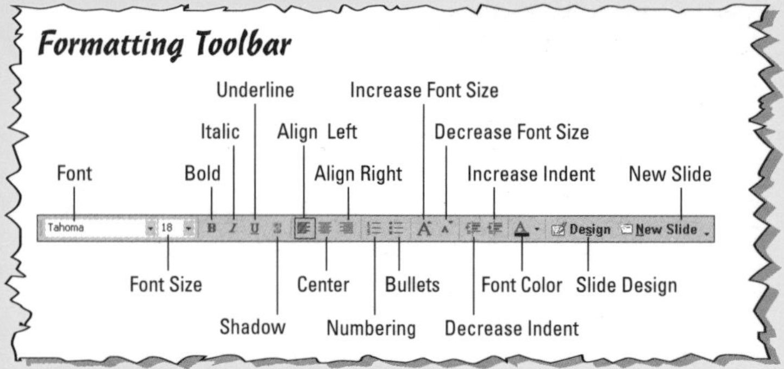

The Standard Toolbar

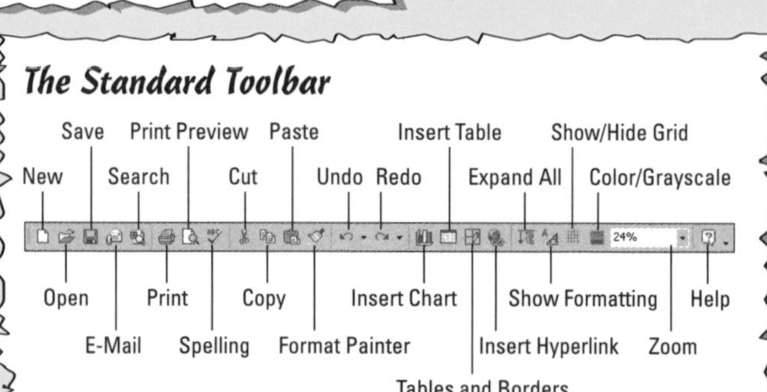

Slide Show Shortcuts

To	Use This
Advance to the next slide	N
Perform the next animation	Enter, Page Down, right arrow, down arrow, or space bar
Go back to the previous slide	P
Repeat the previous animation	Page Up, left arrow, up arrow, or backspace key
Go to a specific slide	Type the slide number and then press Enter
Display a black screen	B
Display a white screen	W
End a slide show	Escape
Go to the next hidden slide	H
Display a pen pointer	Ctrl+P
Display an arrow pointer	Ctrl+A
Hide the pointer	Ctrl+H

Item 0817-2.
For more information about Wiley Publishing, Inc. call 1-800-762-2974.

For Dummies: Bestselling Book Series for Beginners

PowerPoint® 2002 FOR DUMMIES®

PowerPoint® 2002 FOR DUMMIES®

by Doug Lowe

Wiley Publishing, Inc.

PowerPoint® 2002 For Dummies®

Published by
Wiley Publishing, Inc.
909 Third Avenue
New York, NY 10022
www.wiley.com

For general information on our other products and services or to obtain technical support, please contact our Customer Care Department within the U.S. at 800-762-2974, outside the U.S. at 317-572-3993, or fax 317-572-4002.

Wiley also publishes its books in a variety of electronic formats. Some content that appears in print may not be available in electronic books.

Library of Congress Cataloging-in-Publication Data:

Library of Congress Control Number: 2001086301

ISBN: 0-7645-0817-2

Manufactured in the United States of America

10 9 8 7 6 5

About the Author

Doug Lowe has written enough computer books to line all the birdcages in California. His most recent books (other than this one, of course) are *Office 2002 Quick Reference For Dummies, Internet Explorer 5.5 For Dummies,* and *Networking For Dummies,* Fifth Edition.

Although Doug has yet to win a Pulitzer prize, he remains cautiously optimistic. He is hopeful that George Lucas will pick up the film rights to this book and suggests *PowerPoint Episode 1: The Phantom Presentation* as a working title.

Doug lives in sunny Fresno, California, where the motto is "Give Us Electricity or Give Us . . . Uh, No . . . Just Give Us Electricity!" with his wife Debbie, a trio of daughters (Rebecca, Sarah, and Bethany), and a pair of female Golden Retrievers (Nutmeg and Ginger, the original Spice Girls, pictured in Figure 30-4 of this book).

Author's Acknowledgments

To Debbie, Rebecca, Sarah, and Bethany.

Dedication

I'd like to thank all of the good people at Hungry Minds, Inc., who whipped this book into shape and picked up all the loose ends when things got crazy: Steve Hayes for getting the project rolling, project editor/copy editor Andrea Boucher for seeing it through, technical editor Garrett Pease for making it accurate, and everyone else who pitched in.

I'd also like to thank everyone who helped out with previous editions of this book: Kel Oliver, Nancy DelFavero, Grace Jasmine, Garret Pease, Rev Mengle, Tina Sims, Pam Mourouzis, Leah Cameron, Jim McCarter, Kezia Endsley, Becky Whitney, and Michael Partington.

Publisher's Acknowledgments

We're proud of this book; please send us your comments through our online registration form located at `www.dummies.com/register/`.

Some of the people who helped bring this book to market include the following:

Acquisitions, Editorial, and Media Development

Project Editor: Andrea C. Boucher

(Previous Edition: Kelly Oliver, Nancy DelFavero)

Sr. Acquisitions Editor: Steven H. Hayes

Technical Editor: Garrett Pease

Editorial Manager, Freelance: Constance Carlisle

Media Development Manager: Laura Carpenter

Media Development Supervisor: Richard Graves

Editorial Assistants: Amanda Foxworth, Jean Rogers

Production

Project Coordinator: Maridee Ennis

Layout and Graphics: Jackie Nicholas, Jill Piscitelli, Brian Torwelle, Jeremey Unger

Proofreaders: John Greenough, Andy Hollandbeck, Charles Spencer, TECHBOOKS Production Services

Indexer: TECHBOOKS Production Services

General and Administrative

Wiley Technology Publishing Group: Richard Swadley, Vice President and Executive Group Publisher; Bob Ipsen, Vice President and Group Publisher; Joseph Wikert, Vice President and Publisher; Barry Pruett, Vice President and Publisher; Mary Bednarek, Editorial Director; Mary C. Corder, Editorial Director; Andy Cummings, Editorial Director

Wiley Manufacturing: Carol Tobin, Director of Manufacturing

Wiley Marketing: John Helmus, Assistant Vice President, Director of Marketing

Wiley Composition Services: Gerry Fahey, Vice President, Production Services; Debbie Stailey, Director of Composition Services

Contents at a Glance

Part VI: The Part of Tens 299

Index 341

Cartoons at a Glance

By Rich Tennant

The 5th Wave
By Rich Tennant
"No, it's not a pie chart, it's just a corn chip that got scanned into the document."

page 111

The 5th Wave
By Rich Tennant
BUNGCO
BUNGEE CABLE
COMPANY
"Come on Walt—time to freshen the company Web page."

page 263

The 5th Wave
By Rich Tennant
WHAT'S THE DIGITAL BATHROOM SCALE DOING IN MY LAPTOP CASE?
...PROMPT...?

page 299

The 5th Wave
By Rich Tennant
Gesundheit.

page 7

The 5th Wave
By Rich Tennant
DAD ADDS MULTIMEDIA SOUND AND GRAPHICS TO THE TRADITIONAL CAMPFIRE GHOST STORY.

page 235

The 5th Wave
By Rich Tennant
FIRED
YOU
"NIFTY CHART, FRANK, BUT NOT ENTIRELY NECESSARY."

page 183

Cartoon Information:

Fax: 978-546-7747

E-Mail: richtennant@the5thwave.com

World Wide Web: www.the5thwave.com

Table of Contents

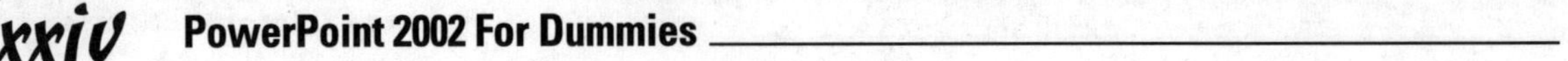

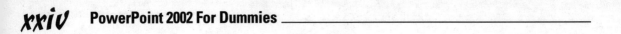

Introduction

Welcome to *PowerPoint 2002 For Dummies,* the book written especially for those who are forced to use PowerPoint at gunpoint and want to find out just enough to save their necks.

Do you ever find yourself in front of an audience, no matter how small, flipping through flip charts or shuffling through a stack of handwritten transparencies? You need PowerPoint! Have you always wanted to take your notebook computer with you to impress a client at lunch, but you don't know what to do with it between trips to the salad bar? Have you ever spent an entire afternoon stuck in an airport, realizing that weather conditions were making you miss a major meeting and that if you could phone in your presentation, you would finally get that promotion you have deserved for the past year? You *really* need PowerPoint!

Or maybe you're one of those folks who bought Microsoft Office because it was such a bargain and you needed a Windows word processor and spreadsheet anyway, and hey, you're not even sure what PowerPoint is, but it was free. Who can resist a bargain like that?

Whichever way, you're holding the perfect book right here in your formerly magic-marker-stained hands. Help is here, within these humble pages.

This book talks about PowerPoint in everyday — and often irreverent — terms. No lofty prose here; the whole thing checks in at about the fifth-grade reading level. I have no Pulitzer expectations for this book. My goal is to make an otherwise dull and lifeless subject at least tolerable, and maybe kind of fun.

About This Book

This isn't the kind of book that you pick up and read from start to finish as though it were a cheap novel. If I ever see you reading it at the beach, I'll kick sand in your face. This book is more like a reference, the kind of book you can pick up, turn to just about any page, and start reading. It has 30 chapters, each one covering a specific aspect of using PowerPoint — such as printing, changing colors, or using clip art.

Each chapter is divided into self-contained chunks, all related to the major theme of the chapter.

For example, the chapter on using clip art contains nuggets like these:

- Dropping in some clip art
- Moving, sizing, and stretching pictures
- Boxing, shading, and shadowing a picture
- Editing a clip art picture
- Inserting pictures without using the Clip Organizer

You don't have to memorize anything in this book. It's a "need-to-know" book: You pick it up when you need to know something. Need to know how to create an organization chart? Pick up the book. Need to know how to override the Slide Master? Pick up the book. Otherwise, put it down and get on with your life.

How to Use This Book

This book works like a reference. Start with the topic you want to find out about: To get going, look for it in the Table of Contents or in the Index. The Table of Contents is detailed enough that you should be able to find most of the topics you look for. If not, turn to the Index, where you find even more detail.

When you find your topic in the Table of Contents or the Index, turn to the area of interest and read as much or as little as you need or want. Then close the book and get on with it.

This book is loaded with information, of course, so if you want to take a brief excursion into your topic, you're more than welcome. If you want to know all about Slide Masters, read the chapter on templates and masters. If you want to know all about color schemes, read the chapter on color schemes. Read whatever you want. This is *your* book, not mine.

On occasion, this book directs you to use specific keyboard shortcuts to get things done. When you see something like

Ctrl+Z

it means to hold down the Ctrl key while pressing the Z key and then release both together. Don't type the plus sign.

Sometimes I tell you to use a menu command, like this:

File⇨Open

This line means to use the keyboard or mouse to open the File menu and then choose the Open command. (The underlined letters are the keyboard *hot keys* for the command. To use them, first press the Alt key. In the preceding example, you press and release the Alt key, press and release the F key, and then press and release the O key to achieve the action of opening a file.)

Whenever I describe a message or information that you see on-screen, it looks like this:

```
Are we having fun yet?
```

Anything you are instructed to type appears in bold like so: Type **a:setup** in the Run dialog box. You type exactly what you see, with or without spaces.

Another nice feature of this book is that whenever I discuss a certain button that you need to click to accomplish the task at hand, the button appears in the margin. This way, you can easily locate it on your screen.

This book rarely directs you elsewhere for information — just about everything you need to know about using PowerPoint is right here. On occasion, I suggest that you turn to Andy Rathbone's *Windows 98 For Dummies* (Hungry Minds, Inc.) for more specific information about wildebeests and dilithium mining techniques — oops — I mean Windows 98.

What You Don't Need to Read

Some parts of this book are skippable. I carefully place extra-technical information in self-contained sidebars and clearly mark them so that you can give them a wide berth. Don't read this stuff unless you just gots to know. Don't worry; I won't be offended if you don't read every word.

Foolish Assumptions

I make only three assumptions about you:

- You use a computer.
- You use Windows 95 or a later version.
- You use or are thinking about using PowerPoint 2002 for Windows.

Nothing else. I don't assume that you're a computer guru who knows how to change a controller card or configure memory for optimal use. These types of computer chores are best handled by people who like computers. Hopefully, you are on speaking terms with such a person. Do your best to stay there.

How This Book Is Organized

Inside this book are chapters arranged in six parts. Each chapter is broken down into sections that cover various aspects of the chapter's main subject. The chapters have a logical sequence, so it makes sense to read them in order if you want. But you don't have to read the book that way; you can flip it open to any page and start reading.

Here's the lowdown on what's in each of the six parts:

Part I: Basic PowerPoint 2002 Stuff

In this part, you review the basics of using PowerPoint. This is a good place to start if you're clueless about what PowerPoint is, let alone how to use it.

Part II: Making Your Slides Look Mahvelous

The chapters in this part show you how to make presentations that look good. Most important are the chapters about templates and masters, which control the overall look of a presentation. Get the template right, and everything else falls into place.

Part III: Neat Things You Can Put on Your Slides

The chapters in this part show you how to spice up an otherwise dreary presentation with clip art, graphs, drawings, organization charts, sealing wax, and other fancy stuff.

Part IV: The Special Effects Department

The chapters in this part show you how to add sizzle to your slides by using sound, video, and animation.

Part V: PowerPoint and the Net

The chapters in this part show you how to use the new Web features of PowerPoint 2002, which are designed to let you create presentations that are connected to one another with special linkages called *hyperlinks*. Such presentations can be saved as Web pages to be used on the Internet's World Wide Web. Also in this part, you find lots of cool things you can do online. For example, you can collaborate in real time, talking to colleagues and marking up presentations internationally, or you can use the PowerPoint 2002 nifty new Presentation Broadcast to give the same kind of multimedia presentations you give in your conference room, but now, to a worldwide audience.

Part VI: The Part of Tens

This wouldn't be a *...For Dummies* book without lists of interesting snippets: the ten PowerPoint commandments, ten tips for creating readable slides, ten things that often go wrong, ten PowerPoint shortcuts, ten new features of PowerPoint 2002, and more! Sorry, no Ginsu knives.

Icons Used in This Book

As you're reading all this wonderful prose, you occasionally see the following icons. They appear in the margins to draw your attention to important information. They are defined as follows:

Watch out! Some technical drivel is just around the corner. Read it only if you have your pocket protector firmly attached.

Pay special attention to this icon — it tells you that some particularly useful tidbit is at hand, perhaps a shortcut or a way of using a command that you may not have considered.

Danger! Danger! Danger! Stand back, Will Robinson!

Did I tell you about the memory course I took?

Where to Go from Here

Yes, you can get there from here. With this book in hand, you're ready to charge full speed ahead into the strange and wonderful world of desktop presentations. Browse through the table of contents and decide where you want to start. Be bold! Be courageous! Be adventurous! Above all else, have fun!

Dealing with older versions

I have good news and I have bad news. The good news is that Microsoft added a bunch of new features to PowerPoint 2002 that make the program easier to use and enable you to create flashier presentations. You may remember that in PowerPoint 97, Microsoft changed the file format it used to store presentation files. In that last version of PowerPoint, you couldn't go backwards; in other words, PowerPoint 97 presentations were not compatible with presentations created by earlier versions. Because this had users ripping off their toupees at every turn, PowerPoint (as well as other applications in the suite) now has backward compatibility. Rest easy, Bill is listening to you.

Not only can PowerPoint 2002 read all your old PowerPoint 2000 or 97 presentations, but you can also save presentations in earlier versions.

And for the bad news? Oh yes, I was kidding. There is no bad news.

Part I

Basic PowerPoint 2002 Stuff

In this part . . .

Once upon a time, the term *presentation software* meant poster board and marker pens. But now, programs such as Microsoft PowerPoint 2002 enable you to create spectacular presentations on your computer.

The chapters in this part comprise a bare-bones introduction to PowerPoint 2002. You learn exactly what PowerPoint is and how to use it to create simple presentations. More advanced stuff such as adding charts or using fancy text fonts is covered in later parts. This part is just the beginning. As a great king once advised, begin at the beginning and go on until you come to the end; then stop.

Chapter 1

Opening Ceremonies

In This Chapter

- What exactly is PowerPoint, anyway?
- Introducing PowerPoint
- Starting PowerPoint
- How much should I tip?
- Help me, Wizard!
- What is all this stuff? (Making sense of the PowerPoint screen)
- Viewing the whole slide
- Editing text
- Moving from slide to slide
- Fifty ways to add a new slide
- Outline that for me!
- Printing that puppy
- Saving and closing your work
- Retrieving a presentation from disk
- Exiting PowerPoint

This chapter is a grand and gala welcoming ceremony for PowerPoint. It's kind of like the opening ceremony for the Olympics, in which all the athletes march in and parade around the track waving their flags and famous people you've never heard of make speeches in French. In this chapter, I parade the features of PowerPoint around the track so you can see what they look like. I may even make a few speeches.

I Give Up . . . What Is PowerPoint?

PowerPoint is the oddball program that comes with Microsoft Office. Most people buy Microsoft Office because it's a great bargain: You get Word and Excel for less than it would cost to buy them separately. As an added bonus, you get a bunch of extra stuff thrown in: Outlook, Access, PowerPoint, a complete set of Ginsu knives, and a Binford VegaPneumatic Power Slicer and Dicer (always wear eye protection).

You know what Word is — it's the world's most loved and most hated word processor; perfect for concocting letters, term papers, and great American novels. Excel is a spreadsheet program used by bean counters the world over. But what the heck is PowerPoint? Does anybody know or care?

PowerPoint is a *presentation* program, and it's one of the coolest programs I know. If you've ever flipped a flip chart, headed over to an overhead projector, or slipped on a slide, you're going to love PowerPoint. With just a few clicks of the mouse, you can create presentations that bedazzle your audience and instantly sway them to your point of view, even if you're selling real estate on Mars, season tickets for the Mets, or a new Medicare plan to congress.

Okay, not everybody buys PowerPoint as part of Microsoft Office. Some people buy it separately. I figured that if you bought PowerPoint by itself, you probably did it on purpose, so it's safe to assume that you already know what PowerPoint is (at least sort of). Heck, you didn't need to read this section anyway. I wrote this little section for the millions of innocent victims who bought Microsoft Office just to get Word and Excel and have no idea what to do with PowerPoint other than to use it as a bookend.

Here are some of the many uses of PowerPoint:

- PowerPoint is a great time-saver for anyone who makes business presentations, whether you've been asked to speak in front of hundreds of people at a shareholders' convention, a group of sales reps at a sales conference, or your own staff or coworkers at a business planning meeting.
- If you're an insurance salesman, you can use PowerPoint to create a presentation about the perils of not owning life insurance, then show it to potential clients on your laptop computer.
- PowerPoint is also great for teachers or conference speakers who want to back up their lectures with slides or overheads.
- PowerPoint is a great program to do your homework on, especially those big semester projects that count for half your grade.
- PowerPoint is also used at churches to display song lyrics on big screens at the front of the church so everyone can sing. If your church still uses hymnals, tell the minister to join the twenty-first century.
- You can use PowerPoint to set up a computerized information kiosk that people can walk up to and use. For example, you can create a museum exhibit about the history of your town or set up a trade-show presentation to provide information about your company and products.

- How about creating a presentation that you can broadcast over the Internet so people can join in on the fun without having to leave the comfort of their own homes or offices? The latest version of PowerPoint has features designed specifically for this task.

PowerPoint Presentations

PowerPoint is similar to a word processor like Word, except that it's geared toward creating *presentations* rather than *documents*. Just as a Word document consists of one or more pages, a PowerPoint presentation consists of one or more *slides*. Each slide can contain text, graphics, and other information. You can easily rearrange the slides in a presentation, delete slides you don't need, add new slides, or modify the contents of existing slides.

You can use PowerPoint both to create your presentations and to actually present them.

A presentation is kind of like those Kodak Carousel slide trays your father used to load up with 35mm slides of your family trip to the Grand Canyon. The main difference is that you don't have to worry about dumping all the slides in your PowerPoint presentation out of the tray and onto the floor.

You can use several different types of media to actually show your presentation:

- Your computer monitor, either a tabletop CRT monitor or the LCD display on a laptop computer. Computer monitors are suitable when you are showing your presentation to just one or two other people.
- A computer projector, which projects an image of your computer monitor onto a screen so larger audiences can view it.
- Web pages on the Internet or on a company intranet.
- Overhead transparencies, which you can show using an overhead projector.
- Printed pages, which allows you to distribute a printed copy of your entire presentation to each member of your audience. (When you print your presentation, you can print one slide per page, or you can print several slides on each page to save paper.)
- 35mm slides. For a fee, you can have your presentation printed onto 35mm slides either by a local company or over the Internet. Then, your presentation really is like a Kodak Carousel slide tray! (For more information, refer to Chapter 30.)

Presentation files

A presentation is to PowerPoint what a document is to Word or a worksheet is to Excel. In other words, a presentation is a file that you create with PowerPoint. Each presentation you create is saved on disk as a separate file.

PowerPoint presentations have the special extension `.ppt` added to the end of their file names. For example, Sales `Conference.ppt` and `History Day.ppt` are both valid PowerPoint file names. When you type the file name for a new PowerPoint file, you don't have to type the `.ppt` extension because PowerPoint automatically adds the extension for you. And PowerPoint often hides the .ppt extension, so a presentation file named `Conference.ppt` often appears as just `Conference`.

PowerPoint is set up initially to save your presentation files in the My Documents folder, but you can store PowerPoint files in any folder on your hard disk you want. And you can store a presentation on a diskette if you want to take it home with you to work on it over the weekend or if you want to give the presentation to someone else so they can use it on their computer.

What's In a Slide?

PowerPoint presentations are made up of one or more slides. Each slide can contain text, graphics, and other elements. A number of PowerPoint features work together to help you easily format attractive slides, as described in the following paragraphs:

- **Slide layouts:** Every slide has a slide layout that controls how information is arranged on the slide. A slide layout is simply a collection of one or more placeholders, which set aside an area of the slide to hold information. Depending on the layout you choose for a slide, the placeholders can hold text, graphics, clip art, sound or video files, tables, charts, graphs, diagrams, or other types of content.
- **Background:** Every slide has a background, which provides a backdrop for the slide's content. The background can be a solid color, a blend of two colors, a subtle texture such as marble or parchment, a pattern such as diagonal lines, bricks, or tiles, or a picture. Each slide can have a different background, but you usually want to use the same background for every slide in your presentation to provide a consistent look.
- **Color scheme:** PowerPoint has built-in color schemes that make it easy for anyone to create attractive slides that don't clash. You can stray from the color schemes if you want, but you should do so only if you have a better eye than the design gurus who work for Microsoft.

- **Slide Master:** The Slide Master controls the basic design and formatting options for slides in your presentation. The Slide Master includes the position and size of basic title and text placeholders, the background and color scheme used for the presentation, as well as font settings such as typefaces, colors, and sizes. In addition, the Slide Master can contain graphic and text objects that you want to appear on every slide.

  You can edit the Slide Master to change the appearance of all the slides in your presentation at once. This helps ensure that the slides in your presentation have a consistent appearance.

- **Design template:** A design template is simply a presentation file that contains a predesigned slide master that you can use to create presentations that look like they were designed by a professional graphic artist. When you create a new presentation, you can base it on one of the presentations that comes with PowerPoint. PowerPoint comes with a collection of design templates you can use, and you can get additional templates from the Microsoft Web site. You can also create your own design templates.

All the features described in the previous paragraphs work together to control the appearance of your slides in much the same way that style sheets and templates control the appearance of Word documents. You can customize the appearance of individual slides by adding any of the following elements:

- **Title and body text:** Most slide layouts include placeholders for title and body text. You can type any text you want into these placeholders. By default, PowerPoint formats the text according to the Slide Master, but you can easily override this formatting to use any font, size, style, or text color you want.
- **Text boxes:** You can add text anywhere on a slide by drawing a text box and then typing text. Text boxes allow you to add text that doesn't fit conveniently in the title or body text placeholders.
- **Shapes:** You can use PowerPoint's drawing tools to add a variety of shapes on your slides. You can use predefined AutoShapes such as rectangles, circles, stars, arrows, and flowchart symbols, or you can create your own shapes using basic line, polygon, and free-hand drawing tools.
- **Pictures:** You can insert pictures onto your slides that you have scanned into your computer or downloaded from the Internet. PowerPoint also comes with a large collection of clipart pictures you can use.
- **Diagrams:** PowerPoint includes a diagramming feature that lets you create several common types of diagrams: Organization Charts, Venn Diagrams, Stacked Pyramid Diagrams, and others.
- **Media files:** You can also add sound clips or video files to your slides.

Introducing PowerPoint 10

The newest version of PowerPoint, known as PowerPoint 10, sports a number of improvements over previous versions of PowerPoint. The following paragraphs summarize the most notable new features:

- Custom animation: Previous versions of PowerPoint let you create slides with crude animations. For example, you could have an object zip in from one side of the slide or drop down from the top. But that was about the extent of PowerPoint's animation capabilities. PowerPoint 10 introduces a whole new array of custom animation features that let you create objects that move around on the slide in just about any way you can imagine. You won't be using PowerPoint to create *Toy Story III*, but you can dazzle your audiences with previously unheard of animation effects. For more information, see Chapter 19.
- Multiple Slide Masters: For years PowerPoint users have been frustrated by the fact that a presentation can have only one Slide Master, which meant that the only way to create slides that deviated from the master layout was to manually override the slide master for each deviant slide. Now, PowerPoint lets you create two or more slide masters in a single presentation. You find out all you need to know about Slide Masters in Chapter 12.
- Diagrams: The new Diagram Gallery lets you create Organization Charts and other types of diagrams, such as Venn Diagrams and Pyramid Diagrams. For more information, see Chapter 15.
- Speech: If you have the right kind of microphone hooked up to your computer, you can talk to PowerPoint. Speech recognition is one of the major new features of Office 10. Speech recognition allows you to dictate text onto your slides or speak commands to PowerPoint. For example, you can say "File New" to create a new file or "Insert Picture From File" to add a picture to a slide.
- Side Pane: One of the most noticeable new features in Office 10 is the Side Pane, an area on the right side of the screen that is used for common tasks. In PowerPoint, you use the Side Pane to create new presentations or open existing presentations, to insert clip art, to change the slide layout, to change the slide design template or color scheme, and to set slide animations and transitions.
- Print Preview Command: PowerPoint now has a Print Preview command just like Word and Excel. Print Preview allows you to see exactly how your slides will appear before you commit them to paper. This feature is especially useful if your printer is located down the hall rather than on your desk.

Starting PowerPoint

Here's the procedure for starting PowerPoint:

1. **Get ready.**

   Light some votive candles. Take two Tylenol. Put on a pot of coffee. If you're allergic to banana slugs, take an antihistamine and an allergy pill. Sit in the lotus position facing Redmond, Washington, and recite the Windows creed three times:

Bill Gates is my friend. Resistance is futile. You will be assimilated.

2. **Rev up your engines (turn your computer on).**

   You have to flip only one switch to do that (I hope). But if your computer, monitor, and printer are plugged in separately, you have to turn each one on separately.

3. **Click the Start button.**

   The Start button is ordinarily found at the lower-left corner of the Windows display. After you click it, a menu magically appears out of nowhere. The Start button works pretty much the same whether you're using Windows 95, Windows 98, or Windows Millennium Edition.

   If you can't find the Start button, try moving the mouse pointer all the way to the bottom edge of the screen and holding it there a moment. With luck on your side, you see the Start button appear. If not, try moving the mouse pointer to the other three edges of the screen: top, left, and right. Sometimes the Start button hides behind these edges.

   If you're not sure what I mean by *click,* read the sidebar "The mouse is your friend" later in this chapter.

4. **Point to Programs on the Start menu.**

   After you click the Start button to reveal the Start menu, move the mouse pointer up to the word Programs and hold it there a moment. Yet another menu appears, revealing a bevy of commands.

5. **Click Microsoft PowerPoint on the Programs menu.**

   Your computer whirs and clicks and possibly makes other unmentionable noises while PowerPoint comes to life.

Which Way Is Up? (Or, What Is All That Stuff on the Screen?)

When you start PowerPoint, it greets you with a screen that's so cluttered with stuff that you're soon ready to consider newsprint and markers as a viable alternative for your presentations. The center of the screen is mercifully blank, but all around the edges and tucked into every corner are little icons and buttons and menus and whatnot. What is all that stuff?

Figure 1-1 shows the basic PowerPoint screen in all its cluttered glory. The following paragraphs point out the more important parts of the PowerPoint screen.

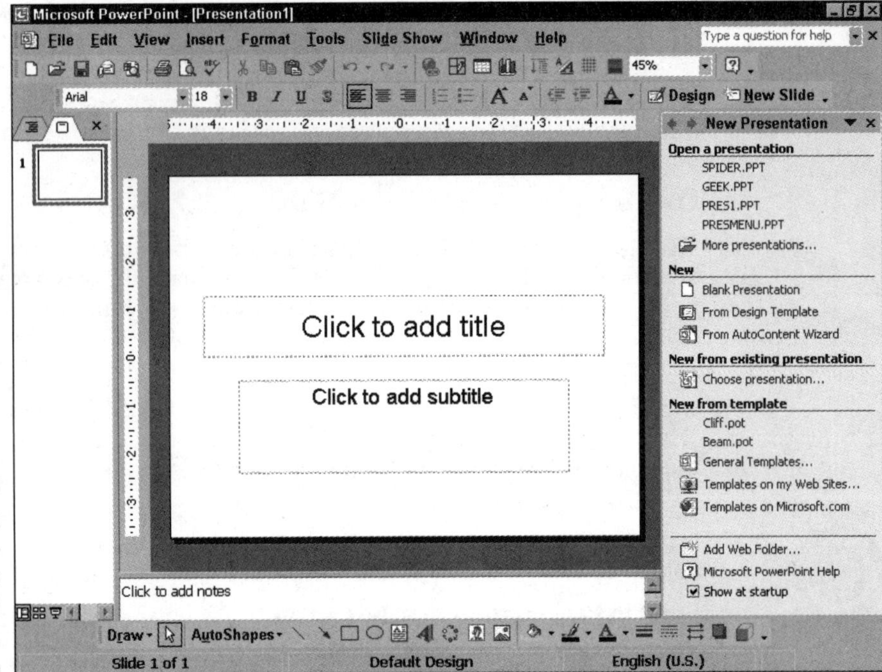

Figure 1-1: PowerPoint's cluttered screen.

- Across the top of the screen, just below the Microsoft PowerPoint title, is the *menu bar.* The deepest and darkest secrets of PowerPoint are hidden on the menu bar. Wear a helmet when exploring it.

  PowerPoint's menus have a nasty habit of changing as you use them. They start out by showing only those commands that the programmers at Microsoft think you'll use most often. The less frequently used commands are hidden beneath the double down-facing arrow that appears at the bottom of each menu. As you use PowerPoint, the commands you use most often show up on the menus so you don't have to click the down-arrow to access them.

  The bottom line is that if you can't find a menu command, don't give up. Just click the double down arrow at the bottom of the menu. Or, just stare at the menu for a few seconds. Eventually, PowerPoint realizes that you can't find what you're looking for, and the missing menu commands magically appear.

- Just below the menu bar are two of the many *toolbars* PowerPoint offers you in an effort to make its most commonly used features easy to use. Each toolbar consists of a bunch of buttons that you can click to perform common functions. The toolbar on the top is the Standard toolbar; immediately beneath it is the Formatting toolbar.

If the two toolbars pictured below the menu bar are jammed together on one line on your computer, you can put them on separate lines by choosing Tools⇨Customize to bring up the Customize dialog box, and then clicking the Options tab, checking the Show Standard and Formatting Buttons on Two Rows option, and clicking OK.

- Down near the bottom of the screen is the Drawing toolbar. It has buttons that let you draw pictures on your slides.

If you're not sure about the function of one of the billions and billions of buttons that clutter the PowerPoint screen, place the mouse pointer on the button in question. After a moment, the name of the button appears in a box just below the button.

- Right smack in the middle of the screen is where your current slide appears.
- On the left side of the slide is an area that alternates between two types of views of your presentation. *Slides View*, which is the view shown in Figure 1-1, shows little thumbnail images of your slides. *Outline View* shows your presentation arranged as an outline. You can switch between Slides View and Outline View by clicking the tabs that appear at the top of this area. (For more information on working in Outline View, see Chapter 3.)
- Beneath the slide is a small area called the Notes Pane, which you can use to add notes to your slides. For more information on using this feature, see Chapter 5.
- To the right of the slide is an area called the *Task Pane.* The Task Pane is designed to help you complete common tasks quickly. When you first start PowerPoint, the Task Pane appears with the New Presentation options, which let you create a new presentation or open an existing presentation. As you work with PowerPoint, you'll encounter other options in the Task Pane for common tasks such as searching, changing the slide design, or setting animation options.
- At the very bottom of the screen is the *status bar,* which tells you which slide is currently displayed (in this example, Slide 1 of 1).
- The salad bar is located . . . well, actually, there is no salad bar. You have to pay extra for that.

You'll never get anything done if you feel that you have to understand every pixel of the PowerPoint screen before you can do anything. Don't worry about the stuff that you don't understand; just concentrate on what you need to know to get the job done and worry about the bells and whistles later.

Lots of stuff is crammed into the PowerPoint screen, enough stuff that the program works best if you let it run in *Full Screen* mode. If PowerPoint doesn't take over your entire screen, look for the boxy-looking maximize button near the top-right corner of the PowerPoint window (it's the middle of the three buttons clustered in the top-right corner — the box represents a window maximized to its largest possible size). Click it to maximize the PowerPoint screen. Click it again to restore the PowerPoint screen to its smaller size.

The mouse is your friend

Remember that scene in *Star Trek IV* when Scotty, having been zapped back into the 1990s and forced to use a primitive computer (it was a Macintosh), picked up the mouse, and talked into it like a microphone? "Computer! Hello computer! Hmmph. How quaint."

You don't get very far with PowerPoint (or any other Windows program) until you discover how to use the mouse. You can try picking it up and talking into it if you want, but you won't get any better results than Scotty did.

Most mice have two buttons on top and a ball underneath. When you move the mouse, the ball rolls. The rolling motion is detected by little wheels inside the mouse and sent to your computer, which responds to your mouse movements by moving the mouse cursor on-screen. What will they think of next?

Here's the lowdown on the various acts of mouse dexterity that you are asked to perform as you use PowerPoint:

- To *move* or *point* the mouse means to move it without pressing any mouse buttons so that the mouse cursor moves to a desired screen location. Remember to leave the mouse on the mouse pad as you move it: If you pick it up, the ball doesn't roll and your movement doesn't register. As you move the little creature, you should see a little arrow whiz across the screen in the general direction you are moving the mouse.
- To *click* means to press and release the left mouse button. Usually, you are asked to click something, which means to point to the something and then click the left button.
- To *double-click* means to press and release the left mouse button twice, as quickly as you can.
- To *triple-click* means to press and release the left mouse button three times, as quickly as you can. Right.
- To *right-click* means to click the right mouse button instead of the left. Get used to right-clicking: It's a handy action in PowerPoint.
- To *click and drag* something (also simply called *drag*) with the mouse means to point at it, press the left button (or right button, depending on the task), and move the mouse while holding down the button. When you arrive at your destination, you release the mouse button.
- To *stay* the mouse means to let go of the mouse and give it the command "Stay!" You don't need to raise your voice; speak in a normal but confident and firm tone. If your mouse starts to walk away, say "No," put it back in its original position, and repeat the command "Stay!" (Under no circumstances should you strike your mouse. Remember, there are no bad mice.)

The View from Here Is Great

On the bottom-left edge of the PowerPoint window is a series of View buttons. These buttons enable you to switch among the various *views*, or ways of looking at your presentation. Table 1-1 summarizes what each View button does.

Table 1-1 View Buttons

Button	*What It Does*
[Normal View button]	Switches to Normal View, which shows your slide, outline, and notes all at once. This view is how PowerPoint normally appears.
[Slide Sorter View button]	Switches to Slide Sorter View, which enables you to easily rearrange slides and add slide transitions and other special effects.
[Slide Show View button]	Switches to Slide Show View, which displays your slides in an on-screen presentation.

Creating a New Presentation

When you first start PowerPoint, the New Presentation Pane appears in the right-hand side of the screen. (Refer to Figure 1-1.) The New Presentation Pane provides several ways for you to get started by opening an existing presentation or creating a new one, as described in the following paragraphs:

- **Open a Presentation:** This section of the New Presentation Pane lists the four presentations you have most recently worked on, plus a More Presentations option that lets you open any existing presentation. If the presentation you want to work on is listed, just click it to open the presentation. Otherwise, click More Presentations to locate your presentation. (For more information, see the section "Opening a Presentation" later in this chapter.)
- **New:** This section lists three ways to create a new presentation:
    - Click Blank Presentation to create a new, empty presentation. Use this option only if you're a PowerPoint whiz and you want to start from scratch.
    - Click From Design Template to create a presentation based on one of PowerPoint's many templates.
    - Click From AutoContent Wizard to start a wizard that actually creates a skeleton presentation for you.

  (For more information about the AutoContent Wizard, see the section "Using the AutoContent Wizard" later in this chapter.)
- **New from Existing Presentation:** This section contains a single option, Choose Presentation, which lets you select an existing presentation to use as the basis for a new presentation file. Use this option if you want to create a presentation that is similar to a presentation you have previously created.

- **New from Template:** This section lets you create a new presentation based on one of the templates supplied with PowerPoint. If the template you want to use is listed, just click it. Otherwise, click General Templates to call up a dialog box listing the templates that come with PowerPoint, Templates on My Web Sites to list templates that reside on Internet Web sites, or Templates on Microsoft.com to list templates at Microsoft's Web site.

Using the AutoContent Wizard

The easiest way to create a new presentation, especially for novice PowerPoint users, is to use the AutoContent Wizard. This wizard asks you for some pertinent information, such as your name, the title of your presentation, and the type of presentation you want to create. Then it automatically creates a skeleton presentation that you can modify to suit your needs.

The marketing folks at Microsoft want you to believe that the AutoContent Wizard writes your presentation for you, as if you just click the button and then go play a round of golf while PowerPoint does your research, organizes your thoughts, writes your text, and throws in a few good lawyer jokes to boot. Sorry. All the AutoContent Wizard does is create an outline for a number of common types of presentations. It doesn't do your thinking for you.

To create a presentation using the AutoContent Wizard, follow these steps:

1. **Start PowerPoint.**

   PowerPoint comes to life, as shown in Figure 1-1.

2. **Click From AutoContent Wizard in the New section of the New Presentation Pane.**

   The AutoContent Wizard takes over and displays the dialog box shown in Figure 1-2. You may also notice your office assistant saying something pithy about the AutoContent Wizard; ignore him for now by right-clicking and choosing Hide.

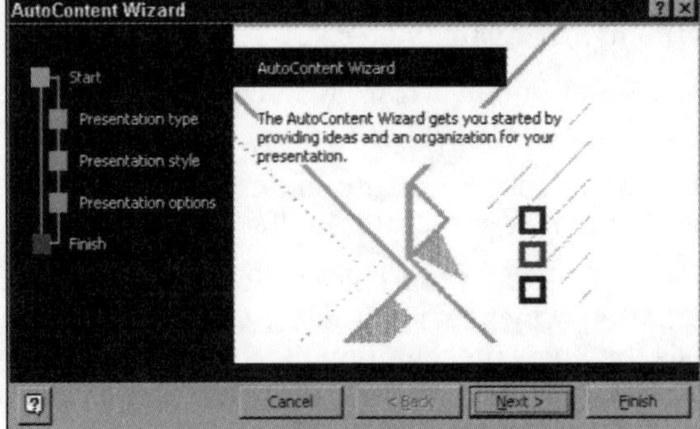

Figure 1-2: The AutoContent Wizard gets under way.

3. **Click Next.**

   The dialog box shown in Figure 1-3 appears.

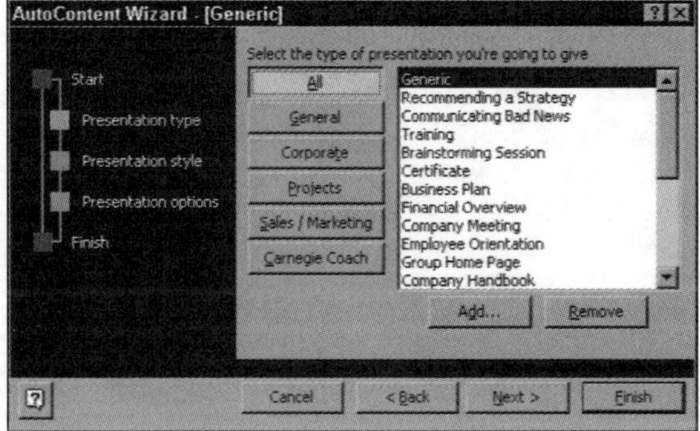

Figure 1-3: The wizard asks what kind of presentation you want to create.

4. **Select the type of presentation that you want to create by clicking one of the presentation types.**

   A variety of presentation types exist in six different categories. Click the category you find the most useful and select a presentation type.

5. **Click Next.**

   When you click Next, the AutoContent Wizard advances to the dialog box shown in Figure 1-4.

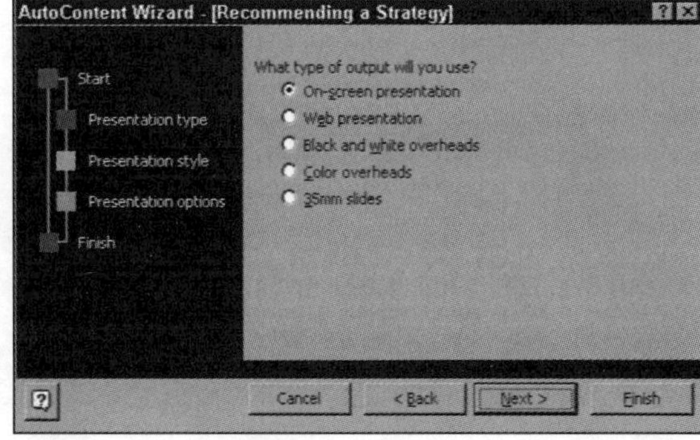

Figure 1-4: The wizard asks what kind of output you are creating.

6. **Indicate the type of output that you want to create.**

   Choose On-Screen Presentation if you are going to use a computer projector to display your slides.

7. **Click Next.**

   The wizard proceeds to the dialog box shown in Figure 1-5.

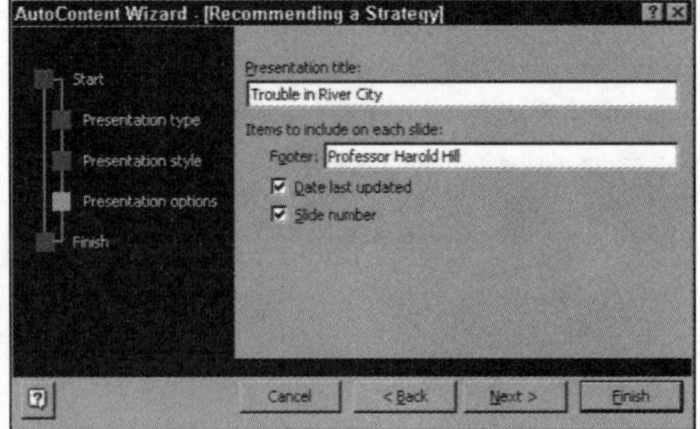

Figure 1-5: Now you have to type in some information.

8. **Type the title of your presentation and footer information, such as your name or company.**

   Note that you get the last-updated presentation by default as well as a slide number. (You can click the check box if you don't feel like having those default settings.)

   For example, in Figure 1-6, I typed *Trouble in River City* as the title and *Professor Harold Hill* as footer information.

9. **Click Next.**

   When you click Next, the wizard moseys on to the dialog box shown in Figure 1-6.

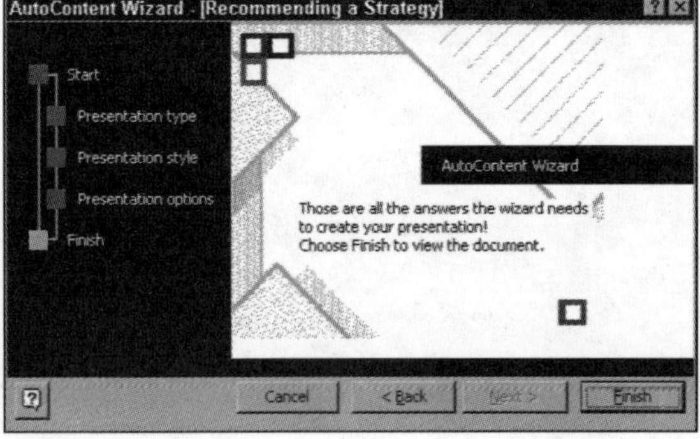

Figure 1-6: Finally! Let's get on with it.

10. **Click Finish.**

    The AutoContent Wizard creates a presentation for you, as shown in Figure 1-7. After the presentation is finished, you can use the editing and formatting techniques described in the rest of this chapter and throughout the book to personalize the presentation.

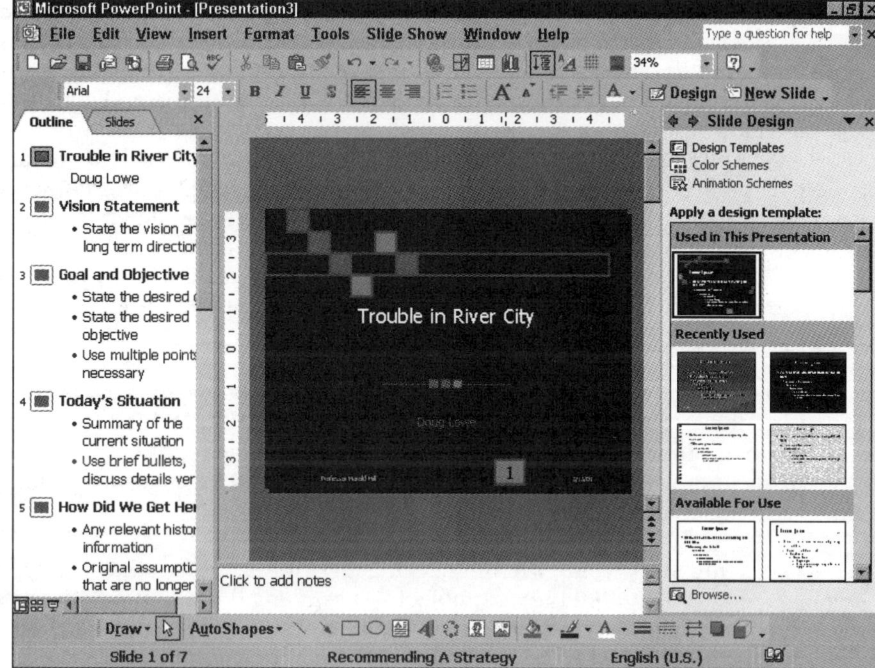

Figure 1-7: A presentation created by the AutoContent wizard.

Zooming In

PowerPoint automatically adjusts its zoom factor so that Slide View displays each slide in its entirety. In Normal View, your slide is at 34 percent if the Task Pane is visible; 48 percent if the Task Pane is hidden. You can change the size of your slide by calling up the View➪Zoom command or by using the Zoom control in the Standard toolbar. This allows you to zoom in close to work on a detailed drawing.

Editing Text

In PowerPoint, slides are blank areas that you can adorn with various types of objects. The most common types of objects are *text objects,* which are rectangular areas that are specially designated for holding text. Other types of objects include shapes such as circles or triangles, pictures imported from clip-art files, and graphs.

Most slides contain two text objects; one for the slide's title, the other for its body text. However, you can add additional text objects if you want, and you can remove the body text or title text object. You can even remove both to create a slide that contains no text.

Whenever you move the mouse cursor over a text object, the cursor changes from an arrow to what's lovingly called the *I-beam,* which you can use to support bridges or build aircraft carriers. Seriously, when the mouse cursor changes to an I-beam, you can click the mouse button and start typing text.

When you click a text object, a box appears around the text and an insertion pointer appears right at the spot where you clicked. PowerPoint then becomes like a word processor. Any characters that you type are inserted into the text at the insertion pointer location. You can use the Delete or Backspace keys to demolish text, and you can use the arrow keys to move the insertion pointer around in the text object. If you press the Enter key, a new line of text begins within the text object.

When a text object contains no text, a placeholder message appears in the object. For a title text object, the message `Click to add title` appears. For other text objects, the placeholder message reads `Click to add text`. Either way, the placeholder message magically vanishes when you click the object and begin typing text.

If you start typing without clicking anywhere, the text that you type is entered into the title text object — assuming that the title text object doesn't already have text of its own. If the title object is not empty, any text that you type (with no text object selected) is simply ignored.

When you're finished typing text, press the Esc key or click the mouse anywhere outside the text object.

In Chapter 2, you find many details about playing with text objects, so hold your horses. You have more important things to attend to first.

Moving from Slide to Slide

You have several ways to move forward and backward through your presentation, from slide to slide:

- Click one of the double-headed arrows at the bottom of the vertical scroll bar. Doing so moves you through the presentation one slide at a time.
- Use the Page Up and Page Down keys on your keyboard. Using these keys also moves one slide at a time.
- Drag the scroll box (the box that appears in the middle of the scroll bar) up or down. As you drag the scroll box, you see a text box that indicates which slide PowerPoint will display when you release the mouse button. Dragging the scroll box is the quickest way to move directly to any slide in your presentation.

- Click the thumbnail for the slide you want to display in the list of slides on the left side of the screen. (If the thumbnails are not visible, click the Slides tab above the outline.)

Fifty Ways to Add a New Slide

The slides created by the AutoContent Wizard may not be adequate for your presentation. Although you may be able to adapt some of the prebuilt slides by editing their titles and text objects, eventually you'll need to add slides of your own.

You're in luck! PowerPoint gives you about 50 ways to add new slides to your presentation. You see only three of them here:

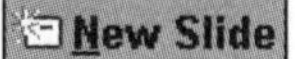

- Click the New Slide button on the standard toolbar.
- Choose the Insert⇨New Slide command.
- Press Ctrl+M.

In all three cases, PowerPoint displays the Slide Layout Pane alongside the new slide, as shown in Figure 1-8. This pane enables you to pick from 27 different types of slide layouts. Just click the mouse on the one you want to use and PowerPoint sets the new slide to the layout of your choosing.

Each slide layout has a name, which you can see by hovering the mouse pointer over the layout for a moment. The layout that's highlighted in Figure 1-9 is called *Title and Text.* The layout name tells you which types of objects are included in the layout. For example, the Text layout includes a text object. *Title, Text & Clip Art* layout includes two objects; one for text, the other for a picture from the PowerPoint clip art gallery. You'll probably use the Text layout most. It's the best format for presenting a topic along with several supporting points. For example, Figure 1-9 shows a typical bulleted list slide, in which a list of bulleted items describes signs that your son is headed down the road toward moral decay.

One of the layouts available in the AutoLayout section of the New Slide dialog box is named *Blank.* This layout doesn't include any objects; it is a blank slate that you can use to create a slide that doesn't fit any of the predefined layouts. All slide layouts except Blank include a single-line text object that serves as a title for the slide. This title is formatted consistently from slide to slide in order to give your presentation a professional look.

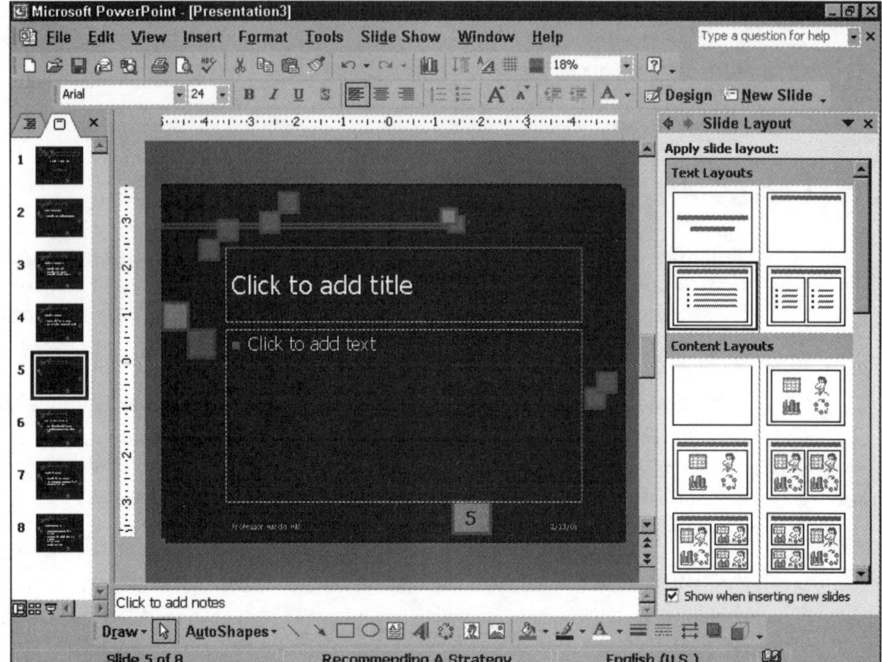

Figure 1-8: The Slide Layout Pane appears when you create a new slide.

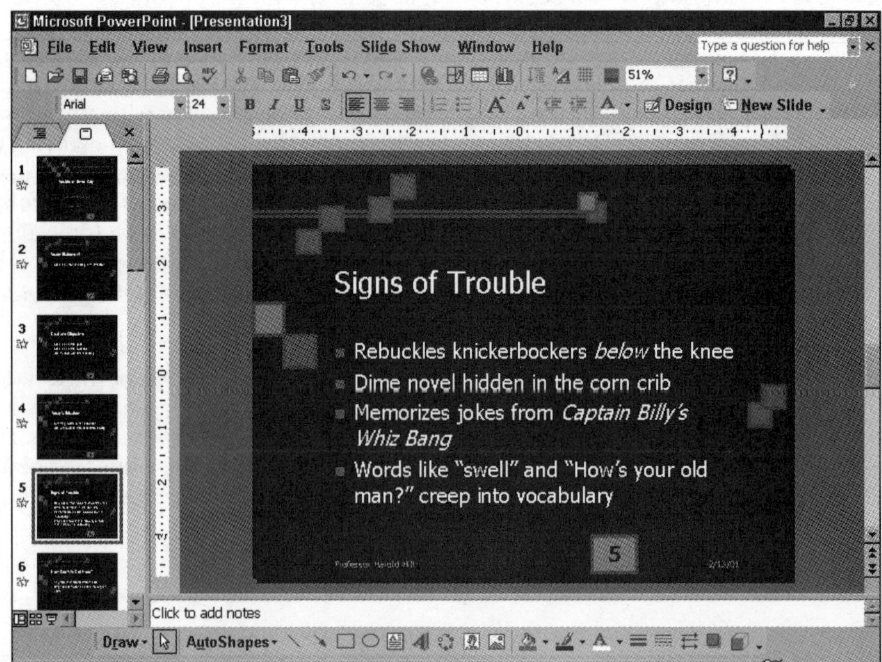

Figure 1-9: A typical Text slide.

Printing That Puppy

After you finish your masterpiece, you may want to print it. Here's the procedure for printing all the slides in your presentation:

1. **Make sure that your printer is turned on and ready to print.**

   Make sure that the *select* or *on-line* light is on. If it isn't, press the Select or On-line button to make it so. Check the paper supply while you're at it.

2. **Click the Print button on the Standard toolbar.**

   If you prefer, use the File➪Print command or press Ctrl+P or Ctrl+Shift+F12. Whichever way you do it, you see the Print dialog box. The Print dialog box has myriad options that you can fiddle with to print your presentation just so, but you can leave them alone if you want to print all the slides in your presentation.

3. **Click the OK button or press the Enter key.**

   Make sure that you say "Engage" in a knowing manner, pointing at your printer as you do so. The secret is to fool your printer into thinking that you know what you're doing.

Printed pages should soon appear on your printer. Check the pages to make sure that they look the way you want. Depending on how complex your slides are and how fast your printer is, your slides may pop right out of your printer before you can say, "I love this program." Or you may be able to take a family vacation to Disneyland while your slides print.

If you're using overhead transparencies, you can load them directly into your laser printer provided that you get transparencies that are designed for laser printers — ordinary transparencies may melt and leave gooey stuff all over your printer's guts and possibly spread radioactive dust throughout the entire tri-state area. Bad idea. Laser transparencies are expensive, though, so printing a proof on plain paper before printing on the transparencies is a good idea.

Similarly, if you use transparencies with an inkjet printer, you should get transparencies that are designed for inkjet printers. Such transparencies have a rough coating on one side that's designed to hold the ink that the printer sprays on. If you use the wrong transparencies or use the right transparencies but load them upside down, you may end up with smeared ink on your hands (and everywhere else).

Tune in to Chapter 6 if you want to know more about printing. If you want your output printed on 35mm slides, check out Chapter 30.

Saving Your Work

Now that you've spent hours creating the best presentation since God gave Moses the Ten Commandments, you can just turn your computer off, right? Wrong-o! All your precious work is held in your computer's fleeting RAM *(random access memory)* until you save your work to a disk file. Turn off your computer before you save your work, and *poof!* your work vanishes as if David Copperfield were in town.

Like everything else in PowerPoint, you have at least four ways to save a document:

- Click the Save button on the Standard toolbar.
- Choose the File⇨Save command.
- Press Ctrl+S.
- Press Shift+F12.

If you haven't yet saved the file to disk, the magical Save As dialog box appears. Type the name that you want to use for the file in the Save As dialog box and click the OK button to save the file. After you save the file once, subsequent saves update the disk file with any changes that you made to the presentation since the last time you saved it.

Some notes to keep in mind when saving files:

- Use your noggin when assigning a name to a new file. The filename is how you can recognize the file later on, so pick a meaningful name that suggests the file's contents.
- When you save a document, PowerPoint displays a bar graph at the bottom of the screen to prove that it's really doing something. See how PowerPoint saves. Save, PowerPoint, save!
- After you save a file for the first time, the name in the presentation window's title area changes from *Presentation* to the name of your file. Still more proof that the file has been saved.

- Don't work on your file for hours at a time without saving it. I've learned the hard way to save my work every few minutes. After all, I live in California so I never know when a rolling blackout will hit my neighborhood. Get into the habit of saving every few minutes, especially after making a significant change to a presentation, like adding a covey of new slides or making a gaggle of complicated formatting changes. It's also a good idea to save your work before printing your presentation.

Opening a Presentation

After you save your presentation to a disk file, you can retrieve it later when you want to make additional changes or to print it. As you may guess, PowerPoint gives you about 40 ways to accomplish the retrieval. Here are the four most common:

- Click the Open button on the Standard toolbar.
- Use the File⇨Open command.
- Press Ctrl+O.
- Press Ctrl+F12.

All four retrieval methods pop up in the Open dialog box, which gives you a list of files to choose from. Click the file that you want, then click the OK button or press the Enter key. PowerPoint reads the file from disk and puts it into your computer's RAM, where you can work on it.

The Open dialog box has controls that enable you to rummage through the various folders on your hard disk in search of your files. If you know how to open a file in any Windows application, you know how to do it in PowerPoint (because the Open dialog box is pretty much the same in any Windows program). If you seem to have lost a file, rummage around in different folders to see whether you can find it. Sometimes you can save a file in the wrong folder by accident. Also, check the spelling of the filename. Maybe your fingers weren't on the home row when you typed the filename, so instead of `River City.ppt`, you saved the file as `Eucwe Xurt`.ppt. I hate it when that happens.

The fastest way to open a file from the Open dialog box is to double-click the file you want to open, point to the file, and click the mouse twice, as fast as you can. This spares you from having to click the file once and then click the OK button. Double-clicking also exercises the fast-twitch muscles in your index finger.

PowerPoint keeps track of the last four files you've opened and displays them on the File menu. To open a file you've recently opened, click the File menu and inspect the list of files at the bottom of the menu. If the file you want is in the list, click it to open it.

The last four files you opened are also listed on the New Presentation Pane, so you can open them quickly if the New Presentation Pane is visible.

Closing a Presentation

Having finished your presentation and printed it just right, you have come to the time to close it. Closing a presentation is kind of like gathering up your papers, putting them neatly in a file folder, and returning the folder to its proper file drawer. The presentation disappears from your computer screen. Don't worry: It's tucked safely away on your hard disk where you can get to it later if you need to.

To close a file, use the File⇨Close command. You also can use the keyboard shortcut Ctrl+W, but you need a mind like a steel trap to remember that Ctrl+W stands for Close.

You don't have to close a file before exiting PowerPoint. If you exit PowerPoint without closing a file, PowerPoint graciously closes the file for you. The only reason you may want to close a file is that you want to work on a different file and you don't want to keep both files open at the same time.

If you've made changes since the last time you saved the file, PowerPoint offers to save the changes for you. Click Yes to save the file before closing or click No to abandon any changes you've made to the file.

If you close all the open PowerPoint presentations, you may discover that most of the PowerPoint commands have been rendered useless (they are grayed on the menu). Fear not. Open a presentation, or create a new one, and the commands return to life.

Exiting PowerPoint

Had enough excitement for one day? Use any of these techniques to shut PowerPoint down:

- Choose the File⇨Exit command.
- Click the X box at the top-right corner of the PowerPoint window.
- Press Alt+F4.

Bammo! PowerPoint is history.

You should know a few things about exiting PowerPoint (or any application):

- PowerPoint doesn't enable you to abandon ship without first considering if you want to save your work. If you've made changes to any presentation files and haven't saved them, PowerPoint offers to save the files for you. Lean over and plant a fat kiss right in the middle of your monitor — PowerPoint just saved you your job.
- Never, never, never, ever, never turn off your computer while PowerPoint or any other program is running. Naughty! Always exit PowerPoint and all other programs that are running before you turn off your computer.

- In fact, you'd best get clean out of Windows before shutting down your computer. Exit all your programs the same way you exited PowerPoint. Then click the Windows Start button and choose the Shut Down command. Select the Shut down your computer option and click Yes. Then wait for Windows to turn off your computer for you or display the message `It's now safe to turn off your computer` before turning off your computer.

Chapter 2

Editing Slides

In This Chapter

- Moving around in a presentation
- Working with objects
- Editing text
- Undoing a mistake
- Deleting slides
- Finding and replacing text
- Rearranging slides

If you're like Mary Poppins ("Practically Perfect in Every Way"), you can skip this chapter. Perfect people never make mistakes, so everything they type in PowerPoint 2002 comes out right the first time. They never have to press Backspace to erase something they typed incorrectly, go back and insert a line to make a point they left out, or rearrange their slides because they didn't add them in the right order to begin with.

If you're more like Jane ("Rather Inclined to Giggle; Doesn't Put Things Away") or Michael ("Extremely Stubborn and Suspicious"), you probably make mistakes along the way. This chapter shows you how to go back and correct those mistakes.

Reviewing your work and correcting it if necessary is called *editing*. It's not a fun job, but it has to be done. A spoonful of sugar usually helps.

This chapter focuses mostly on editing text objects. Many of the techniques apply to editing other types of objects, such as clip art pictures or drawn shapes. For more information about editing other types of objects, see Part III.

Moving from Slide to Slide

The most common way to move around in a PowerPoint presentation is to press the Page Up and Page Down keys on your keyboard:

- **Page Down:** Moves forward to the next slide in your presentation
- **Page Up:** Moves backward to the preceding slide in your presentation

Alternatively, you can move forward or backward through your presentation by clicking the double-headed arrows at the bottom of the vertical scroll bar on the right edge of the presentation window. You also can use the vertical scroll bar on the right edge of the presentation window to move forward or backward through your presentation.

Another way to move quickly from slide to slide is to click the scroll box within the vertical scroll bar on the right side of the window and drag it up or down by holding down the left mouse button. As you drag the box, a little text box pops up next to the slide bar to tell you which slide will be displayed if you release the button at that position.

Dragging the scroll box to move from slide to slide is just one example of the many Windows tasks that are much harder to explain than to actually do. After you read this, you probably will say to yourself, “Huh?” But after you try it, you’ll say, “Oh, I get it! Why didn’t he just say so?”

Working with Objects

In the beginning, the User created a slide. And the slide was formless and void, without meaning or content. And the User said, “Let there be a Text Object.” And there was a Text Object. And there was evening and there was morning, one day. Then the User said, “Let there be a Picture Object.” And there was a Picture Object. And there was evening and there was morning, a second day. This continued for forty days and forty nights, until there were forty objects on the slide, each after its own kind. And the User was laughed out of the auditorium by the audience who could read the slide not.

I present this charming little parable solely to make the point that PowerPoint slides are nothing without objects. Objects are the lifeblood of PowerPoint. Objects give meaning and content to otherwise formless and void slides.

Most of the objects on your slides will be text objects, which let you type text on your slides. For more information about working with text objects, see the section “Editing a Text Object: The Baby Word Processor” later in this chapter.

Every slide has a slide layout that consists of one or more *placeholders*. A placeholder is simply an area on a slide that is reserved for text, clipart, a graph, or some other type of object. For example, if you choose the Title layout, PowerPoint creates a new slide with two placeholders for text objects: one for the title, the other for the subtitle. You can add more objects to the slide later; or you can delete objects, move them around, or resize them if you want. Most of the time, though, you can be content to leave the objects where they are.

There are many other different types of objects you can add, such as clip art, charts, graphs, rectangles, circles, and so on. You can add additional objects to your slide by using one of the tools that appears on the Drawing toolbar at the bottom of the screen. For more information about adding additional objects to your slides, see Chapters 10, 14, 15, 16, and 17.

Each object occupies a rectangular region on the slide. The contents of the object may or may not visually fill the rectangular region, but you can see the outline of the object when you select it (see the section "Selecting objects" later in this chapter).

Objects can overlap. Usually, you don't want them to, but sometimes doing so creates a jazzy effect. You may lay some text on top of some clip art, for example.

Selecting objects

Before you can edit anything on a slide, you have to select the object that contains whatever it is you want to edit. For example, you can't start typing away to edit text on-screen. Instead, you must first select the text object that contains the text you want to edit. Likewise, you must select other types of objects before you can edit their contents.

Here are some guidelines to keep in mind when selecting objects:

- Before you can select anything, make sure that the cursor is shaped like an arrow. If it isn't, click the arrow button on the Drawing toolbar. (This button is officially called the Select Objects button, but it sure looks like an arrow to me.)
- To select a text object so that you can edit its text, move the arrow pointer over the text you want to edit and click the left button. A rectangular box appears around the object, and the background behind the text changes to a solid color to make the text easier to read. A text cursor appears so that you can start typing away.
- Other types of objects work a little differently. Click an object, and the object is selected. The rectangular box appears around the object to let you know that you have hooked it. After you have hooked the object, you can drag it around the screen or change its size, but you cannot edit it. To edit a nontext object, you must double-click it. (Selecting the object first is not necessary. Just point to it with the arrow pointer and double-click.)

- Another way to select an object — or more than one object — is to use the arrow pointer to drag a rectangle around the objects that you want to select. Point to a location above and to the left of the object or objects that you want to select, then click and drag the mouse down and to the right until the rectangle surrounds the objects. When you release the button, all the objects within the rectangle are selected.
- Also, you can press the Tab key to select objects. Press Tab once to select the first object on the slide. Press Tab again to select the next object. Keep pressing Tab until the object that you want is selected.

Pressing Tab to select objects is handy when you can't easily point to the object you want to select. This problem can happen if the object that you want is buried underneath another object or if the object is empty or otherwise invisible and you're not sure of its location.

Resizing or moving an object

When you select an object, an outline box appears around it, as shown in Figure 2-1. If you look closely at the box, you can see that it has *love handles,* one on each corner and one in the middle of each edge. You can use these love handles to adjust the size of an object. And you can grab the box between the love handles to move the object around on the slide.

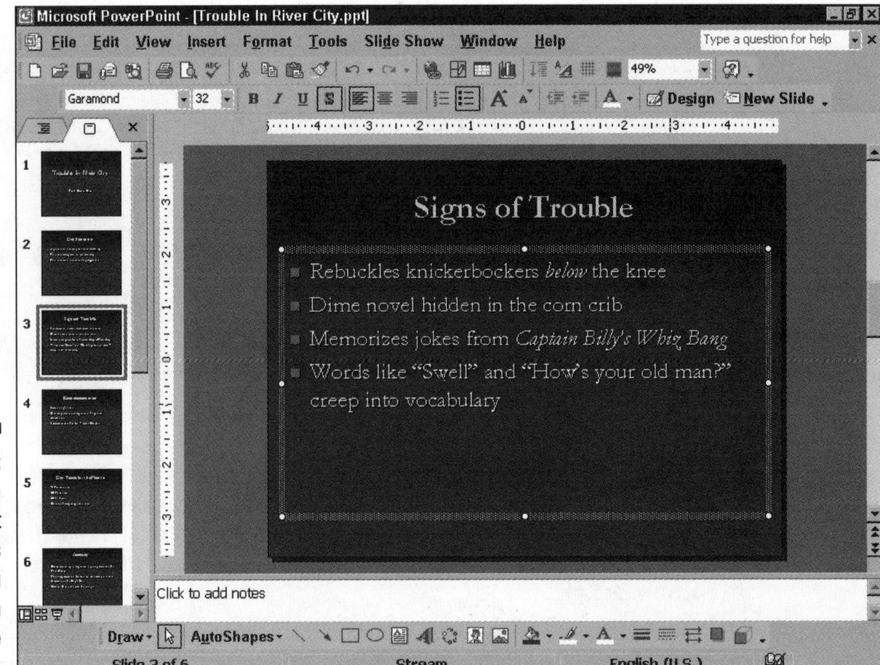

Figure 2-1: The PowerPoint love handles let you adjust an object's size

To change the size of an object, click it to select it and then grab one of the love handles by clicking it with the arrow pointer. Hold down the mouse button and move the mouse to change the object's size.

Why so many handles? To give you different ways to change the object's size. The handles at the corners allow you to change both the height and the width of the object. The handles on the top and bottom edges allow you to change just the object's height. The handles on the right and left edges change just the width.

Changing a text object's size doesn't change the size of the text in the object; it changes only the size of the "frame" that contains the text. Changing the width of a text object is equivalent to changing margins in a word processor: It makes the text lines wider or narrower. To change the size of the text within a text object, you must change the font size. Chapter 9 has the exciting details.

If you hold down the Ctrl key while you drag one of the love handles, the object stays centered at its current position on the slide. Try it, and you can see what I mean. Also, try holding down the Shift key as you drag an object using one of the corner love handles. This combination maintains the object's proportions as you resize it.

To move an object, click anywhere on the outline box except on a love handle, then drag the object to its new locale.

The outline box can be hard to see if you have a fancy background on your slides. If you select an object and have trouble seeing the outline box, try squinting or cleaning your monitor screen. Or, in severe weather, try clicking the Color/Grayscale View button in the Standard toolbar. This button brings up a menu that lets you choose one of three color modes for viewing your slides: Color, which displays slides in full color, Grayscale, which displays colors as shades of gray, and Pure Black and White, which shows the slides in black and white. Viewing the slide in Grayscale or Pure Black and White mode may make the love handles easier to spot. To switch back to full-color view, click the Color/Grayscale button again and choose Color from the menu that appears.

Editing a Text Object: The Baby Word Processor

When you select a text object for editing, PowerPoint transforms itself into a baby word processor. If you're familiar with just about any other Windows word-processing software, including Microsoft Word or even WordPad (the free word processor that comes with Windows), you'll have no trouble working in baby word-processor mode. This section presents some of the highlights, just in case.

PowerPoint automatically splits lines between words so that you don't have to press the Enter key at the end of every line. Press Enter only when you want to begin a new paragraph.

Text in a PowerPoint presentation is usually formatted with a *bullet character* at the beginning of each paragraph. The default bullet character is usually a simple square box, but you can change it to just about any shape that you can imagine (see Chapter 9). The point to remember here is that the bullet character is a part of the paragraph format, not a character you have to type in your text.

Most word processing software enables you to switch between *insert mode* and *typeover mode* by pressing the Insert key on the right side of your keyboard. In insert mode, characters that you type are inserted at the cursor location; in typeover mode, each character that you type replaces the character at the cursor location. However, PowerPoint always works in insert mode, so any text that you type is inserted at the cursor location. Pressing the Insert key has no effect on the way text is typed.

Using the arrow keys

You can move around within a text object by pressing the *arrow keys.* I looked at my computer's keyboard and saw that 13 of the keys have arrows on them — 16, if you count the greater-than (>) and less-than (<) signs and the ubiquitous caret (^), all of which look sort of like arrows. So I have included Figure 2-2, which shows you the arrow keys I'm talking about.

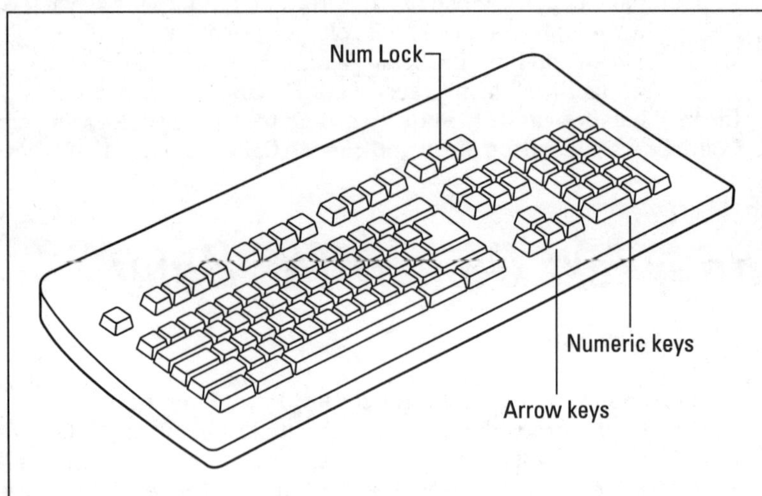

Figure 2-2: The arrow keys I'm talking about.

The arrow keys are sometimes called the *cursor keys* because they move the cursor around the screen. Each key moves the cursor in the direction in which the arrow points, as shown in Table 2-1.

Table 2-1 The Arrow Keys

Keystroke	*Where the Cursor Moves*
↑	Up one line
↓	Down one line
←	One character to the left
→	One character to the right

The arrow keys are duplicated on the 2, 4, 6, and 8 numeric keys on the right side of the keyboard. The function of these keys alternates between numeric keys and cursor-control keys, depending on whether you have pressed the Num Lock key. When you press Num Lock once, the Num Lock light comes on, indicating that the numeric keys create numerals when you press them. When you press Num Lock again, the Num Lock light goes off, which indicates that these keys control the cursor.

Using the mouse can be the fastest way to get somewhere. Point at the exact spot in the text where you want the cursor to appear and click the left button. The cursor magically jumps to that spot.

The left-arrow key looks just like the Backspace key. This evil plot is designed to fool computer novices into fearing that the arrow keys will erase text, just as the Backspace key does. Not so! Pay no attention to those fearmongers! The arrow keys are completely docile. All they do is move the cursor around; they do not destroy text.

Moving around faster

The arrow keys can get you anywhere within a text object, but sometimes they're as slow as molasses. Table 2-2 shows a few tricks for moving around faster.

For the Ctrl+key combinations listed in Table 2-2, first press and hold the Ctrl key and then press the arrow key, the End key, or the Home key. Then release both keys.

Table 2-2 Keyboard Tricks for Moving Around Faster

Keystroke	*Where the Cursor Moves*
Ctrl+↑	To the start of the paragraph, then up one paragraph
Ctrl+↓	Down one paragraph
Ctrl+←	Left one word
Ctrl+→	Right one word
End	To end of line
Home	To beginning of line
Ctrl+End	To end of text object
Ctrl+Home	To beginning of text object

Your keyboard has two Ctrl keys, a lefty and a righty. Either one works. I usually press the one on the left with my little finger and press the arrow key with my right hand. Whatever feels good is okay by me.

As long as the Ctrl key is pressed, you can press any of the arrow keys repeatedly. To move three words to the right, for example, hold down the Ctrl key and press the right-arrow key three times. Then release the Ctrl key. If the cursor is in the middle of a word, pressing Ctrl+← moves the cursor to the beginning of that word. Pressing it again moves the cursor to the beginning of the preceding word.

Deleting text

You delete text by pressing the Delete or Backspace key, both of which work, as shown in Table 2-3.

Table 2-3 Deleting Text

Keystroke	*What It Deletes*
Delete	The character immediately to the right of the cursor
Backspace	The character immediately to the left of the cursor
Ctrl+Delete	Characters from the cursor all the way to the end of the current word
Ctrl+Backspace	Characters from the cursor all the way to the beginning of the current word

You can press Ctrl+Delete to delete an entire word by first pressing Ctrl+← or Ctrl+→ to move the cursor to the beginning of the word you want to delete. Then press Ctrl+Delete.

If you first select a block of text, the Delete and Backspace keys delete the entire selection. If you don't have a clue about what I mean, skip ahead to the following section, "Marking text for surgery."

Another way to delete a word is to double-click anywhere in the middle of the word and then press the Delete key. The double-click marks the entire word, and then the Delete key deletes the marked word.

You can also use the Edit⇨Clear command to delete text permanently. The Delete key is simply a keyboard shortcut for the Edit⇨Clear command.

Marking text for surgery

Some text-editing operations — such as amputations and transplants — require that you first mark the text on which you want to operate. This list shows you the methods for doing so:

- When you use the keyboard, hold down the Shift key while you press any of the cursor-movement keys to move the cursor.
- When you use the mouse, point to the beginning of the text you want to mark and then click and drag the mouse over the text. Release the button when you reach the end of the text you want to mark.

The PowerPoint Automatic Word Selection option tries to guess when you intend to select an entire word. If you use the mouse to mark a block of text, you notice that the selected text jumps to include entire words as you move the mouse. If you don't like this feature, you can disable it by using the Tools⇨Options command (click the Edit tab and then uncheck the Automatic Word Selection check box).

- To mark a single word, point the cursor anywhere in the word and double-click. Click-click.
- To mark an entire paragraph, point anywhere in the paragraph and triple-click. Click-click-click.
- To delete the entire block of text you've marked, press the Delete key or the Backspace key.
- To replace an entire block of text, mark it and then begin typing. The marked block vanishes and is replaced by the text you're typing.
- You can use the Cut, Copy, and Paste commands from the Edit menu with marked text blocks. The following section describes these commands.

Using Cut, Copy, and Paste

Like any good Windows program, PowerPoint uses the standard Cut, Copy, and Paste commands. These commands work on the *current selection.* When you're editing a text object, the current selection is the block of text that you have marked. But if you select an entire object, the current selection is the object itself. In other words, you can use the Cut, Copy, and Paste commands with bits of text or with entire objects.

Cut, Copy, and Paste all work with one of the greatest mysteries of Windows, the *Clipboard.* The Clipboard is where Windows stashes stuff so that you can get to it later. The Cut and Copy commands add stuff to the Clipboard, and the Paste command copies stuff from the clipboard to your presentation.

PowerPoint 10 uses a new clipboard feature called the Office Clipboard, which lets you store not just one bit of information but as many as 24. For more information about using the Office Clipboard, see the section "Using the Office Clipboard" later in this chapter.

The keyboard shortcuts for Cut, Copy, and Paste are the same as they are for other Windows programs: Ctrl+X for Cut, Ctrl+C for Copy, and Ctrl+V for Paste. Because these three keyboard shortcuts work in virtually all Windows programs, memorizing them pays off.

The Copy and Paste commands are often used together to duplicate information. If you want to repeat an entire sentence, for example, you copy the sentence to the Clipboard, place the cursor where you want the sentence duplicated, and then use the Paste command. Or if you want to create a slide that has five identical rectangles on it, start by drawing one rectangle. Then, copy the rectangle to the clipboard and paste it to the slide four times. You'll end up with five rectangles; the original one you drew, plus the four copies you pasted.

The Cut and Paste commands are used together to move stuff from one location to another. To move a sentence from one slide to another, for example, select the sentence and cut it to the Clipboard. Then move to the slide you want to place the sentence on, click where you want the sentence moved, and choose the Paste command.

Cutting or copying a text block

When you cut a block of text, the text is removed from the slide and placed on the Clipboard where you can retrieve it later if you want. Copying a text block stores the text in the Clipboard but doesn't remove it from the slide.

To cut a block, first mark the block you want to cut by using the keyboard or the mouse. Then conjure up the Cut command by using any of these three methods:

- Choose the Edit⇨Cut command from the menu bar.

- Click the Cut button on the Standard toolbar (shown in the margin).
- Press Ctrl+X.

Using any method causes the text to vanish from your screen. Don't worry, though. It's safely nestled away on the Clipboard.

To copy a block, mark the block and invoke the Copy command by using one of these methods:

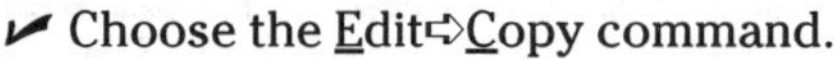
- Choose the Edit⇨Copy command.

- Click the Copy button on the Standard toolbar (shown in the margin).
- Press Ctrl+C.

The text is copied to the Clipboard, but this time the text doesn't vanish from the screen. To retrieve the text from the Clipboard, use the Paste command, as described in the following section.

Pasting text

To paste text from the Clipboard, first move the cursor to the location where you want to insert the text. Then invoke the Paste command by using whichever of the following techniques suits your fancy:

- Choose the Edit⇨Paste command from the menu bar.

- Click the Paste button on the Standard toolbar.

- Press Ctrl+V.

When you paste text into a PowerPoint presentation, PowerPoint automatically reformats the text to match the formatting of the text object you pasted the text into. If you want to retain the original text's formatting, click the Paste Options button (shown in the margin) which appears next to the pasted text, then choose Keep Source Formatting from the menu that appears.

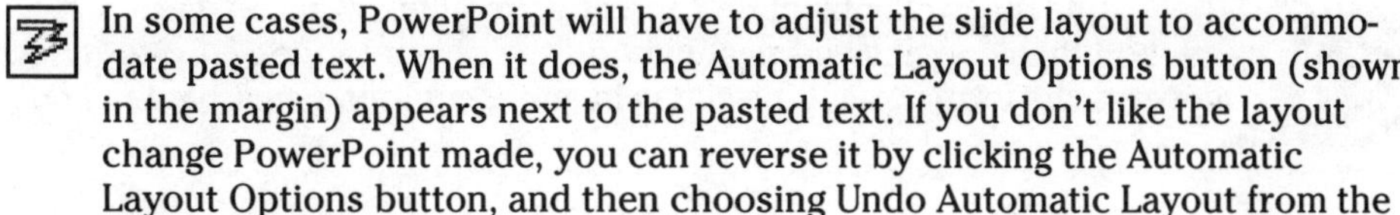

In some cases, PowerPoint will have to adjust the slide layout to accommodate pasted text. When it does, the Automatic Layout Options button (shown in the margin) appears next to the pasted text. If you don't like the layout change PowerPoint made, you can reverse it by clicking the Automatic Layout Options button, and then choosing Undo Automatic Layout from the menu that appears.

Cutting, copying, and pasting entire objects

The use of Cut, Copy, and Paste isn't limited to text blocks; the commands work with entire objects also. Just select the object, copy or cut it to the Clipboard, move to a new location, and paste the object from the Clipboard.

To move an object from one slide to another, select the object and cut it to the Clipboard. Then move to the slide where you want the object to appear and paste the object from the Clipboard.

To duplicate an object on several slides, select the object and copy it to the Clipboard. Then move to the slide that you want the object duplicated on and paste the object.

You can duplicate an object on the same slide by selecting the object, copying it to the Clipboard, and then pasting it. The only glitch is that the pasted object appears on top of the original object, but you can just grab the newly pasted object with the mouse and move it to another location on the slide.

An easier way to duplicate an object is to use the Edit⇨Duplicate command. (The keyboard shortcut for the Edit⇨Duplicate command is Ctrl+D.) It combines the functions of Copy and Paste but doesn't disturb the Clipboard. The best thing about the Edit⇨Duplicate command is that if you duplicate an object once, then move the duplicate to a new location on the slide, PowerPoint automatically places any subsequent duplicates you create.

Try this to see what I mean: On a blank slide, draw a little rectangle. (If you're not sure how, refer to Chapter 14). Select the rectangle and press Ctrl+D to duplicate the rectangle. Then, grab the duplicate rectangle with the mouse and move it to a position that's next to the original instead of on top of it. Now press Ctrl+D again and watch PowerPoint put a third rectangle next to the second!

If you want to blow away an entire object permanently, select it and press the Delete key or use the Edit⇨Clear command. This step removes the object from the slide but doesn't copy it to the Clipboard. It's gone forever. Well, sort of — you can still get it back by using the Undo command, but only if you act fast. See the section, "Oops! I Didn't Mean It (The Marvelous Undo Command)".

To include the same object on each of your slides, you can use a better method than copying and pasting: Add the object to the *Slide Master,* which governs the format of all the slides in a presentation (see Chapter 12).

Using the Office Clipboard

The Office Clipboard is a new feature of all Office programs that lets you gather up to 24 items of text or graphics from any Office program, then selectively paste them into an Office document. The Office Clipboard appears in the Task Pane at the right side of the screen, where it lists all the items you have copied or cut to the Office clipboard. Figure 2-3 shows the Office Clipboard in action.

To paste an item from the Office Clipboard, first summon the Office Clipboard Task Pane by choosing Edit⇨Office Clipboard. Then, click to mark the location in the document where you want to insert the item and click the item in the Office Clipboard that you want to insert.

Items you cut or copy are added to the Office Clipboard only if the Office Clipboard is active. There are several ways to activate the Office Clipboard:

- Choose Edit⇨Office Clipboard.
- Press Ctrl+C twice.
- Copy or cut two items consecutively, without doing anything else in between.

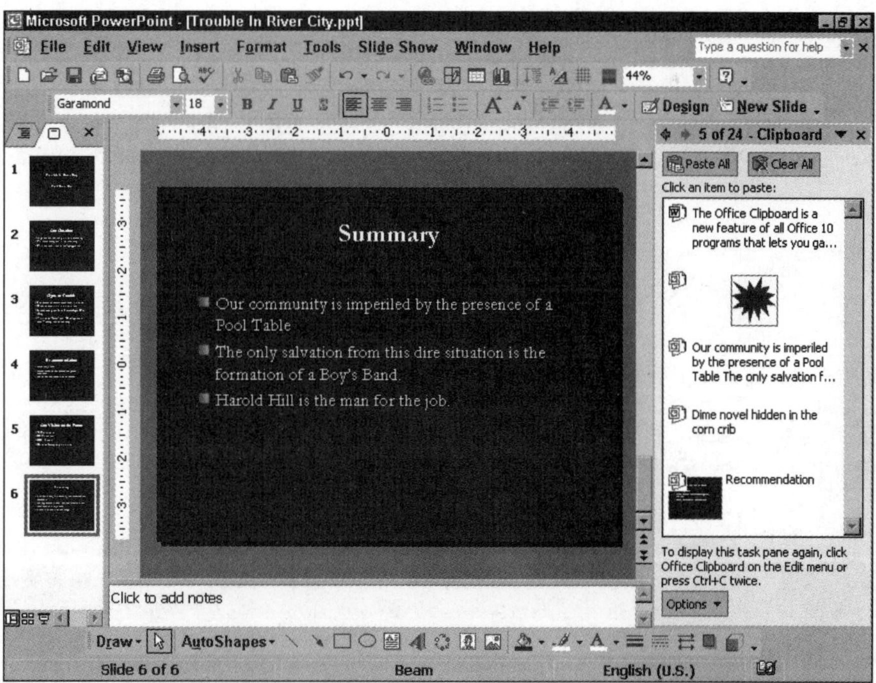

Figure 2-3: The Office Clipboard in action.

The Office Clipboard icon (shown in the margin) appear in the task bar whenever the Office Clipboard is active. As long as this icon appears, items you cut or copy are added to the Office Clipboard, even if the Office Clipboard is not visible in the task bar in the program you are working in.

To remove an item from the Office Clipboard, right-click the item and choose Delete from the menu that appears. You can remove all items from the Office Clipboard by clicking the Clear All button that appears at the top of the Office Clipboard Task Pane.

When you are finished working with the Office Clipboard, you can hide it by clicking the Close button (marked by an "X") located at the top right corner of the Office Clipboard Task Pane.

Oops! I Didn't Mean It (The Marvelous Undo Command)

Made a mistake? Don't panic. Use the Undo command. Undo is your safety net. If you mess up, Undo can save the day.

You have three ways to undo a mistake:

- Choose the Edit⇨Undo command from the menu bar.

- Click the Undo button on the Standard toolbar (shown in the margin). If you can't find it, use the down arrow on the standard toolbar to access it the first time; it will then become a customized toolbar feature.
- Press Ctrl+Z.

Undo reverses whatever you did last. If you deleted text, Undo adds it back in. If you typed text, Undo deletes it. If you moved an object, Undo puts it back where it was. You get the idea.

Undo is such a useful command that committing the Ctrl+Z keyboard shortcut to memory is a good idea. If you want, think of the word "Zip!" to help you remember how to zip away your mistakes.

Undo remembers up to 20 of your most recent actions. However, as a general rule, you should correct your mistakes as soon as possible. If you make a mistake, feel free to curse, kick something, or fall on the floor in a screaming tantrum if you must, *but don't do anything else on your computer!* If you use Undo immediately, you can reverse your mistake and get on with your life.

PowerPoint also offers a Redo command, which is sort of like an Undo for Undo. In other words, if you undo what you thought was a mistake by using the Undo command and then decide that it wasn't a mistake after all, you can use the Redo command. Following are three ways to use the Redo command:

- Choose the Edit➪Redo command from the menu bar.

- Click the Redo button on the Standard toolbar (shown in the margin).
- Press Ctrl+Y.

Deleting a Slide

Want to delete an entire slide? No problem. Move to the slide that you want to delete and use the Edit➪Delete Slide command. Zowie! The slide is history. (If the Delete Slide command doesn't show up on your Edit menu, click the double-down arrow at the bottom of the Edit menu.)

Another way to delete a slide is to click the miniature of the slide in the Slide Preview Pane (on the left side of the screen), then press the Delete key.

Deleted the wrong slide, eh? No problem. Just press Ctrl+Z or choose Edit➪Undo to restore the slide.

Duplicating a Slide

PowerPoint sports a Duplicate Slide command that lets you duplicate an entire slide; text, formatting, and everything else included. That way, after you toil over a slide for hours to get its formatting just right, you can create a duplicate to use as the basis for another slide.

To duplicate a slide, move to the slide that you want to duplicate. Then choose the Insert➪Duplicate Slide. A duplicate of the slide is inserted into your presentation.

If you're a keyboard shortcut fanatic, all you have to do is select the slide you want to duplicate in the Slide Preview Pane (on the left side of the screen), then press Ctrl+D.

Finding Text

You know that buried somewhere in that 60-slide presentation is a slide that lists the options available on the Vertical Snarfblat, but where is it? This sounds like a job for the PowerPoint Find command!

The Find command can find text buried in any text object on any slide. These steps show you the procedure for using it:

1. **Think of what you want to find.**

   Snarfblat will do in this example.

2. **Summon the Edit⇨Find command.**

   The keyboard shortcut is Ctrl+F. Figure 2-4 shows the Find dialog box, which contains the secrets of the Find command.

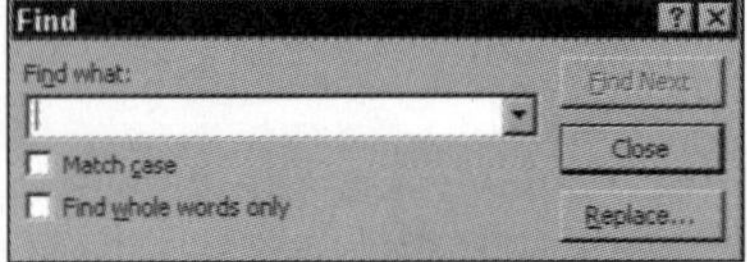

Figure 2-4: The Find dialog box.

3. **Type the text that you want to find.**

   It shows up in the Find What box.

4. **Press the Enter key.**

   Or click the Find Next button. Either way, the search begins.

If the text that you type is located anywhere in the presentation, the Find command zips you to the slide that contains the text and highlights the text. Then you can edit the text object or search for the next occurrence of the text within your presentation. If you edit the text, the Find dialog box stays on-screen to make it easy to continue your quest.

Here are some facts to keep in mind when using the Find command:

- To find the next occurrence of the same text, press Enter or click the Find Next button again.
- To edit the text you found, click the text object. The Find dialog box remains on-screen. To continue searching, click the Find Next button again.
- You don't have to be at the beginning of your presentation to search the entire presentation. When PowerPoint reaches the end of the presentation, it automatically picks up the search at the beginning and continues back to the point at which you started the search.
- You may receive the message:

  ```
  PowerPoint has finished searching the presentation. The
          search item was not found.
  ```

  This message means that PowerPoint has given up. The text you typed just isn't anywhere in the presentation. Maybe you spelled it wrong, or maybe you didn't have a slide about Snarfblats after all.

- If the right mix of uppercase and lowercase letters is important to you, check the Match Case box before beginning the search. This option is handy when you have, for example, a presentation about Mr. Smith the Blacksmith.
- Use the Find Whole Words Only check box to find your text only when it appears as a whole word. If you want to find the slide on which you talked about Smitty the Blacksmith's mitt, for example, type **mitt** for the Find What text and check the Find Whole Words Only box. That way, the Find command looks for *mitt* as a separate word. It doesn't stop to show you the *mitt* in *Smitty.*
- If you find the text you're looking for and decide that you want to replace it with something else, click the Replace button. This step changes the Find dialog box to the Replace dialog box, which is explained in the following section.
- To make the Find dialog box go away, click the Close button or press the Esc key.

Replacing Text

Suppose that the Rent-a-Nerd company decides to switch to athletic consulting, so it wants to change the name of its company to Rent-a-Jock. Easy. Just use the handy Replace command to change all occurrences of the word *Nerd* to *Jock.* The following steps show you how:

1. **Invoke the Edit⇨Replace command.**

   The keyboard shortcut is Ctrl+H. I have no idea why. In any case, you see the Replace dialog box, shown in Figure 2-5.

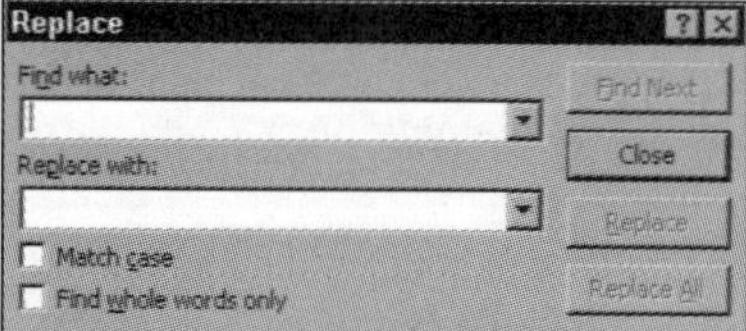

Figure 2-5: The Replace dialog box.

2. **In the Find What box, type the text that you want to find.**

   Enter the text that you want to replace with something else (*Nerd,* in the example).

3. **Type the replacement text in the Replace With box.**

   Enter the text that you want to use to replace the text you typed in the Find What box (*Jock,* in the example).

4. **Click the Find Next button.**

   PowerPoint finds the first occurrence of the text.

5. **Click the Replace button to replace the text.**

   Read the text first to make sure that it found what you were looking for.

6. **Repeat the Find Next and Replace sequence until you're finished.**

   Click Find Next to find the next occurrence, click Replace to replace it, and so on. Keep going until you have finished.

If you're absolutely positive that you want to replace all occurrences of your Find what text with the Replace with text, click the Replace All button. This step dispenses with the Find Next and Replace cycle. The only problem is that you're bound to find at least one spot where you didn't want the replacement to occur. Replacing the word *mitt* with *glove,* for example, results in *Sglovey* rather than *Smitty.* Don't forget that you can also use the Find Whole Words Only option to find and replace text only if it appears as an entire word.

If you totally mess up your presentation by clicking Replace All, you can use the Undo command to restore sanity to your presentation.

Rearranging Your Slides in Slide Sorter View

Normal View is the view you normally work in to edit your slides, move things around, add text or graphics, and so on. But Normal View has one serious limitation: It doesn't give you a big picture of your presentation. You can see the details of only one slide at a time, and the Slide Preview Pane lets you see snapshots of only a few slides. To see an overall view of your presentation, you need to work in Slide Sorter View.

You can switch to Slide Sorter View in two easy ways:

- Click the Slide Sorter View button in the bottom-left corner of the screen.
- Choose the View⇨Slide Sorter command.

The PowerPoint Slide Sorter View is shown in Figure 2-6.

The following list tells you how to rearrange, add, or delete slides from Slide Sorter View:

- To move a slide, click and drag it to a new location. Point to the slide and then press and hold down the left mouse button. Drag the slide to its new location and release the button. PowerPoint adjusts the display to show the new arrangement of slides.

- To delete a slide, click the slide to select it and then press the Delete key. The Delete key works on an entire slide only in Slide Sorter View. You also can use the Edit⇨Delete Slide command.
- To add a new slide, click the slide you want the new slide to follow and then click the New Slide button. The Slide Layout Task Pane appears so that you can choose the layout for the new slide. To edit the contents of the slide, return to Slide or Outline View by using the view buttons (located at the bottom-left corner of the screen) or the View command.

66%

If your presentation contains more slides than fit on-screen at one time, you can use the scroll bars to scroll through the display. Or you can change the zoom factor to make the slides smaller. Click the down arrow next to the zoom size in the Standard toolbar and choose a smaller zoom percentage, or just type a new zoom size into the toolbar's zoom control box. (The Zoom control is shown in the margin.)

Slide Sorter View may seem kind of dull and boring, but it's also the place where you can add jazzy transitions, build effects, or add cool animation effects to your slides. For example, you can make your bullets fall from the top of the screen like bombs and switch from slide to slide by using strips, wipes, or blinds. Chapter 19 describes all this cool stuff.

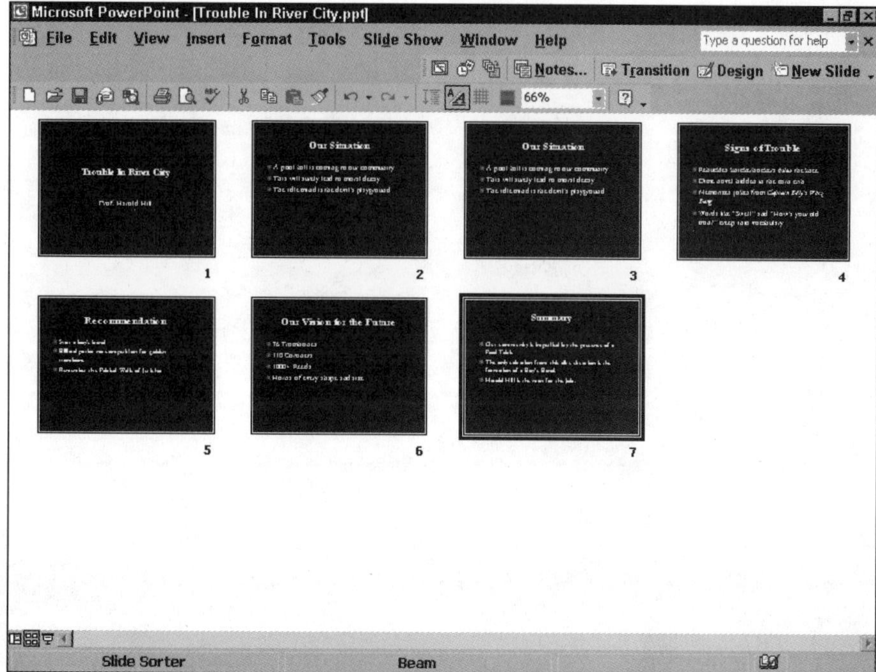

Figure 2-6: Slide Sorter View lets you see the big picture.

Chapter 3

Outlining Your Presentation

In This Chapter

- Understanding the Outline
- Focusing on substance, not form
- Adding a slide in the Outline tab — the many ways
- Promoting, demoting, and the lateral arabesque
- Collapsing and expanding the outline
- Expanding a slide
- Creating a summary slide

You probably have already noticed that most presentations consist of slide after slide of bulleted lists. You may see a chart here or there and an occasional bit of clip art thrown in for comic effect, but the bread and butter of presentations is the bulleted list. It sounds boring, but it's the best way to make sure that your message gets through.

For this reason, presentations lend themselves especially well to outlining. Presentations are light on prose but heavy in the point and subpoint department — and that's precisely where outlines excel. The Outline tab that appears to the left of your slides in Normal View lets you focus on your presentation's main points and subpoints. In other words, it enables you to focus on content without worrying about appearance.

Calling Up the Outline

In Normal View, the left-hand side of the screen shows little thumbnail previews of the slides in your presentation. Above these thumbnails is a pair of tabs that lets you switch between the thumbnails and an outline of your presentation. The Outline tab shows your presentation as an outline, with each slide a separate heading at the highest level of the outline and the text on each slide as lower-level headings subordinate to the slide headings.

To summon the outline, click the Outline tab that appears above the thumbnails. (The Outline tab contains the icon shown in the margin.) The outline appears, as shown in Figure 3-1.

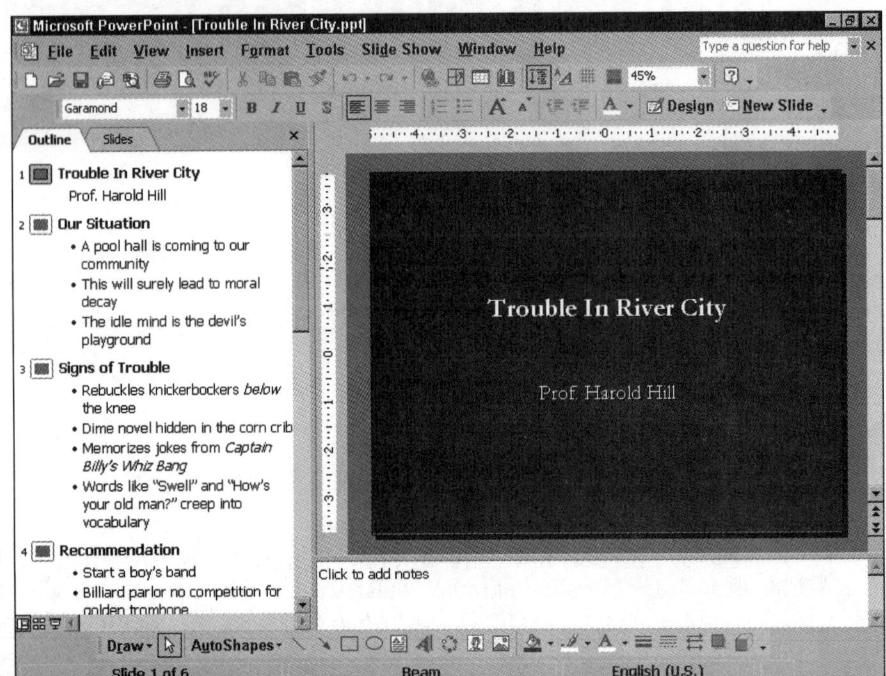

Figure 3-1: Viewing the outline.

You can expand the area devoted to the outline by clicking and dragging the border of the Outline Pane.

The following list highlights a few important things to notice about the outline:

- The outline is made up of the titles and body text of each slide. Any other objects that you add to a slide — such as pictures, charts, and so on — are not included in the outline. Also, if you add any text objects to the slide in addition to the basic title and body text objects that are automatically included when you create a new slide, the additional text objects are not included in the outline.

- Each slide is represented by a high-level heading in the outline. The text of this heading is drawn from the slide's title, and an icon that represents the entire slide appears next to the heading (this icon is shown in the margin). Also, the slide number appears to the left of the slide icon.

- Each text line from a slide's body text appears as an indented heading, subordinate to the slide's main title heading.
- An outline can contain subpoints that are subordinate to the main points on each slide. PowerPoint enables you to create as many as five heading levels on each slide, but your slides probably will get too complicated if you go beyond two headings. You can find more about working with heading levels in the section "Promoting and Demoting Paragraphs" later in this chapter.

Using the Outlining Toolbar

PowerPoint includes a special Outlining toolbar that contains special buttons for working with outlines. You can summon this toolbar by choosing View⇨Toolbars⇨Outlining. The Outlining toolbar appears to the left of the outline.

Table 3-1 summarizes what each button does.

Table 3-1 Buttons on the Outlining Toolbar

Button	Name	What It Does
	Promote	Promotes the paragraph to a higher outline level
	Demote	Demotes the paragraph to a lower outline level
	Move Up	Moves the paragraph up
	Move Down	Moves the paragraph down
	Collapse	Collapses the selected slide or slides
	Expand	Expands the selected slide or slides
	Collapse All	Collapses an entire presentation
	Expand All	Expands an entire presentation
	Summary Slide	Creates a summary slide
	Show Formatting	Shows or hides text formatting

You can perform all the functions provided by the Outlining toolbar's buttons without calling up the toolbar. The Outlining toolbar is a leftover from previous versions of PowerPoint, in which you had to switch to a separate view to work with the outline. If you're used to working with the Outlining toolbar because you started with an older version of PowerPoint, feel free to continue using the Outlining toolbar. But otherwise, I wouldn't bother with the toolbar.

Selecting and Editing an Entire Slide

When you work in Outline View, you often have to select an entire slide. PowerPoint provides three ways to do that:

- Click the slide's Slide icon (shown in the margin).
- Click the slide's number.
- Triple-click anywhere in the slide's title text.

When you select an entire slide, the slide title and all its body text are highlighted. In addition, any extra objects such as graphics that are on the slide are selected as well, even though those objects don't appear in the outline.

To delete an entire slide, select it and then press the Delete key.

To cut or copy an entire slide to the Clipboard, select it and then press Ctrl+X (Cut) or Ctrl+C (Copy). You can then move the cursor to any location in the outline and press Ctrl+V to paste the slide from the Clipboard.

To duplicate a slide, select it and then invoke the Edit⇨Duplicate command or press Ctrl+D. This step places a copy of the selected slide immediately after the selected slide. (Actually, you don't have to select the entire slide to duplicate it. Just click anywhere in the slide's title or body text.)

Selecting and Editing One Paragraph

You can select and edit an entire paragraph along with all its subordinate paragraphs. Just click the bullet next to the paragraph that you want to select or triple-click anywhere in the text. To delete an entire paragraph along with its subordinate paragraphs, select it and then press the Delete key.

To cut or copy an entire paragraph to the Clipboard along with its subordinates, select it and then press Ctrl+X (Cut) or Ctrl+C (Copy). You can then press Ctrl+V to paste the paragraph anywhere in the presentation.

Promoting and Demoting Paragraphs

To *promote* a paragraph means to move it up one level in the outline. If you promote the "Memorizes jokes from *Captain Billy's Whiz Bang*" line in Figure 3-1, for example, that line becomes a separate slide rather than a bullet paragraph under "Signs of Trouble."

To *demote* a paragraph is just the opposite: The paragraph moves down one level in the outline. If you demote the "Dime novel hidden in the corn crib" paragraph in Figure 3-1, it becomes a subpoint under "Rebuckles knickerbockers *below* the knee" rather than a separate main point.

Promoting paragraphs

To promote a paragraph, place the cursor anywhere in the paragraph and then perform any of the following techniques:

- Click the Promote button (shown in the margin) on the Outlining toolbar.
- Press the Shift+Tab key.
- Use the keyboard shortcut Alt+Shift+←.

Or just click and drag the paragraph's bullet to the left. For more information about this method, see the section "Dragging paragraphs to new levels" later in this chapter.

You can't promote a slide title. Slide title is the highest rank in the outline hierarchy.

Demoting paragraphs

To demote a paragraph, place the cursor anywhere in the paragraph and then do one of the following:

- Click the Demote button (shown in the margin) on the Outlining toolbar.
- Press the Tab key.
- Use the keyboard shortcut Alt+Shift+→.

Or just click and drag the paragraph's bullet to the right. For more information about this method, see next section, "Dragging paragraphs to new levels."

If you demote a slide title, the entire slide is subsumed into the preceding slide. In other words, the slide title becomes a main point in the preceding slide.

Be sensitive when you demote paragraphs. Being demoted can be an emotionally devastating experience.

Dragging paragraphs to new levels

When you move the mouse pointer over a bullet (or the slide button), the pointer changes from a single arrow to a four-cornered arrow. This arrow is your signal that you can click the mouse to select the entire paragraph (and any subordinate paragraphs). Also, you can use the mouse to promote or demote a paragraph along with all its subordinates.

To promote or demote with the mouse, follow these steps:

1. **Point to the bullet that you want to demote or promote.**

   The mouse pointer changes to a four-cornered arrow, as shown in the margin. To demote a slide, point to the slide button. (Remember that you can't promote a slide. It's already at the highest level.)

2. **Click and hold the mouse button down.**

3. **Drag the mouse to the right or left.**

   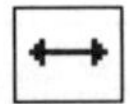

   The mouse pointer changes to a double-pointed arrow (as shown in the margin), and a vertical line appears that shows the indentation level of the selection. Release the button when the selection is indented the way you want. The text is automatically reformatted for the new indentation level.

If you mess up, press Ctrl+Z or click the Undo button to undo the promotion or demotion. Then try again.

Adding a New Paragraph

To add a new paragraph to a slide using the outline, move the cursor to the end of the paragraph that you want the new paragraph to follow and then press the Enter key. PowerPoint creates a new paragraph at the same outline level as the preceding paragraph.

If you position the cursor at the beginning of a paragraph and press the Enter key, the new paragraph is inserted to the left of the cursor position. If you position the cursor in the middle of a paragraph and press the Enter key, the paragraph is split in two.

After you add a new paragraph, you may want to change its level in the outline. To do that, you must promote or demote the new paragraph. To create a subpoint for a main point, for example, position the cursor at the end of the main point and press the Enter key. Then demote the new paragraph by pressing the Tab key.

Adding a New Slide

You can add a new slide in many ways when you're working with the outline. This list shows the most popular methods:

- Promote an existing paragraph to the highest level. This method splits a slide into two slides. In Figure 3-1, for example, you can create a new slide by promoting the "The idle mind is the devil's playground" paragraph. That step splits the "Our Situation" slide into two slides.
- Add a new paragraph and then promote it to the highest level.
- Place the cursor in a slide's title text and press the Enter key. This method creates a new slide before the current slide. Whether the title text stays with the current slide, goes with the new slide, or is split between the slides depends on the location of the cursor within the title when you press Enter.
- Place the cursor anywhere in a slide's body text and press Ctrl+Enter. This method creates a new slide immediately following the current slide. The position of the cursor within the existing slide doesn't matter; the new slide is always created after the current slide. (The cursor must be in the slide's body text for this method to work, though. If you put the cursor in a slide title and press Ctrl+Enter, the cursor jumps to the slide's body text without creating a new slide.)

New Slide

- Place the cursor anywhere in the slide and invoke the Insert➪New Slide command. Or, use the keyboard, Ctrl+M, or click the New Slide button (shown in the margin).
- Select an existing slide by clicking the slide's icon or triple-clicking the title and then duplicate it by using the Edit➪Duplicate command or its keyboard shortcut, Ctrl+D.

Because the outline focuses on slide content rather than on layout, new slides receive the basic Bulleted List layout, which includes title text and body text formatted with bullets. If you want to change the layout of a new slide, you must call up the Slide Layout Task Pane by choosing the Format➪Slide Layout command. (The Slide Layout Task Pane automatically appears if you create the slide by using the Insert➪New Slide command, the Ctrl+M keyboard shortcut, or the New Slide button.)

Moving Text Up and Down

The outline is a handy way to rearrange your presentation. You can easily change the order of individual points on a slide, or you can rearrange the order of the slides.

Moving text the old-fashioned way

To move text up or down, first select the text that you want to move. To move just one paragraph (along with any subordinate paragraphs), click its bullet. To move an entire slide, click its slide button.

To move the selected text up, use either of the following techniques:

- Click the Move Up button (shown in the margin) on the Outline toolbar on the left side of the screen.
- Press Alt+Shift+↑.

To move the selected text down, use either of the following techniques:

- Click the Move Down button (shown in the margin) on the Outline toolbar on the left side of the screen.
- Press Alt+Shift+↓.

Moving text the dragon drop way

To move text up or down by using the mouse, follow these steps:

1. **Point to the bullet next to the paragraph that you want to move.**

   The mouse pointer changes to a four-cornered arrow (shown in the margin). To move a slide, point to the slide button.

2. **Click and hold the mouse button down.**
3. **Drag the mouse up or down.**

   The mouse pointer changes again to a double-pointed arrow (shown in the margin), and a horizontal line appears, showing the horizontal position of the selection. Release the mouse when the selection is positioned where you want it; in other words, drag and drop.

Be careful when you're moving text in a slide that has more than one level of body text paragraphs. Notice the position of the horizontal line as you drag the selection; the entire selection is inserted at that location, which may split up subpoints. If you don't like the result of a move, you can always undo it by pressing Ctrl+Z or clicking the Undo button.

Expanding and Collapsing the Outline

If your presentation has many slides, you may find that grasping its overall structure is difficult, even when looking at the Outline. Fortunately, PowerPoint enables you to *collapse* the outline so that only the slide titles are shown. Collapsing an outline doesn't delete the body text; it merely hides the body text so that you can focus on the order of the slides in your presentation.

Expanding a presentation restores the collapsed body text to the outline so that you can once again focus on details. You can collapse and expand an entire presentation, or you can collapse and expand one slide at a time.

Collapsing an entire presentation

To collapse an entire presentation, you have two options:

- Click the Collapse All button (shown in the margin) on the Outlining toolbar.
- Press Alt+Shift+1.

Expanding an entire presentation

To expand an entire presentation, try one of these methods:

- Click the Expand All button (shown in the margin) on the Outlining toolbar.
- Press Alt+Shift+9.

Collapsing a single slide

To collapse a single slide, position the cursor anywhere in the slide that you want to collapse. Then do one of the following:

- Click the Collapse button (shown in the margin) on the Outline toolbar.
- Press Alt+Shift+– (the minus sign).

Expanding a single slide

To expand a single slide, position the cursor anywhere in the title of the slide that you want to expand. Then perform one of the following techniques:

- Click the Expand button (shown in the margin) on the Outlining toolbar.
- Press Alt+Shift++ (the plus sign).

Creating a Summary Slide

A nifty feature that was first introduced in PowerPoint 97 and is still around for PowerPoint 10 is the Summary Slide button, which automatically creates a summary slide that shows the titles of some or all the slides in your presentation. To use the Summary Slide feature, follow these steps:

1. **Select the slides whose titles you want to appear on the summary slide.**

   To include the entire presentation, press Ctrl+A to select all the slides.

2. **Click the Summary Slide button. You can find the Summary Slide button on the Outlining toolbar.**

   If the Outlining toolbar is not visible, summon it by choosing View⇨Toolbars⇨Outlining.

   A summary slide is created at the beginning of the selected slides, as shown in Figure 3-2.

3. **Type a title for the summary slide.**

   Unless, of course, you like the boring title "Summary Slide."

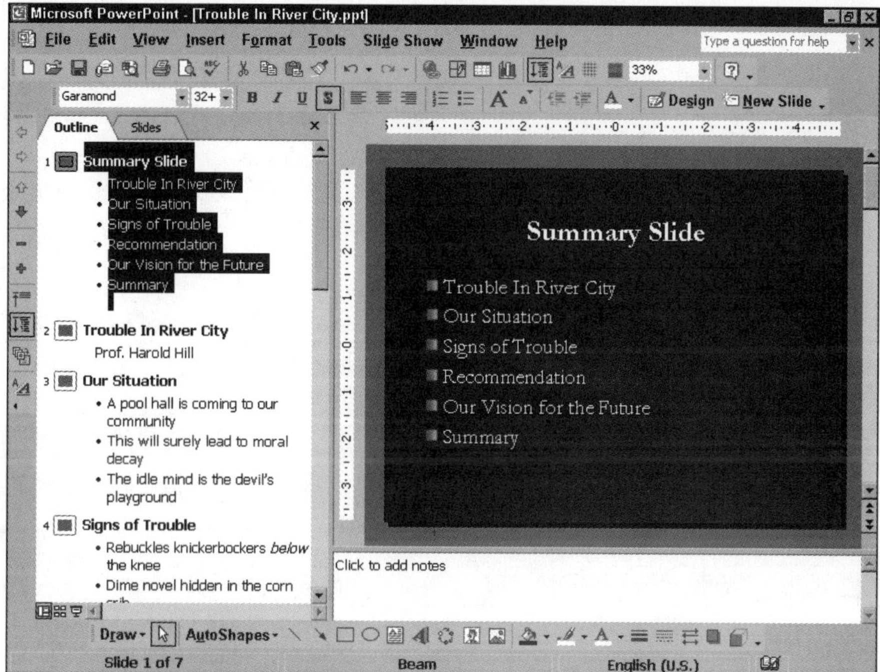

Figure 3-2: A summary slide.

Chapter 4

Doing It with Style

In This Chapter

- Checking your presentation for embarrassing stylistic mistakes
- Checking your spelling
- Capitalizing and punctuating correctly
- Using the AutoCorrect feature

I was voted Worst Speller in the sixth grade. Not that being Worst Speller qualifies me to run for vice-president or anything, but it shows how much I appreciate computer spell checkers. Spelling makes no sense to me. I felt a little better after watching *The Story of English* on public television. Now at least I know whom to blame for all the peculiarities of English spelling — the Anglos, the Norms (including the guy from *Cheers*), and the Saxophones.

Fortunately, PowerPoint has a pretty decent spell checker. In fact, the spell checker in PowerPoint is so smart that it knows that you've made a spelling mistake almost before you make it. The spell checker watches over your shoulder as you type and helps you correct your spelling errors as you work.

PowerPoint also has a nifty style checker that helps catch innocent typographical errors before you show your presentation to a board of directors. The style checker can fix your capitalization (capital idea, eh?), make sure that you punctuate your bullet points consistently, warn you about using too many fonts, and catch other embarrassing style gaffes.

The Over-the-Shoulder Spell Checker

Spelling errors in a word-processing document are bad, but at least they're small. In a PowerPoint presentation, spelling errors are small only until you use a projector to throw your presentation onto a 20-foot screen. Then they get all blown out of proportion. Nothing is more embarrassing than a 2-foot-tall spelling error. And if you're like me, you probably try to look for mistakes in people's Web pages just for yuks. Thank goodness for PowerPoint's on-the-fly spell checker.

The PowerPoint spell checker doesn't make you wait until you finish your presentation and run a special command to point out your spelling errors. It boldly points out your mistakes right when you make them by underlining any mistake that you make with a wavy colored line, as shown in Figure 4-1.

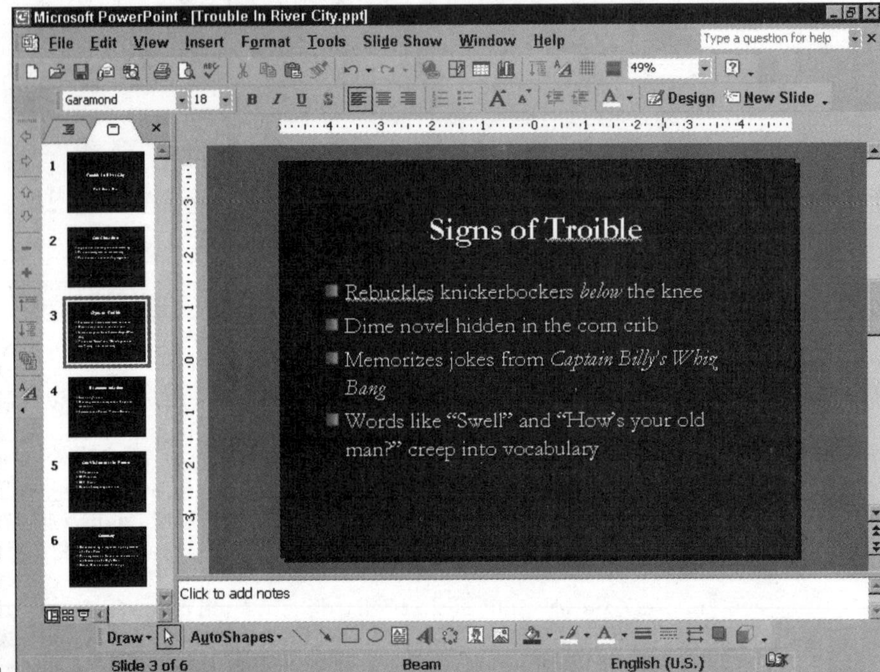

Figure 4-1: PowerPoint usually knows before you do that you've misspelled a word.

In Figure 4-1, two words have been marked as misspelled: *Troible* and *Rebuckles*. When you see the telltale wavy colored line, you have several options:

- You can retype the word using the correct spelling.
- You can click the word with the right mouse button to call up a menu that lists any suggested spellings for the word. In most cases, PowerPoint can figure out what you meant to type and suggests the correct spelling. To replace the misspelled word with the correct spelling, just click the correctly spelled word in the menu.
- You can ignore the misspelling. Sometimes, you want to misspell a word on purpose (for example, if you run a restaurant named "The Koffee Kup"). More likely, the word is correctly spelled, but PowerPoint just doesn't know about the word (for example, *Rebuckles* in Figure 4-1).

After-the-Fact Spell Checking

If you prefer to ignore the constant nagging by PowerPoint about your spelling, you can always check your spelling the old-fashioned way: by running the spell checker after you have finished your document. The spell checker works its way through your entire presentation, looking up every word in its massive list of correctly spelled words and bringing any misspelled words to your attention. It performs this task without giggling or snickering. As an added bonus, the spell checker even gives you the opportunity to tell it that you're right and it's wrong and that it should discern how to spell words the way you do.

The following steps show you how to check the spelling for an entire presentation:

1. **If the presentation that you want to spell check is not already open, open it.**
2. **Fire up the spell checker.**

   Click the Spelling button on the Standard toolbar (shown in the margin), press F7, or choose the Tools⇨Spelling command.
3. **Tap your fingers on your desk.**

   PowerPoint is searching your presentation for embarrassing spelling errors. Be patient.
4. **Don't be startled if PowerPoint finds a spelling error.**

   If PowerPoint finds a spelling error in your presentation, it switches to the slide that contains the error, highlights the offensive word, and displays the misspelled word along with a suggested correction, as shown in Figure 4-2.

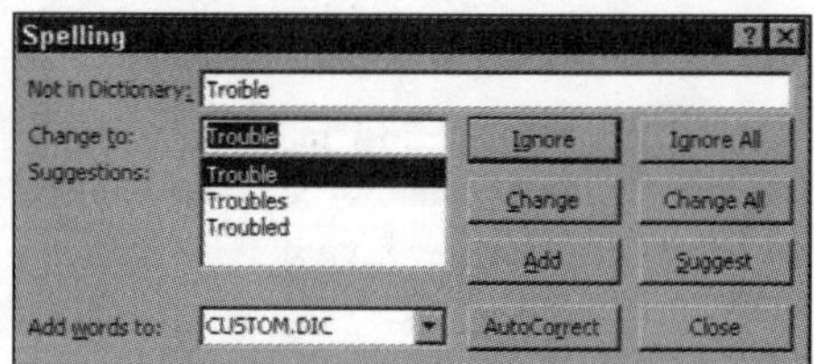

Figure 4-2: The PowerPoint spell checker points out a boo-boo.

5. **Choose the correct spelling or laugh in PowerPoint's face.**

   If you agree that the word is misspelled, scan the list of corrections that PowerPoint offers and click the one you like. Then click the Change button. If you like the way that you spelled the word in the first place (maybe it's an unusual word that isn't in the PowerPoint spelling dictionary, or maybe you like to spell like Chaucer did), click the Ignore button. Watch as PowerPoint turns red in the face.

6. **Repeat Steps 4 and 5 until PowerPoint gives up.**

   When you see the following message:

   ```
   The spelling check is complete
   ```

   You're finished.

PowerPoint always checks spelling for the entire presentation, beginning with the first slide unless you specify a single word or group of words by highlighting them first. PowerPoint checks the spelling of titles, body text, notes, and text objects added to slides. It doesn't check the spelling for embedded objects, however, such as charts or graphs.

If PowerPoint cannot come up with a suggestion or if none of its suggestions are correct, you can type your own correction and click the Change button. If the word you type isn't in the dictionary, PowerPoint asks you whether you're sure that you know what you're doing. Double-check and click OK if you really mean it.

If you want PowerPoint to ignore all occurrences of a particular misspelling, click the Ignore All button. Likewise, if you want PowerPoint to correct all occurrences of a particular misspelling, click the Change All button.

If you get tired of PowerPoint always complaining about a word that's not in its standard dictionary (such as *rebuckles*), click Add to add the word to the custom dictionary. If you cannot sleep at night until you know more about the custom dictionary, read the following sidebar titled "Don't make me tell you about the custom dictionary."

Don't make me tell you about the custom dictionary

The PowerPoint spell checker uses two spelling dictionaries: a standard dictionary, which contains untold thousands of words all reviewed for correctness by Noah Webster himself (just kidding), and a custom dictionary, which contains words you have added by clicking the Add button when the spell checker found a spelling error.

The custom dictionary lives in a file named CUSTOM.DIC, which makes its residence in the \WINDOWS\APPLICATION DATA\MICROSOFT\PROOF folder. Other Microsoft programs that use spell checkers — most notably Microsoft Word — share the same custom dictionary with PowerPoint. So if you add a word to the custom dictionary in Word, the PowerPoint spell checker knows about the word, too.

What if you accidentally add a word to the dictionary? Then you have a serious problem. You have two alternatives. You can petition Noah Webster to have your variant spelling officially added to the English language, or you can edit the CUSTOM.DIC file, search through the file until you find the bogus word, and delete it. CUSTOM.DIC automatically defaults to Notepad, the jiffy editor that comes free with Windows.

The speller cannot tell the difference between *your* and *you're, ours* and *hours, angel* and *angle,* and so on. In other words, if the word is in the dictionary, PowerPoint passes it by regardless of whether you used the word correctly. The PowerPoint spell checker is no substitute for good, old-fashioned proofing. Print your presentation, sit down with a cup of cappuccino, and *read* it.

Capitalizing Correctly

The PowerPoint Change Case command enables you to capitalize the text in your slides properly. These steps show you how to use it:

1. **Select the text that you want to capitalize.**
2. **Choose the Format⇨Change Case command.**

   The Change Case dialog box appears, as shown in Figure 4-3.

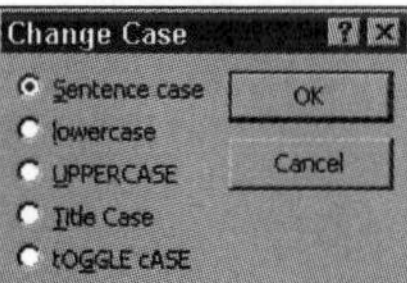

Figure 4-3: The Change Case dialog box.

3. **Study the options for a moment and then click the one you want.**

   The case options follow:

   - **Sentence case:** The first letter of the first word in each sentence is capitalized. Everything else is changed to lowercase.
   - **lowercase:** Everything is changed to lowercase.
   - **UPPERCASE:** Everything is changed to capital letters.
   - **Title Case:** The first letter of each word is capitalized. PowerPoint is smart enough to leave certain words, such as "a" and "the," lowercase, but you should double-check to ensure that it worked properly.
   - **tOGGLE cASE:** This option turns capitals into lowercase and turns lowercase into capitals, for a ransom-note look.

4. **Click OK or press Enter and check the results.**

Always double-check your text after using the Change Case command to make sure that the result is what you intended.

Slide titles almost always should use title case. The first level of bullets on a slide can use title or sentence case. Lower levels usually should use sentence case.

Avoid uppercase if you can. It's harder to read and looks like you're SHOUTING.

Using Style Checker Options

PowerPoint's spell checker does more than check your spelling: It also checks your style, letting you know if you've used punctuation and capitalization consistently, warning you about slides that contain too many bullets or text that's too small, and so on.

Unfortunately, PowerPoint's style checking features are turned off by default. But you can activate them by following these steps:

1. **Choose the Tools⇨Options command, then click the Spelling and Style tab.**

   The dialog box shown in Figure 4-4 appears.

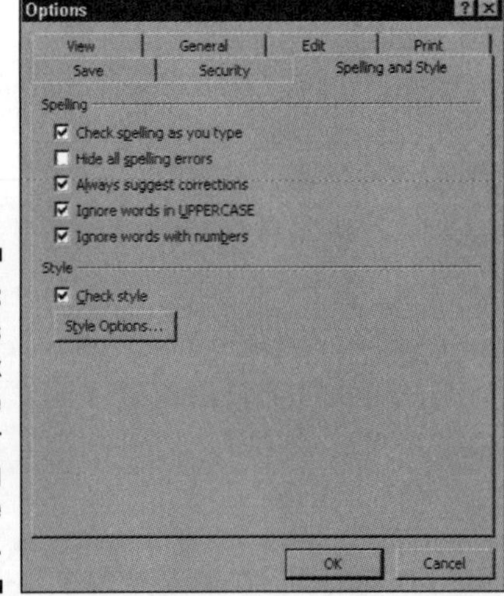

Figure 4-4: The Options dialog box contains the settings for the spelling and style checker.

2. **Check the Check Style option.**

   If this option is not already checked, click it to select it.

3. **Click the Style Options button and adjust the style settings to your liking.**

The Style Options dialog box has two tabs with options for checking the following style element.

- **Case and End Punctuation:** These settings, shown in Figure 4-5, make sure that your capitalization and punctuation are consistent.
- **Visual clarity:** These options, shown in Figure 4-6, check for visual clarity and warn you about slides that have too many fonts, titles, and body text that is too small to read or too long, slides that have too many bullets, or slides that have text that runs off the page. Note that there are default numbers here. It's up to you if you prefer to change maximum font sizes or whatever, but realize these defaults usually work pretty well.

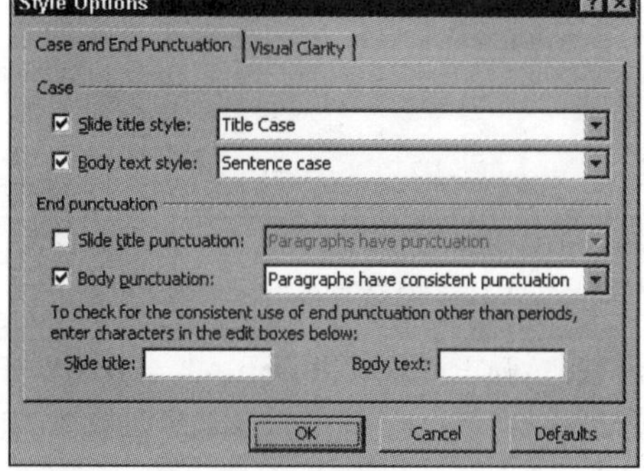

Figure 4-5: The Case and End Punctuation settings.

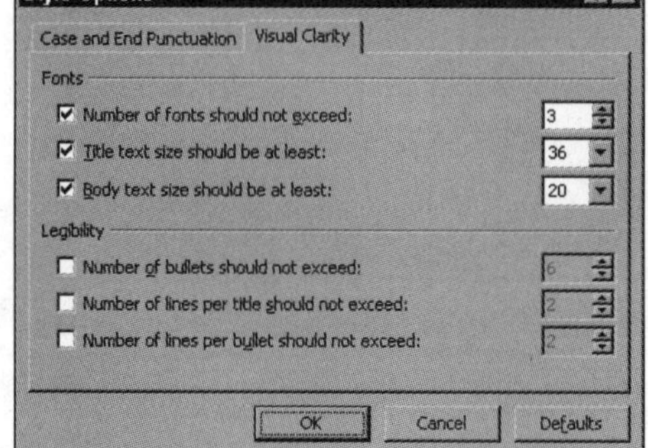

Figure 4-6: The Visual Clarity settings.

4. **Click OK if you like all this stuff and move on!**

Now, whenever PowerPoint detects a style problem, a light-bulb icon appears next to the text with questionable style (as shown in the margin). Click this icon to call up the Office Assistant (see Chapter 7), who cheerfully explains the problem and offers several possible solutions.

The style checker works only if you have the Office Assistant turned on.

Using the AutoCorrect Feature

PowerPoint includes an AutoCorrect feature that can automatically correct spelling errors and style errors as you type them. For example, if you accidentally type `teh`, PowerPoint automatically changes your text to `the`. And if you forget to capitalize the first word of a sentence, PowerPoint automatically capitalizes it for you.

Any time PowerPoint makes a correction you don't like, just press Ctrl+Z (or choose the Edit⇨Undo command) to undo the correction. For example, if you really intended to type `teh`, press Ctrl+Z immediately after PowerPoint corrects it to `the`.

If you move the insertion pointer back to a word that has been corrected (or if you click the word), a small blue line appears beneath the first letter of the word. Point the mouse at this blue line and the button shown in the margin appears. You can then click this button to bring up a menu that enables you to undo the correction that was made, tell PowerPoint to stop making that type of correction, or summon the AutoCorrect options dialog box to adjust your AutoCorrect settings.

To control PowerPoint's AutoCorrect feature, choose the Tools⇨AutoCorrect Options command. This brings forth the dialog box shown in Figure 4-7.

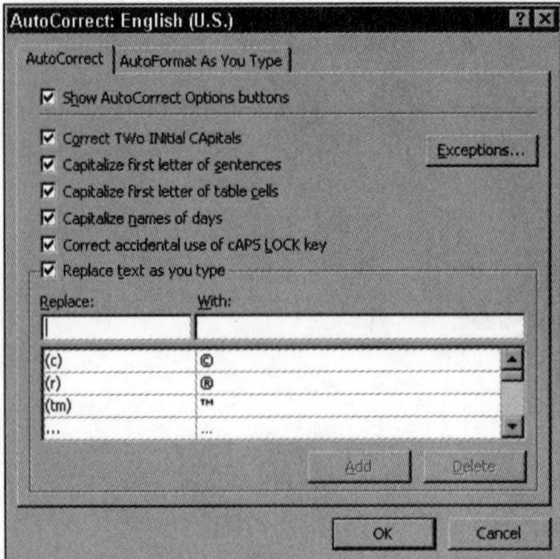

Figure 4-7: The AutoCorrect Options dialog box.

As you can see, the AutoCorrect Options dialog box contains check boxes for a variety of options that govern how AutoCorrect works:

- **Show AutoCorrect Options buttons:** This option displays the AutoCorrect button beneath words that were changed by the AutoCorrect feature, which allows you to undo the change or tell PowerPoint to stop making that particular type of correction.
- **Correct TWo INitial CApitals:** Looks for words with two initial capitals and changes the second one to lowercase. For example, if you type `BOther`, PowerPoint changes it to `Bother`. However, if you type three or more capitals in a row, PowerPoint assumes you did it on purpose so no correction is made.
- **Capitalize first letter of sentences:** Automatically capitalizes the first word of a new sentence if you forget.
- **Capitalize first letter of table cells:** Automatically capitalizes the first word in table cells.
- **Capitalize names of days:** You know, Monday, Tuesday, Wednesday, etc.
- **Correct accidental use of the cAPS LOCK key:** This is an especially cool feature. If PowerPoint notices that you're capitalizing everything backwards, it assumes you accidentally pressed the Caps Lock key. So it turns off Caps Lock and corrects the words that you capitalized backwards.
- **Replace text as you type:** This option is the heart of the AutoCorrect feature. It consists of a list of words that are frequently typed wrong, along with the replacement word. For example, `teh` is replaced by `the` and `adn` is replaced by `and`. The AutoCorrect list also contains some shortcuts for special symbols. For example, `(c)` is replaced by the copyright symbol (©) and `(tm)` is replaced by the TradeMark symbol (™).

You can add your own words to this list. Type the word you want PowerPoint to watch for in the Replace text box and the word you want PowerPoint to substitute for the first word in the With text box, then click the Add button.

The AutoCorrect feature also includes several formatting options that can automatically apply formats as you type. To set these options, click the AutoFormat As You Type tab. The options shown in Figure 4-8 appear. These options let you control formatting options such as automatically converting straight quotes to curly quotes, changing fractions such as `1/2` to actual fraction symbols such as ½, and so on.

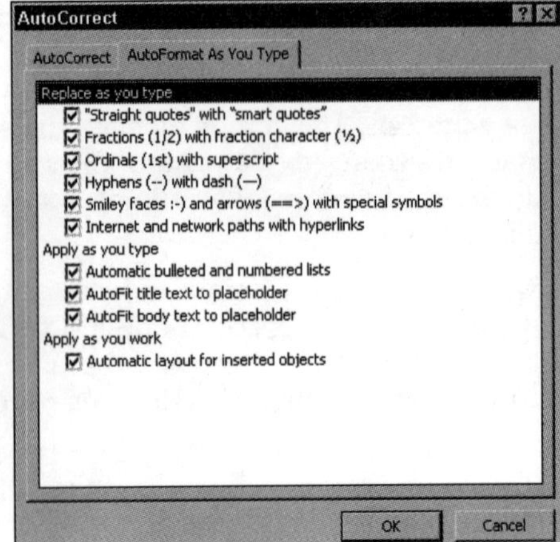

Figure 4-8: The AutoFormat As You Type options.

Chapter 5

Don't Forget Your Notes!

In This Chapter

- Creating speaker notes to get you through your presentation
- Adjusting the notes page to make long notes fit
- Adding a new slide from Notes Pages View
- Printing your notes pages

Ever had the fear — or maybe the actual experience — of showing a beautiful slide, complete with snappy text and perhaps an exquisite chart, and suddenly forgetting why you included the slide in the first place? You stumble for words. "Well, as you can see, this is a beautiful chart, and, uh, this slide makes the irrefutable point that, uh, well, I'm not sure — are there any questions?"

Fear not! One of the slickest features in PowerPoint is its ability to create speaker notes to help you get through your presentation. You can make these notes as complete or as sketchy as you want or need. You can write a complete script for your presentation or just jot down a few key points to refresh your memory.

The best part about speaker notes is that you're the only one who sees them. They don't actually show up on your slides for all the world to see. Instead, notes pages are printed separately. There's one notes page for each slide in the presentation, and each notes page includes a reduced version of the slide so that you can keep track of which notes page belongs to which slide.

One great feature of PowerPoint is that, assuming your computer has the hardware to pull it off, you can display your slides on a computer projector and your notes on a separate monitor so only you can see them. For more information about this feature, see the section "Displaying Notes on a Separate Monitor" later in this chapter.

Don't you think that it's about time for a short chapter? Although notes pages are one of the slickest features in PowerPoint, creating notes pages isn't all that complicated — hence the brevity of this chapter.

Understanding Notes

Notes are like an adjunct attachment to your slides. They don't appear on the slides themselves, but are displayed separately. Each slide in your presentation has its own page of notes.

In Normal View, the notes are hidden at the bottom of the screen in a separate Notes Pane. To work with notes in Normal View, you must first enlarge the Notes area to give yourself some room to work. For more information, see the section "Adding Notes to a Slide" later in this chapter.

PowerPoint also has a separate view designed for working with notes pages, called (you guessed it) Notes Page View. To call up Notes Page View, choose the View⇨Notes Page command. Figure 5-1 shows a slide in Notes Page View. Each notes page consists of a reduced version of the slide and an area for notes.

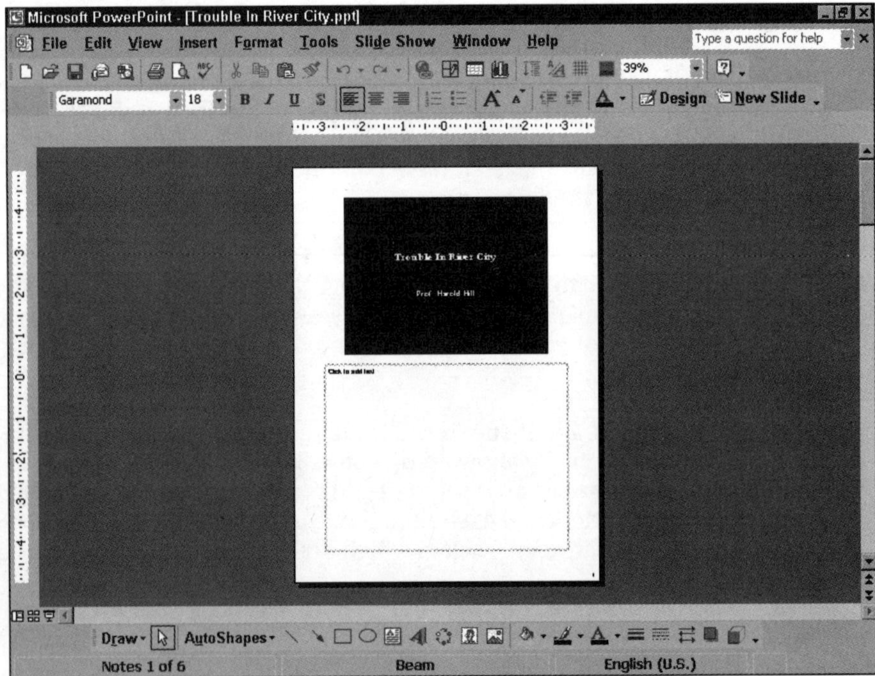

Figure 5-1: Notes Page View lets you see your notes.

Of course, these notes are too small to see or work with in Notes Page View unless you increase the zoom setting. If you want to work in Notes Page View, you'll need to zoom in so you can see your work.

Unfortunately, no keyboard shortcut is available to switch directly to Notes Page View. In earlier versions of PowerPoint, there was a button alongside the other view buttons in the lower-left corner of the screen. But for some mysterious reason, Microsoft decided to omit this button from PowerPoint 10. So the only way to get to Notes Page View now is to choose the View⇨Notes Page command.

Adding Notes to a Slide

To add notes to a slide, follow this procedure:

1. **In Normal view, move to the slide to which you want to add notes.**
2. **Click and drag the Notes Pane border, if necessary, to bring the notes text into view.**
3. **Click the notes text object, where it reads** `Click to add notes.`
4. **Type away.**

The text you type appears in the notes area. As you create your notes, you can use any of the PowerPoint standard word-processing features, such as cut, copy, and paste. Press the Enter key to create new paragraphs.

Figure 5-2 shows a slide with the Notes Pane enlarged to a comfortable size and some notes typed.

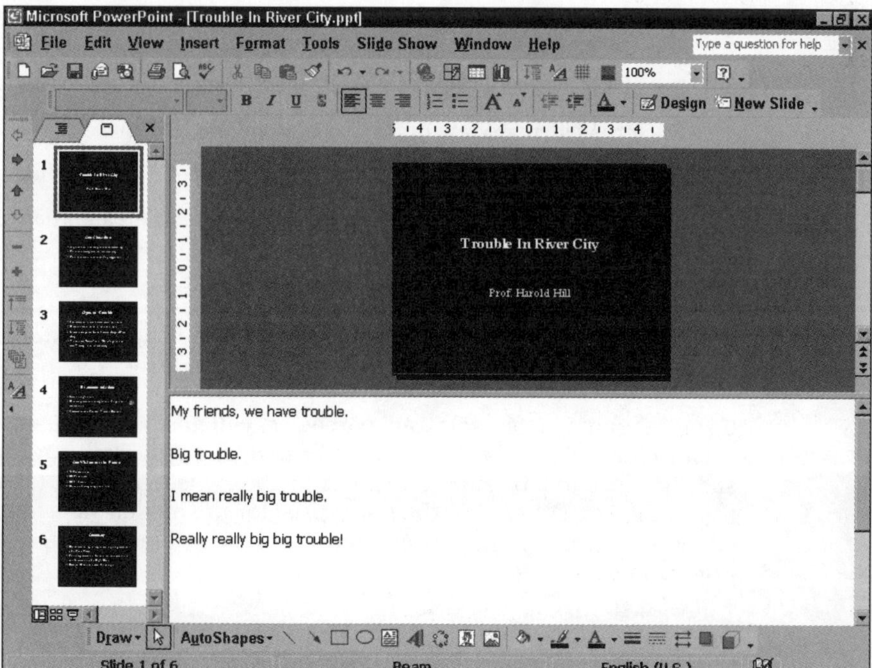

Figure 5-2: A slide with notes.

Adding an Extra Notes Page for a Slide

PowerPoint doesn't provide a way to add more than one page of notes for each slide. But these steps show a trick that accomplishes essentially the same thing:

1. **Create a duplicate slide immediately following the slide that requires two pages of notes.**

   To duplicate the slide, move to the slide you want to duplicate in Normal View, then choose the Insert⇨Duplicate Slide command.

2. **Switch to the Notes Page View.**

   The Notes Page for the new duplicate slide appears.

3. **Delete the slide object at the top of the duplicate notes page.**

   To do so, click the slide object at the top of the page and press the Delete key.

4. **Extend the notes text area up so that it fills the page.**

   To extend the notes area, just drag the top-center love handle of the notes area up.

5. **Type the additional notes for the preceding slide on this new notes page.**

   Add a heading, such as "Continued from slide 23," at the top of the text to help you remember that this portion is a continuation of notes from the preceding slide.

6. **Return to Normal View.**

   Click the Normal View button or choose View⇨Normal.

5. **Use the Slide Show⇨Hide Slide command to hide the slide.**

   The Hide Slide command hides the slide, which means that it isn't included in an on-screen slide show.

The result of this trick is that you now have two pages of notes for a single slide, and the second notes page doesn't have an image of the slide on it and is not included in your slide show.

If you're printing overhead transparencies, you may want to uncheck the Print Hidden Slides check box in the Print dialog box. That way, the hidden slide isn't printed. Be sure to recheck the box when you print the notes pages, though. Otherwise, the notes page for the hidden slide isn't printed either — and the reason you created the hidden slide in the first place was to print a notes page for it!

Think twice before creating a second page of notes for a slide. Do you really have that much to say about a single slide? Maybe the slide contains too much to begin with and should be split into two slides.

Adding a New Slide from Notes Page View

If you're working in Notes Page View and realize that you want to create a new slide, you don't have to return to Normal View. Just click the New Slide button on the Standard toolbar or use the Insert⇨New Slide menu command to add the new slide.

If you want to work on the slide's appearance or contents, however, you must switch back to Normal View. You can't modify a slide's appearance or contents from Notes Page View.

Printing Notes Pages

If you don't have a computer that can show your slides on a projector and your notes on a separate monitor, you can always print your notes on paper, then use the printed notes while you give your presentation. These steps show you how to print your notes:

1. **Choose the File⇨Print command.**

   The Print dialog box appears.

2. **Use the Print What list box to choose the Notes Pages option.**
3. **Make sure that the Print Hidden Slides box is checked if you want to print notes pages for hidden slides.**
4. **Click the OK button or press the Enter key.**

If you have just printed slides on overhead transparencies, don't forget to reload your printer with plain paper. You probably don't want to print your speaker notes on transparencies!

More information about printing is in Chapter 6.

Displaying Notes on a Separate Monitor

If you're lucky enough to have a computer that can use two monitors, you can display your notes on one monitor and connect a projector as the other monitor to show your slides. That way, you can see your notes on the monitor while your audience sees only the projected slides.

To enable this feature, call up the Slide Show⇨@Set Up Show command. This summons the Set Up Show dialog box. In the Multiple Monitors section of the dialog box, change the Display Slide Show On setting to Secondary Monitor. You switch to Notes View on the primary monitor to view your notes, and then start the slide show on the secondary monitor to show the slides on the projector.

Random Thoughts about Notes

This section provides some ideas that may help you make the most of your notes pages.

- If you're giving an important presentation for a large audience, you may want to consider using notes pages to write a complete script for your presentation. For less formal presentations, more succinct notes are probably better.
- Use notes pages to jot down any anecdotes, jokes, or other asides you want to remember to use in your presentation.
- If you prefer to handwrite your notes, you can print blank notes pages. Don't bother adding notes to your presentation, but use the File⇨Print command to print notes pages. The resulting notes pages have a reduced image of the slide at the top and a blank space in which you can handwrite your notes later.
- You may also consider providing blank notes pages for your audience. The File⇨Print command can print audience handouts that contain two, three, or six slides per page, but these handout pages leave no room for the audience members to write notes.

Chapter 6

Printing Your Presentation

In This Chapter

- Printing slides
- Printing handouts
- Printing speaker notes
- Printing an outline
- Previewing your output
- Troubleshooting

The Print command. The Printmeister. Big presentation comin' up. Printin' some slides. The Printorama. The Mentor of de Printor. Captain Toner of the Good Ship Laseroo.

Don't worry — when you print a PowerPoint Presentation, no one's waiting to ambush you with annoying one-liners like that guy who used to be on *Saturday Night Live*. Just a handful of boring dialog boxes with boring check boxes. Point-point, click-click, print-print. (Hey, humor me, okay? The French think that I'm a comic genius!)

The Quick Way to Print

The fastest way to print your presentation is to click the Print button found in the Standard toolbar. Clicking this button prints your presentation without further ado using the current settings for the Print dialog box, which I explain in the remaining sections of this chapter. Usually, this results in printing a single copy of all the slides in your presentation. But if you have altered the Print dialog box settings, clicking the Print button uses the altered settings automatically.

Using the Print Dialog Box

For precise control over how you want your presentation printed, you must conjure up the Print dialog box. You can do so in more ways than the government can raise revenue without calling it a tax, but the three most common are shown in this list:

- Choose the File➪Print command.
- Press Ctrl+P.
- Press Ctrl+Shift+F12.

Any of these actions summons the Print dialog box, shown in Figure 6-1. Like the genie in the Disney movie *Aladdin,* this box grants you three wishes, but with two limitations: It can't kill anyone ("ix-nay on the illing-kay"), and it can't make anyone fall in love with you.

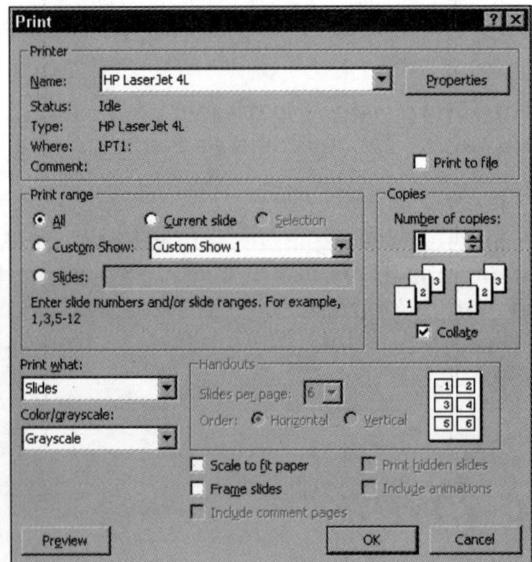

Figure 6-1: Behold the Print dialog box.

After you unleash the Print dialog box, click OK or press Enter to print all the slides in your presentation. Or fiddle around with the settings to print a select group of slides, print more than one copy, or print handouts, speaker notes, or an outline. This section shows you the treasures that lie hidden in this dialog box.

Printing can be es-el-oh-double-ewe. PowerPoint politely displays a status box to keep you informed of its progress, so at least you know that the darn program hasn't gone AWOL on you.

Don't panic if your printer doesn't start spewing forth pages immediately after the Print dialog box goes away. PowerPoint printouts tend to demand a great deal from the printer, so sometimes the printer has to work for a while before it can produce a finished page. Be patient. The Printer wizard has every intention of granting your request.

Oh, by the way, if you see a vague error message that says something like "Put paper in the printer, silly," try putting paper in the printer.

Changing printers

If you're lucky enough to have two or more printers at your disposal, you can use the Name field to pick which printer you want to use. Each printer must first be successfully installed in Windows 98 — a topic that's beyond the reach of this humble book, but that you will find plenty of information about in the appropriate version of Andy Rathbone's *Windows 98 For Dummies* (published by Hungry Minds, Inc.).

Even if your computer doesn't have two printers physically attached to it, your computer may be connected to a computer network that does have two or more printers. In that case, you can use the Name field to select one of these networked printers to print your presentation.

The Properties button calls forth the Windows Printer Properties dialog box, which lets you fuss with various printer settings. Avoid it if you can.

Printing part of a presentation

When you first use the Print command, the All option is checked so that your entire presentation prints. The other options in the Print Range portion of the Print dialog box enable you to tell PowerPoint to print just part of your presentation. In addition to All, you have four options:

- **Current slide**: Prints just the current slide. Before you invoke the Print command, you should move to the slide you want to print. Then check this option in the Print dialog box and click OK. This option is handy when you make a change to one slide and don't want to reprint the entire presentation.

- **Selection:** Prints just the portion of the presentation that you selected before invoking the Print command. This option is easiest to use in Outline or Slide Sorter View. First, select the slides you want to print by dragging the mouse to highlight them. Then invoke the Print command, click the Selection box, and click OK. (Note that if you don't select anything before you call up the Print dialog box, this field is grayed out, as shown in Figure 6-1.)
- **Custom Show:** If you have used the Slide Show⇨Custom Shows command to create custom slide shows, you can use this option to select the show you want to print.
- **Slides:** Enables you to select specific slides for printing. You can print a range of slides by typing the beginning and ending slide numbers, separated by a hyphen, as in *5-8* to print slides 5, 6, 7, and 8. Or you can list individual slides, separated by commas, as in *4,8,11* to print slides 4, 8, and 11. And you can combine ranges and individual slides, as in *4,9-11,13* to print slides 4, 9, 10, 11, and 13.

To print a portion of a presentation, first call up the Print dialog box. Next, select the Slide Range option you want. Then click OK or press Enter.

Printing more than one copy

The Number of Copies field in the Print dialog box enables you to tell PowerPoint to print more than one copy of your presentation. You can click one of the arrows next to this field to increase or decrease the number of copies, or you can type directly in the field to set the number of copies.

Below the Number of Copies field is a check box labeled Collate. If this box is checked, PowerPoint prints each copy of your presentation one at a time. In other words, if your presentation consists of ten slides and you select three copies and check the Collate box, PowerPoint first prints all ten slides of the first copy of the presentation, and then all ten slides of the second copy, and then all ten slides of the third copy. If you don't check the Collate box, PowerPoint prints three copies of the first slide, followed by three copies of the second slide, followed by three copies of the third slide, and so on.

The Collate option saves you from the chore of manually sorting your copies. If your presentation takes forever to print because it's loaded down with heavy-duty graphics, however, you probably can save time in the long run by unchecking the Collate box. Why? Because many printers are fast when it comes to printing a second or third copy of a page. The printer may spend ten minutes figuring out how to print a particularly complicated page, but after it figures it out, the printer can chug out umpteen copies of that page without hesitation. If you print collated copies, the printer must labor over each page separately for each copy of the presentation it prints.

What do you want to print?

The Print What field in the Print dialog box enables you to select which type of output that you want to print. The following choices are available:

- **Slides:** Prints slides. Note that if you have used build effects in the presentation, this option doesn't appear. Instead, it's replaced with two similar options: Slides (with Builds) and Slides (without Builds). If you don't know what builds are — and there's no reason you should, unless you've been reading ahead — just ignore the next two options.
- **Notes pages:** Prints speaker notes pages, which are covered in Chapter 5.
- **Handouts (With Slides per Page):** Prints audience handout pages. Select the number of slides you would like to appear on each handout page by clicking the Slides per Page box. You can also order the slides to appear horizontally or vertically on the handout.
- **Outline View:** Prints an outline of your presentation.

Select the type of output that you want to print and then click OK or press Enter. Off you go!

When you're printing slides to be used as overhead transparencies, print a proof copy of the slides on plain paper before committing the output to transparencies. Transparencies are too expensive to print on until you're sure that your output is just right.

To change the orientation of your printed output from Landscape to Portrait mode (or vice versa), use the File⇨Slide Setup command.

To print handouts with two, three, or six slides per page, PowerPoint naturally must shrink the slides to make them fit. Because slides usually have outrageously large type, the handout slides are normally still readable, even at their reduced size.

What are all those other controls?

The Print command has several additional controls, which hide out near the bottom of the dialog box, hoping to slip by unnoticed. This list shows you what they do:

- **Color/grayscale:** This drop-down list box lets you choose whether to print your slides in color, black and white, or with shades of gray.

Note: Microsoft considered licensing TurnerVision technology to colorize slides printed with the Black & White option, but decided against it when it was discovered that most audiences dream in black and white when they fall asleep during a boring presentation.

- **Scale to fit paper:** Adjusts the size of the printed output to fit the paper in the printer. Leave this option unchecked to avoid bizarre printing problems.
- **Frame slides:** Draws a thin border around the slides.
- **Include comment pages:** If you've added comments to your slides, you can print the comments on separate pages by choosing this option. This option is grayed out if the presentation has no comments.
- **Print hidden slides:** You can hide individual slides by way of the Tools➪Hide Slide command. After a slide is hidden, it does not print unless you check the Print Hidden Slides option in the Print dialog box. This option is grayed out if the presentation has no hidden slides.
- **Include Animations:** If you used animation effects to build slide show text and you check the Include Animations box, a separate page prints for each bulleted item on the slide. The first page has just the first bulleted item; the second page shows the first and second bullets; and so on. This option is grayed out if the presentation does not use animation.

Using the Print Preview Command

After many years, PowerPoint 10 has now been blessed with a command that other Office programs (such as Word and Excel) have had for years: Print Preview, which lets you see how your pages will appear before committing them to paper (or transparencies). To use the Print Preview feature, choose File➪Print Preview or click the Print Preview button (shown in the margin). A preview of the printed page appears, as shown in Figure 6-2.

From the Print Preview screen, you can zoom in to examine the preview more closely by clicking anywhere in the preview area. Or, you can scroll through the pages using the scroll bar, the Page Up and Page Down keys, or the Prev Page and Next Page buttons located at the top-left corner of the screen (shown in the margin).

When you're satisfied that the printout will be satisfactory, click the Print button to print the presentation. If you discover a mistake in the preview, click Close to return to PowerPoint so you can correct the mistake before printing your slides.

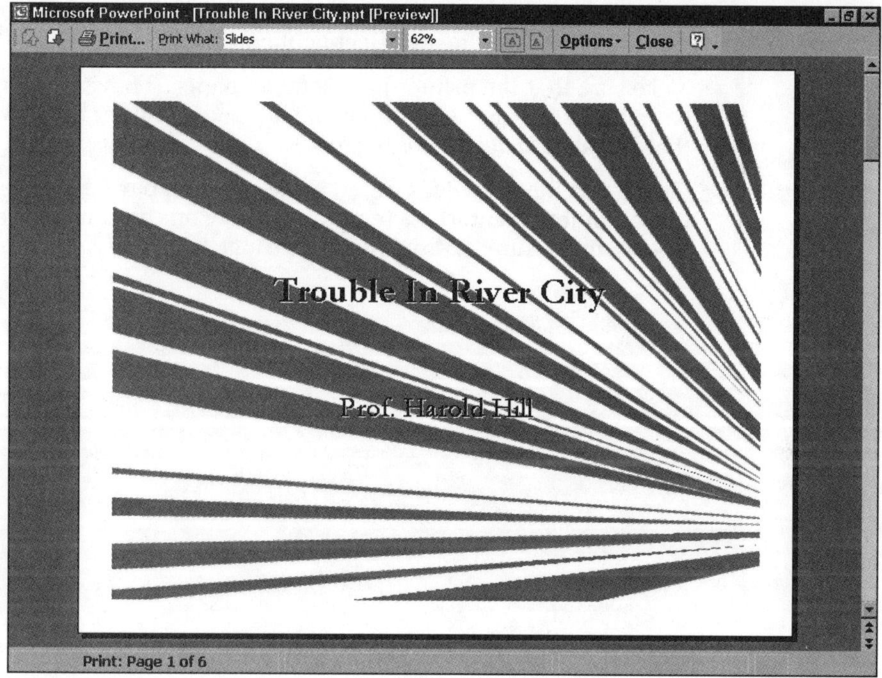

Figure 6-2: Previewing your printed output.

Printing Boo-Boos

On the surface, printing seems as though it should be one of the easiest parts of using PowerPoint. After all, all you have to do to print a presentation is click the Print button, right? Well, usually. Unfortunately, all kinds of things can go wrong between the time you click the Print button and the time gorgeous output bursts forth from your printer. If you run into printer trouble, check out the things discussed in this section.

Your printer must be ready and raring to go before it can spew out printed pages. If you suspect that your printer is not ready for action, this list presents some things to check:

- Make sure that the printer's power cord is plugged in and that the printer is turned on.
- The printer cable must be connected to both the printer and the computer's printer port. If the cable has come loose, turn off both the computer and the printer, reattach the cable, and then restart the computer and the printer. (You know better, of course, than to turn off your computer without first saving any work in progress, exiting from any active application programs, and shutting down Windows. So I won't say anything about it. Not even one little word.)

- If your printer has a switch labeled On-line or Select, press it until the corresponding On-line or Select light comes on.
- Make sure that the printer has plenty of paper. (I have always wanted to write a musical about a printer that ate people rather than paper. I think that I'll call it *Little DOS of Horrors.*)
- If you're using an ink-jet printer, make sure you have plenty of ink. PowerPoint presentations tend to be heavy on the color. For a laser printer, make sure that the toner cartridge has plenty of life left in it.

Chapter 7

Show Time!

In This Chapter

- Running a slide show
- Getting the John Madden effect
- Using the Meeting Minder
- Using custom shows

You can play some really slick tricks during an on-computer slide show with PowerPoint 2002. You can use the mouse (or keyboard) to move from slide to slide, to go back to a slide that you've already shown, or to skip a slide. And you can use the mouse to doodle on your slides, underlining or circling key points as you go (I call this the "John Madden Effect," in honor of the former football coach who circles plays with great relish on telecasts). This chapter shows you how to employ these nifty tricks to bedazzle your audience.

But before you go to the play-by-play section of this chapter, consider your audience. PowerPoint culture is changing as Internet and intranet broadcasting becomes more common and as projection devices become staples in everyone's office. There are really three ways you can present an on-computer slide show:

- In a one-on-one meeting.
- In a large group setting with a computer data projector.
- Using Presentation Broadcast (explained in Chapter 20).

For all three types of slide show there are many similarities. This chapter focuses on live presentations. For presentations on your intranet or Internet, see Chapter 21. Whichever method you use, however, you first have to set up your show.

Setting Up a Slide Show

To set up a slide show so it can be presented on your computer, first open the presentation you want to set up, then choose the Slide Show⇨Set Up Show command. This summons the Set Up Show dialog box, shown in Figure 7-1. With this dialog box, you can twiddle with the various options that are available for presenting slide shows.

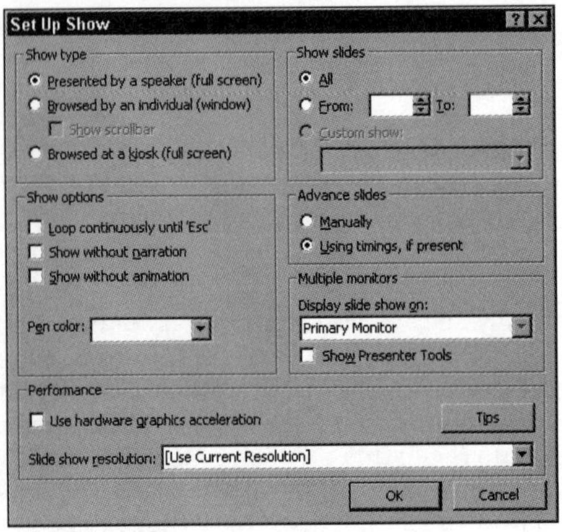

Figure 7-1: The Set Up Show dialog box.

With the options on the Set Up Show dialog box, you can do the following:

- Configure the presentation for one of three basic slide show types: Presented by a Speaker (Full Screen), Browsed by an Individual (Window), or Browsed at a Kiosk (Full Screen).
- Choose Loop Continuously until Esc if you want the show to run indefinitely. If you enable this setting, the show jumps back to the first slide after the last slide is shown, and continues to repeat until you press the Esc key.
- Choose to show the slide show without narrations or animations if you want to simplify the presentation by not playing narrations you've recorded or animations you've created.
- Select the color to use for the pen. (See "The John Madden Effect" later in this chapter for more information about using the pen.)
- Choose All to include all slides in the slide show, or choose From and supply starting and ending slide numbers if you want to display just some of the slides in the presentation.
- Choose Custom Show if you have set up any custom shows within your presentation. (See the section "Using Custom Shows" later in this chapter for more information.)

- Choose Manually to advance from slide to slide by pressing the Enter key, pressing the spacebar, or clicking the mouse button. Or, if you want the show to proceed automatically, choose Using Timings, if present.
- If your computer has two monitors, select the monitor to use for the slide show using the drop-down list in the Multiple Monitors section.

Starting a Slide Show

When you start a slide show in a one-on-one or small group setting without a projector, beginning is just a click away.

To start a slide show immediately, click the Slide Show button (shown in the margin). If you have set up a full-screen slide show, PowerPoint replaces the entire screen with the first slide of the slide show. To advance to the next slide, click the mouse, press Enter, the down arrow, the Page Down key, or the spacebar. You can also start a slide show by choosing the View⇨Slide Show command or the Slide Show⇨View Show command.

To start the slide show from the first slide, make sure the first slide of the show is selected. (Press Ctrl+Home to call up the first slide.)

You can also start a slide show by using the keyboard shortcut, F5, or by choosing the View⇨Slide Show command or the Slide Show⇨View Show command.

If you've configured PowerPoint to display the slide show on a secondary monitor, the slide show runs on the secondary monitor. The primary monitor still displays the presentation in Normal View. If you want, you can switch to Notes View on the primary monitor to display your notes while the slides are displayed on the Secondary monitor. (For more information about displaying notes on one monitor and slides on another, refer to Chapter 5.)

Setting Up a Projector

If you're going to present your show using a computer projector and a laptop computer, you need to know how to connect the computer to your laptop computer as well as how to set up the projector, turn it on, focus it, and so on. Most of these details vary from one projector to the next, so you'll have to consult the manual that came with the projector or bribe someone to set the projector up for you. The following paragraphs describe a few general tips that may help:

- Most laptop computers have an external video port on the back, and most projectors have a video input connection. A standard VGA monitor cable works to connect the computer to the projector.

- To use the laptop with a projector, you must first activate the external video port. Some laptops have a key you can press to do this; others require that you twiddle with the display settings to activate the external video port. If you can't figure out how to make the switch, try right-clicking an empty area of the desktop and choosing Properties from the menu that appears. Click the Settings tab, then click the Advanced button and look for a setting to enable the external video port. (On my Toshiba laptop, this setting is located in the Display Device tab of the dialog box that appears when I click the Advanced button.)
- Most projectors can accept input from more than one source. For example, you may be able to connect a computer and a VCR to the projector. The projector should have some buttons or perhaps a menu setting that lets you select the input that is used to display the projected image. If you connect your computer to the projector and everything else seems okay but you still don't get a picture, make sure the projector is set to the correct input.
- If you want to use the projector's remote control to operate your presentation, you'll need the appropriate cable to connect the projector to your laptop computer's mouse port. The correct cable should come with the projector.
- Finally, if your presentation has sound, you'll need to connect your computer's sound outputs to a set of amplified speakers or, if you're showing the presentation in a large auditorium, a PA system. The correct cable to connect to a PA system depends on the PA system, but a cable with a mini-stereo plug on one end and a ¼" plug on the other will probably do the trick.

Keyboard and Mouse Tricks for Your Slide Show

During an on-screen slide show, you can use the keyboard and mouse to control your presentation. Tables 7-1 and 7-2 list the keys and clicks you can use.

Table 7-1 Keyboard Tricks for Your Slide Show

To Do This	*Press Any of These Keys*
Display next slide	Enter, spacebar, Page Down, N
Display preceding slide	Backspace, Page Up, P
Display first slide	1+Enter
Display specific slide	Slide number+Enter

To Do This	Press Any of These Keys
Toggle screen black	B, period
Toggle screen white	W, comma
Show or hide pointer	A, = (equals sign)
Erase screen doodles	E
Stop or restart automatic show	S, + (plus sign)
Display next slide even if hidden	H
Display specific hidden slide	Slide number of hidden slide+Enter
Change pen to arrow	Ctrl+A
Change arrow to pen	Ctrl+P
End slide show	Esc, Ctrl+Break (the Break key doubles as the Pause key), – (minus)

Table 7-2 Mouse Tricks for Your Slide Show

To Do This	Do This
Display next slide or build	Click
Move through slides	Roll the wheel on your mouse (if your mouse has one)
Call up menu of actions	Right-click
Display first slide	Hold down both mouse buttons for two seconds
Doodle	Press Ctrl+P to change the mouse arrow to a pen and then draw on-screen like John Madden

The John Madden Effect

If you've always wanted to diagram plays on-screen the way John Madden does, try using the pen during a slide show. Here's how:

1. **Start a slide show.**
2. **When you want to doodle on a slide, press Ctrl+P.**

   The mouse arrow pointer changes to a pen shape.

3. **Draw away.**

   Figure 7-2 shows an example of a doodled-upon slide.

4. **To erase your doodles, press E.**

Drawing doodles like this requires good mouse dexterity. With practice, you can create all kinds of interesting doodles. Work on circling text or drawing exclamation or question marks, smiley faces, and so on.

Keep these tasty tidbits in mind when doodling:

- To hide the mouse pointer temporarily during a slide show, press *A* or the equal sign (=). The pointer returns the moment you move the mouse, or you can press *A* or (=*)* again to summon it back.
- If you use the pen, be sure to say "Bam" and "Pow" a lot.
- To turn off the Doodle button, press the equals sign (=) on your keyboard.

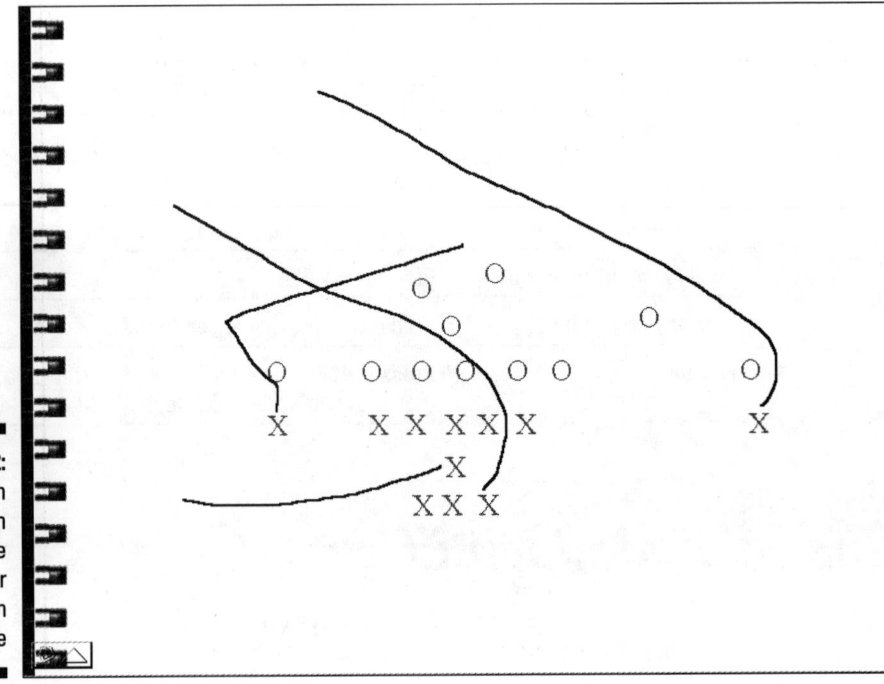

Figure 7-2: John Madden would love Power Point's Pen feature

You can also right-click the mouse for a floating menu of these choices; however, this may be a little more distracting for your audience than the keystrokes as the audience will suddenly be privy to all your fancy footwork. But, do notice that the menu allows you to change pen colors and a few other tricks. You can set up the pen color before you begin your presentation so as not to distract via the Slide Show⇨Set Up Show command. If you have a remote mouse and you won't have access to your keyboard during your presentation, I suggest you investigate the floating menu method.

Rehearsing Your Slide Timings

You can use the PowerPoint Rehearsal feature to rehearse your presentation. The rehearsal lets you know how long your presentation takes, and it can even set slide timings so that the slides automatically advance based on the timings you set during the rehearsal.

To rehearse a slide show, summon the Slide Show⇨Rehearse Timings command. This starts the slide show, with a special Rehearsal dialog box visible, as shown in Figure 7-3.

Figure 7-3: Rehearsing a slide show.

Now rehearse your presentation. Click the mouse or use keyboard shortcuts to advance slides. As you rehearse, PowerPoint keeps track of how long you display each slide and the total length of your presentation.

When you dismiss the final slide, PowerPoint displays a dialog box that gives you the option of applying the timings recorded during the rehearsal to the slides in the presentation or ignoring the rehearsal timings. If you were satisfied with the slide timings during the rehearsal, click Yes.

If you mess up during a rehearsal, click the Repeat button (shown in the margin). Clicking this button restarts the rehearsal from the beginning.

The Meeting Minder

PowerPoint includes a nifty feature called the Meeting Minder, which allows you to take notes during a presentation. To use the Meeting Minder, right-click the mouse during a slide show and choose the Meeting Minder command. The dialog box shown in Figure 7-4 appears.

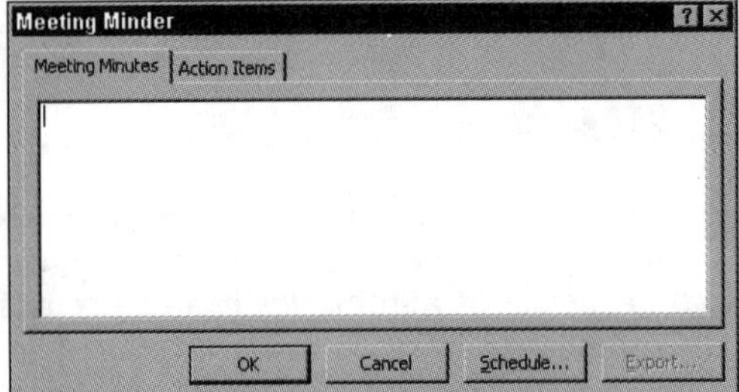

Figure 7-4: Mind your own meetings with the Meeting Minder.

As you can see, the Meeting Minder has two tabbed areas. You can use these areas as follows:

- **Meeting Minutes:** Click the Meeting Minutes tab to keep minutes during a meeting. When you are finished, you can then click the Export button and convert the minutes to a Word document.
- **Action Items:** Click the Action Items tab to record items that require action following the meeting. Anything you type here is added to the last slide of the presentation, titled "Action Items." That way, the action items are automatically displayed at the end of the presentation.

Running a Presentation over a Network

PowerPoint allows you to run presentation conferences over a computer network, which basically means that you can run a slide show and invite other network users to view the slide show on their computers. Because this feature uses Web technology to give it its "oomph," all viewers around the world or down the hall need to view your broadcast is a browser. For more information about this Presentation Broadcast Web phenomenon, check out Chapter 20.

Using Custom Shows

Custom Shows is a PowerPoint feature that lets you create several similar slide shows stored in a single presentation file. For example, suppose you are asked to give presentations about company benefits to management and non-management staff. You can create a presentation containing slides for all the company benefits and then create a custom show containing only those slides describing benefits that are available to non-management staff. This custom slide show can leave out slides such as "Executive Washrooms," "Golf Days," and "Boondoggles." You may then show the complete presentation to management, but show the custom show to non-management staff.

A presentation can contain as many custom shows as you want. Each custom show is simply a subset of the complete presentation — made up of selected slides from the complete presentation.

Creating a custom show

To create a custom show, follow these steps:

1. **Choose the Slide Show⇨Custom Shows command.**

   This displays the Custom Shows dialog box.

2. **Click the New button.**

   The Define Custom Show dialog box appears, as shown in Figure 7-5.

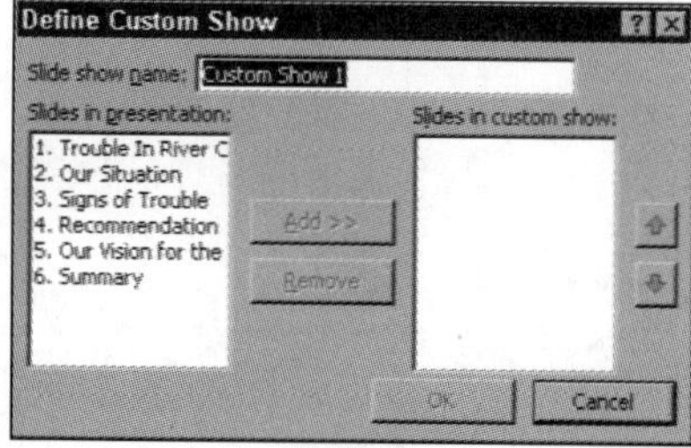

Figure 7-5: Defining a custom show.

3. **Type a name for the custom show in the Slide Show Name field.**

4. **Add the slides you want to appear in the custom slide show.**

   All the slides available in the presentation are listed in the list box on the left side of the Define Custom Show dialog box. To add a slide to the custom show, click the slide you want to add, and then click Add. The slide you added appears in the list box on the right side of the Define Custom Show dialog box.

You don't have to add slides to the custom show in the same order that the slides appear in the presentation. Slides for a custom show can appear in any order you want. You can also include a slide from the original presentation more than once in a custom show.

To remove a slide you've added by mistake, click the slide you want to remove in the list box on the right side of the Define Custom Show dialog box, and then click Remove.

5. **Click OK.**

   You return to the Custom Shows dialog box.

6. **Click Close to dismiss the Custom Shows dialog box.**

Showing a custom show

To show a custom show, first open the presentation that contains the custom show. Then, choose the Slide Show⇨Custom Shows command to summon the Custom Shows dialog box. Click the custom show you want, and then click the Show button.

You can also call up a custom show during a slide show by right-clicking the mouse anywhere in the presentation, choosing the Go⇨Custom Shows command, and clicking the custom show you want to display.

Chapter 8

Help!

In This Chapter

- Using the Office Assistant
- Accessing Help
- Finding help that holds your hand
- Searching for specific Help topics
- Getting help on the Internet
- Fixing PowerPoint problems

The ideal way to use PowerPoint would be to have a PowerPoint expert sitting patiently at your side, answering your every question with a straightforward answer, gently correcting you when you make silly mistakes, and otherwise minding his or her own business. All you'd have to do is occasionally toss the expert a Twinkie and let him or her outside once a day.

The good news is that PowerPoint has such an expert built in. This expert is referred to as the Office Assistant, and he works not just with PowerPoint, but with other Microsoft Office programs, including Word, Excel, Access, and Outlook. You don't even have to feed the Office Assistant, unlike a real guru.

Meet the Assistant

Alexander Graham Bell had Watson, Batman had Robin, and Dr. Frankenstein had Igor. Everybody needs an Assistant, and Office users are no exception. That's why Microsoft decided to bless Office with the Office Assistant, a handy fellow who offers helpful assistance as you work with Office programs, including PowerPoint.

The Office Assistant is an animated persona who suddenly morphs onto your desktop with sage advice and suggestions and even a little idea light that gives you a clue that you can use a clue! You can also ask the Office Assistant a question when you're not sure what to do, and the Assistant thoroughly searches the PowerPoint online Help database to provide the answer.

When you first start PowerPoint, the Office Assistant appears, as shown in Figure 8-1. As you can see, my Office Assistant resembles a cute little pooch. As it turns out, this one — named Rocky — is but one of seven Assistants that you can choose from. See the section "Changing Assistants" later in this chapter for instructions on how to switch to a different Assistant.

Figure 8-1: Meet Rocky, an Office Assistant.

The fun thing about the Assistant is that he is animated. Watch the Assistant on-screen as you work. Every once in a while he blinks, and on occasion he dances or makes a face. The Assistant often responds to commands that you choose in PowerPoint. For example, if you call up the Find command (Edit⇨Find or Ctrl+F), the Assistant makes a gesture as if he is searching for something. And when you print your presentation, the Assistant does some cute little printer schtick. Microsoft went to a lot of trouble to make sure that the Assistant is entertaining, and the results are sometimes amusing. When you ask the Assistant for help, he sits down, plops his feet up on a desk, and takes copious notes — don't you wish real people cared so much!

Notice that the Assistant has a special type of dialog box called a *balloon*, which includes an area for you to type a question and several buttons that you can click. The balloon functions like any other dialog box, but it has a special appearance that's unique to the Assistant.

PowerPoint used to have Help topics that you simply clicked and used, but now Help is driven by the user interacting with the Assistant. Most of the time, if you type in your question nicely and ask pretty-please, the Assistant answers with information on the appropriate Help subject.

When you click any topic presented by the Assistant, you see two boxes at the bottom of the Assistant's balloon — one that says Options, and another that says Search. If you choose Options, a dialog box appears that allows you to turn off the Assistant. If you do turn off the Assistant, the Help functions behave differently (a topic I cover later in this chapter in "Help the Old-Fashioned Way").

Summoning the Assistant

You can summon the Assistant in several ways when you need help. In many cases, the Assistant is already on the screen, so all you need to do to get his attention is click the Assistant. This action pops up the balloon dialog box so that you can ask a question.

If the Assistant isn't visible on-screen, you can summon him quickly by using one of the following three methods:

- Choose the Help⇨Microsoft PowerPoint Help command from the menu.
- Press F1, the magic Help key.
- Click the Help button in the Standard toolbar.

Sometimes the Assistant figures out that you're struggling with something and offers some helpful assistance all on its own. For example, if you try to select an object that's on the slide master (which you can only select in Slide Master View), the Assistant tells you why you can't select the object, as shown in Figure 8-2. The Assistant offers to take you to the master view so you can select the background object, or to tell you more about masters.

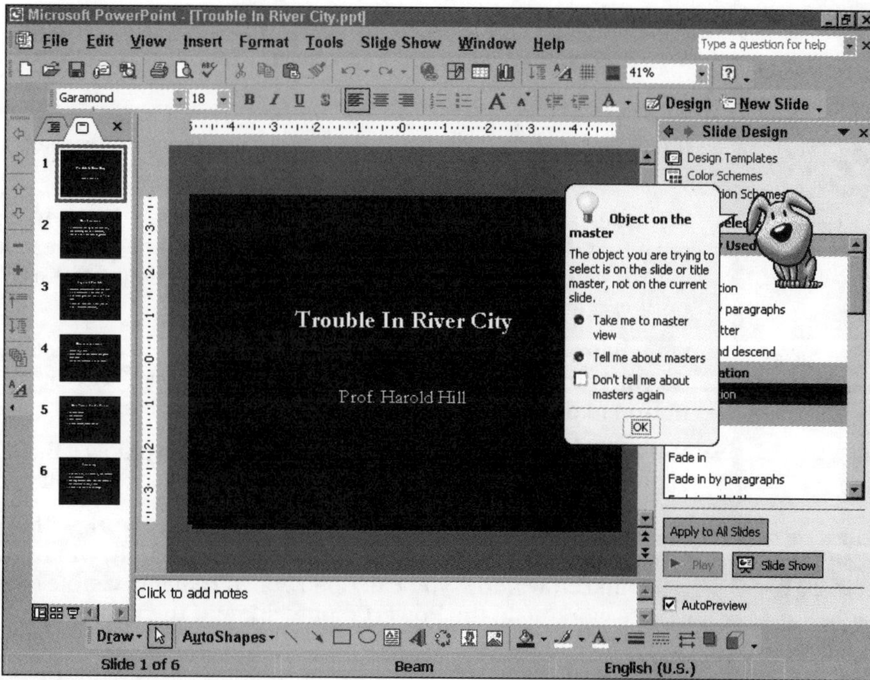

Figure 8-2: The Assistant offers friendly advice.

If you click on the option to tell you more about masters, a help screen such as the one shown in Figure 8-3 appears. As you can see, the Help topic in Figure 8-3 explains what masters are and provides information about using them.

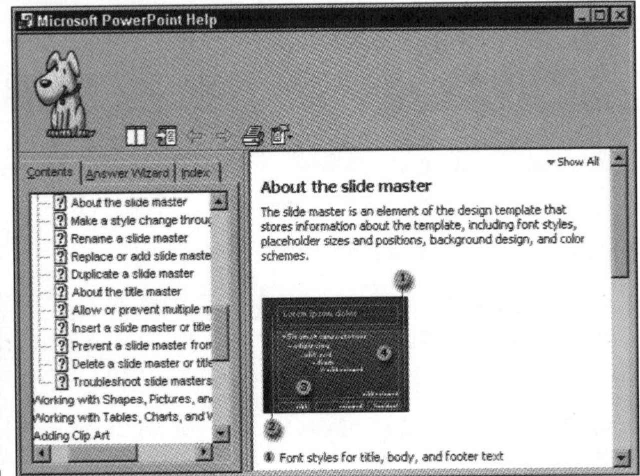

Figure 8-3: A Help topic about working with masters.

After you get yourself this deep into Help, you need to heed the following advice to find your way around and get out when you find out what you want to know:

- If you find a Help topic that you consider uncommonly useful, click the Print button and print the darn thing.
- If you see an underlined word or phrase, you can click it to zip to a Help page that describes that word or phrase. By following these underlined words, you can bounce your way around from Help page to Help page until you eventually find the help you need.
- Sometimes, Help offers several choices under a heading such as "What do you want to do?" Each choice is preceded by a little button; click the button to display step-by-step help for that choice.
- You can retrace your steps by clicking the Help window's Back button. You can use Back over and over again, retracing all your steps if necessary.

- Help operates as a separate program, so you can work within PowerPoint while the Help window remains on-screen. The Help window appears as a minimized window you can open which remains visible even when you're working in the PowerPoint window. If the Help window gets in the way, you can move it out of the way by dragging it by the title bar. Or you can minimize it by clicking the minimize button in the top-right corner of the window.

- When you've had enough of Help, you can dismiss it by pressing Esc or clicking the close button in the upper-right corner of the Help window.

Take-You-by-the-Hand Help

Many PowerPoint Help screens include a special Show Me button. Click this button, and the Assistant actually helps you accomplish the task at hand. For example, if you click the Show Me button from the Change the Way Text Looks topic page, the Assistant delivers you straight to the Font dialog box, where you can select the text options you want.

Asking a Question

If none of the Help topics offered by the Assistant seem to be what you're looking for, you can type a question right in the Assistant's balloon dialog box to look for help on a specific dialog box. For example, if you want to know how to change the background color of a slide, type **How do I change the background color of a slide?** in the text box and then click the Search button or press Enter. The Assistant responds by displaying Help topics that relate to your question, as shown in Figure 8-4.

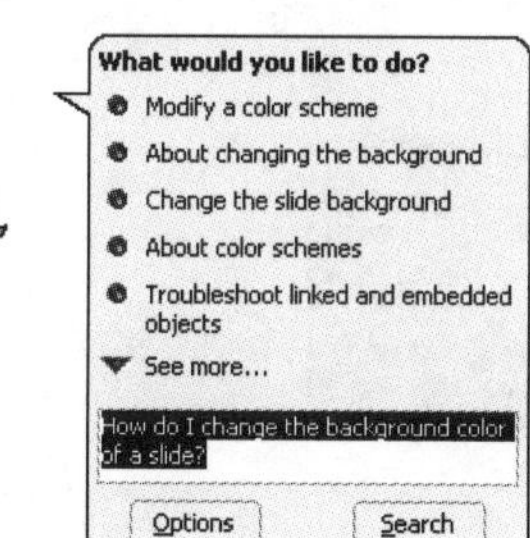

Figure 8-4: The Assistant answers a question.

If one of the topics looks promising, click it. Or click See more to see whether the Assistant can come up with other topics related to your question.

If none of the topics seem related to the question you asked, try rephrasing the question and clicking Search again.

You don't actually have to phrase your question as a question. You can eliminate words such as *How do I,* and you can also usually eliminate "noise words" such as *a, an, the, of, in,* and *so on*. Thus, the brief question "change background color slide" yields exactly the same result as the more verbose "How do I change the background color of a slide?"

Getting a Tip

As I mention earlier, every once in a while, a light bulb appears in the Assistant's word balloon, or even in the middle of your slide. When this light bulb appears, you can click it to see a tip that the Assistant thinks may be useful. If the tip is worthwhile, plant a big fat kiss on the Assistant (not literally!) and be thankful. If not, feel free to roll your eyes and act annoyed.

Changing Assistants

Rocky, the friendly and loyal cyberpup Assistant, is but one of seven Assistants that you can choose from. To select a different Assistant, summon the Assistant by clicking the Help button or pressing F1. Then click the Options button to display the Office Assistant dialog box. Click the Gallery tab located at the top of this dialog box. The Assistant Gallery is displayed, as shown in Figure 8-5.

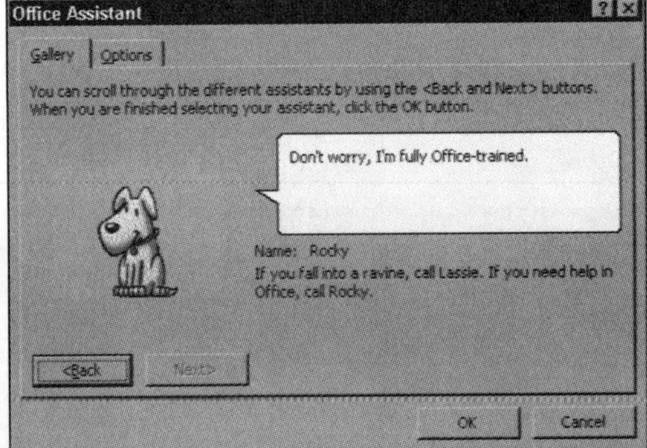

Figure 8-5: The Assistant Gallery

To change to a different Assistant, click the Next button. Keep clicking the Next button to work your way through all the Assistants. When you find the one that you want to use, click OK.

After you've clicked the Next button once, you can use the Back button to move backwards through the list of Assistants. Figure 8-6 shows all the Assistants.

These Assistants differ only in appearance, not in their ability to offer assistance with using PowerPoint features.

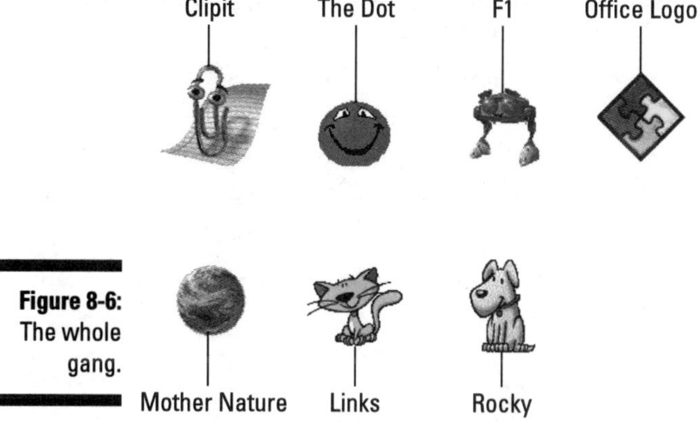

Figure 8-6: The whole gang.

Setting Assistant Options

You can configure the Assistant with several options that alter the way it works. To change these options, summon the Assistant and click the Options button to summon the dialog box shown in Figure 8-7. Change whatever options you want to change and then click OK.

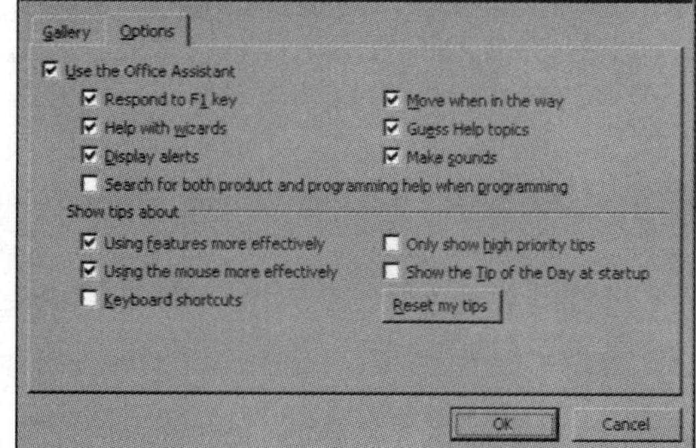

Figure 8-7: Changing the Office Assistant options.

The following list describes each of the Office Assistant options:

- **Use the Office Assistant:** Turns the Assistant on or off until further notice.
- **Respond to F1 key:** Summons the Office Assistant whenever you press F1.
- **Help with wizards:** Activates the Office Assistant whenever you use a PowerPoint Wizard.

- **Display alerts:** Uses the Assistant to display warnings about saving your file before exiting PowerPoint and so on.
- **Move when in the way:** Automatically moves the Assistant dialog box whenever it obscures what you're working on.
- **Guess Help topics:** Attempts to guess what topics you need help with.
- **Make sounds:** If you want the Assistant to make noises to get your attention, select this option.
- **Search for both product and programming help when programming:** If you're a programmer, check this option. Otherwise, leave it blank.
- **Show tips about:** Offers five categories of tips that Assistant can provide: using features, using the mouse, using keyboard shortcuts showing only high priority tips, (so that minor tips don't appear), and showing a Tip of the Day automatically when you start PowerPoint.

Help the Old-Fashioned Way

The Assistant isn't the only way to get help in PowerPoint 2002. PowerPoint 2002 still offers help the old-fashioned Windows way through the traditional Help interface.

To summon old-fashioned topic menu Help, first turn off the Assistant by summoning the Assistant Options dialog box and unchecking the Use the Office Assistant check box, as described in the previous section. Then press F1 or choose the Help➪Microsoft PowerPoint Help command. This summons the Help table of contents, shown in Figure 8-8.

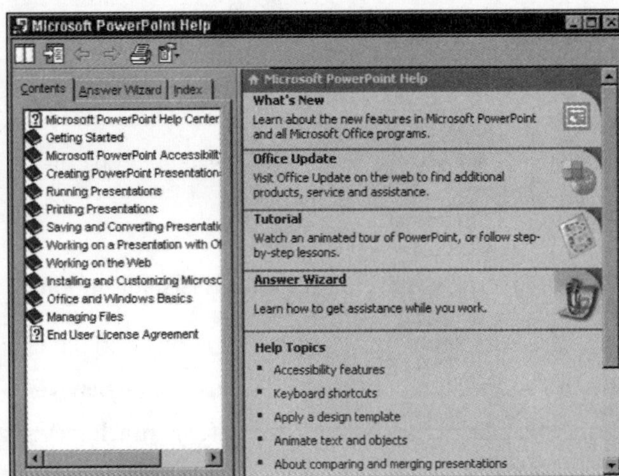

Figure 8-8: Good old-fashioned help.

To display help on one of the topics listed in the Help table of contents, just double-click the topic. Doing so expands the Help Contents to show the help that's available for a specific topic. For example, Figure 8-9 shows the expanded Help Contents for Creating PowerPoint Presentations.

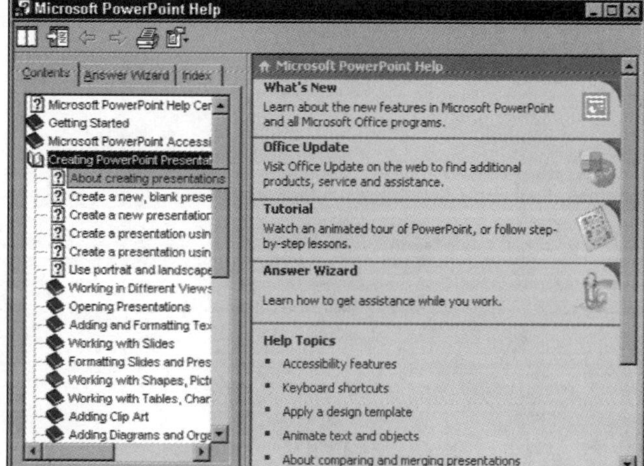

Figure 8-9: Looking up Help topics in the table of contents.

To display a particular Help topic, double-click the topic title in the contents list.

Searching for Lost Help Topics

If you can't find help for a nasty problem by browsing through the Help Contents, try using the Help Index. It lets you browse through an alphabetical listing of all the Help topics that are available. With luck, you can quickly find the help you're looking for.

When you click the Index tab in the Help topics dialog box, the screen shown in Figure 8-10 appears. Here you can type the text that you want to search for to zip quickly through the list to the words that you want to find.

If you see a match that looks as if it may be helpful, double-click it. Doing so takes you directly to help for that topic or displays a list of related topics. Double-click the topic that you want to display.

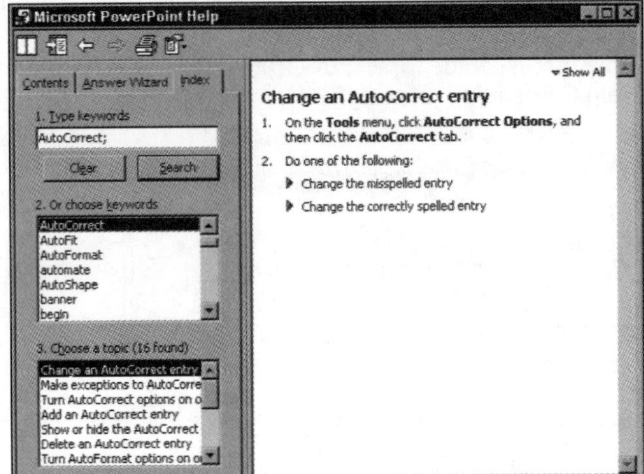

Figure 8-10: Help's Index.

Getting Help on the Internet

In addition to the help that's built in to PowerPoint, you can also get PowerPoint help from the Internet. All you need is an Internet connection. (If you don't have an Internet connection, get a copy of my book, *Internet Explorer 5.5 For Windows For Dummies,* published by Hungry Minds, Inc. That book shows you how to access the Internet using the popular Microsoft Internet Explorer program.)

To seek help on the Internet, choose the Help➪Office on the Web command. PowerPoint in turn launches Internet Explorer, the Microsoft program for accessing the Internet, provided free with PowerPoint and Office. Internet Explorer then politely connects to the Internet and displays the Microsoft support page. On the PowerPoint support page, you can ask your question through a search engine.

You may want to check out the Microsoft PowerPoint home page for the variety of downloads and bells and whistles that can make your PowerPoint application the Master of the Universe. (You can even find tie-dyed template backgrounds for your presentation if you're a throwback or just artistic.)

Repairing a Broken Office

If PowerPoint doesn't seem to be working right — for example, if it locks up your computer when you use certain commands or if features seem to be missing — you can use the built-in Office repair tool to detect and correct problems. To use the repair tool, first locate your PowerPoint or Office Setup CD. Then, choose the Help⇨Detect and Repair command. Follow the instructions that appear on the screen. If the repair tool needs to retrieve any files from the installation CD, it asks you to insert the CD in your computer's CD drive.

Part II

Making Your Slides Look Mahvelous

"No, it's not a pie chart, it's just a corn chip that got scanned into the document."

In this part . . .

It is widely believed that Californians indulge in cosmetic surgery more often than Floridians complain about hanging chads. The chapters in this part are all about cosmetic surgery for your presentations. You learn how to perform such procedures as typosuction, clip-art lifts, and color tucks.

Chapter 9

Fabulous Text Formats

In This Chapter

- Using bold, italics, underlining, and other character effects
- Changing the text font and size
- Using bullets and colors
- Lining things up
- Tabbing and indenting
- Spacing things out

A good presentation should be like a fireworks show: At every new slide, the audience gasps, "O-o-o-h. A-a-a-h." The audience is so stunned by the spectacular appearance of your slides that no one really bothers to read them.

This chapter gets you on the road toward ooohs and aaahs by showing you how to format text. If you use PowerPoint's templates as the basis for your presentations, your text is already formatted acceptably. But to really pull out the pyrotechnic stops, you have to know a few basic formatting tricks.

Many PowerPoint text-formatting capabilities work the same as Microsoft Word. If you want to format text a certain way and you know how to do it in Word, try formatting the same way in PowerPoint. Odds are that it works.

If you find that the Standard and Formatting toolbars are jammed together on one line so that you can't get to the formatting buttons you use often, choose View➪Toolbars➪Customize command to summon the Customize dialog box. Then click the Options tab to bring up the toolbar options and check the Show Standard and Formatting Toolbars on Two Rows checkbox.

Changing the Look of Your Characters

PowerPoint enables you to change the look of individual characters in subtle or drastic ways. You can control all character attributes by way of the Font dialog box, which you summon by using the Format➪Font command (see Figure 9-1).

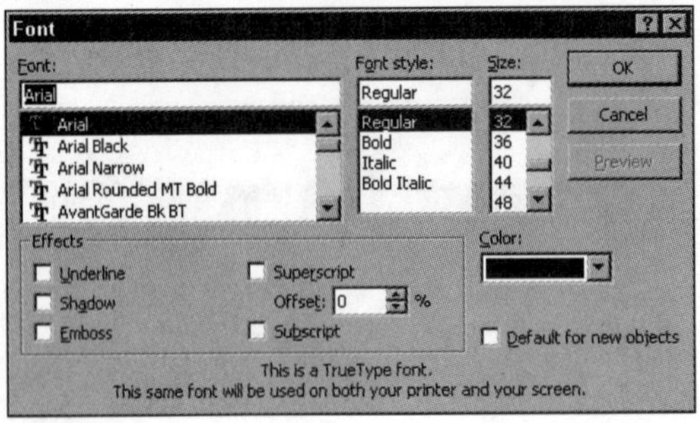

Figure 9-1: The Font dialog box.

The Font dialog box is a bit cumbersome to use, but fortunately PowerPoint provides an assortment of shortcuts for your formatting pleasure. These shortcuts are listed in Table 9-1; the procedures for using them are described in this section.

Table 9-1 Character-Formatting Shortcuts

Button	*Keyboard Shortcut*	*Format*
B	Ctrl+B	**Bold**
I	Ctrl+I	*Italic*
U	Ctrl+U	Underline
S	(none)	Text shadow
(none)	Ctrl+spacebar	Normal
Arial	Ctrl+Shift+F	Font
32	Ctrl+Shift+P	Change font size
A	Ctrl+Shift+>	Increase font size
A	Ctrl+Shift+<	Decrease font size
A	(none)	Font color

It's true — PowerPoint has many keyboard shortcuts for character formatting. You don't have to learn them all, though. The only ones I know and use routinely are for bold, italic, underline, and normal. Learn those and you'll be in good shape. You get the added bonus that these keyboard shortcuts are the same as the shortcuts that many other Windows programs use. And if you are mouse-happy and keyboard-annoyed, click away for goodness sakes. What matters most is that you can easily find and use what you need.

If you want, you can instruct these formats to gang-tackle some text. In other words, text can be bold, italic, and underlined for extra, extra emphasis. You can gang-tackle text with any combination of formats that you want.

You also can remove all text formats in one fell swoop by highlighting the text and pressing Ctrl+spacebar.

Most of the formatting options covered in this chapter are available only in Normal View. If you try to apply a format in Notes Page or Slide Sorter View you notice you can't. However, just double-click on your slide in Notes Page View or Slide Sorter View and you return instantly to Normal View.

Another way to summon the Font dialog box is to highlight the text you want to format and right-click the mouse. A menu appears. Choose the Font option from the menu and voilà! — the Font dialog box appears.

To boldly go . . .

Want to emphasize a point? Make it bold. Remember: Martin Luther said that if you must sin, sin boldly.

To make existing text bold, follow these steps:

1. **Highlight the text you want to make bold.**

2. **Press Ctrl+B or click the Bold button (shown in the margin) on the Formatting toolbar.**

To type new text in boldface, follow these steps:

B

1. **Press Ctrl+B or click the Bold button on the Formatting toolbar.**
2. **Type some text.**

   Make a bold effort.

3. **Press Ctrl+B or click the Bold button to return to typing normal text.**

You can use the Format⇨Font command to make text bold, but who wants to mess with a cumbersome dialog box when you can click the Bold button or press Ctrl+B instead? The rule is to use whatever is easiest for you.

You can remove the bold attribute also by highlighting the bold text and pressing Ctrl+spacebar. This technique removes not only the bold attribute but also other character attributes, such as italics and underlining. In other words, Ctrl+spacebar returns the text to normal.

Italics

Another way to emphasize a word is to italicize it. To italicize existing text, follow these steps:

1. **Highlight the text you want to italicize.**

2. **Press Ctrl+I or click the Italic button (shown in the margin) on the Formatting toolbar.**

To type new text in italics, follow these steps:

1. **Press Ctrl+I or click the Italic button on the Formatting toolbar.**
2. **Type some text.**

   Don't be afraid, Luke.

3. **Press Ctrl+I or click the Italic button to return to typing normal text.**

The cumbersome Format⇨Font command has an italic option, but why bother? Ctrl+I and the Italic button are too easy to ignore.

Pressing Ctrl+spacebar removes italics along with any other character formatting that you apply. Use this key combination to return text to normal or, as NASA would say, to "reestablish nominal text."

Underlines

Back in the days of typewriters, underlining was the only way to add emphasis to text. You can underline text in PowerPoint, but you wouldn't want to appear antiquated. Also, in these Web-savvy days folks may think the underline is actually a hyperlink, (especially if you are publishing your PowerPoint presentation on the Web). Underlining usually looks out of place in today's jazzy presentations, unless you're shooting for a nostalgic effect.

To underline existing text, follow these steps:

1. **Highlight the text you want to underline.**

2. **Press Ctrl+U or click the Underline button (shown in the margin) on the Formatting toolbar.**

To type new text and have it automatically underlined, follow these steps:

1. **Press Ctrl+U or click the Underline button on the Formatting toolbar.**
2. **Type some text.**

3. **Press Ctrl+U or click the Underline button to return to typing normal text.**

The Format➪Font command enables you to underline text, but Ctrl+U or the Underline button is easier to use.

You can remove the underlines and all other character formats by highlighting the text and pressing Ctrl+spacebar.

Big and little characters

If text is hard to read or you simply want to draw attention to it, you can make part of the text bigger than the surrounding text.

To increase or decrease the font size for existing text, follow these steps:

1. **Highlight the text whose size you want to change.**

2. **To increase the font size, press Ctrl+Shift+> or click the Increase Font Size button (shown in the margin) on the Formatting toolbar.**

   To decrease the font size, press Ctrl+Shift+< or click the Decrease Font Size button (shown in the margin) on the Formatting toolbar.

   To set the font to a specific size, press Ctrl+Shift+P or click the Font Size text box (shown in the margin) on the Formatting toolbar and type the point size you want.

To type new text in a different font size, change the font size by using a method from Step 2. Then type away. Change back to the original font size when you are finished.

Again, you can use the Format➪Font command to change the point size, but why bother when the controls are right there on the Formatting toolbar? Only a masochist would mess with the Format➪Font command.

Text fonts

If you don't like the looks of a text font, you can easily switch to a different font. To change the font for existing text, follow these steps:

1. **Highlight the text that is in the font you can't stand.**
2. **Click the arrow next to the Font control on the Formatting toolbar. A list of available fonts appears. Click the one you want to use.**

   Or press Ctrl+Shift+F and then press the down-arrow key to display the font choices.

If you have set the Formatting and Standard toolbars to display on the same row, you may not see the Font Type dialog box and will get no reaction from the keyboard shortcut. Don't forget to look for more buttons by checking the down arrows on the toolbar or by separating the two toolbars when you run PowerPoint. If you read this book in beginning-to-end order, you'll remember that I advised you to separate those toolbars while working through this book.

To type new text in a different font, change the font as described in Step 2 and begin typing. Change back to the original font when you're finished.

Sure, you can change the font with the Format⇨Font command. But the Font control on the Formatting toolbar is not only more convenient, but it also has a major advantage over the Font dialog box. The Formatting toolbar's Font control displays each of your fonts using the font itself, so you can see what each font looks like before you apply it to your text. In contrast, the Font dialog box displays the name of each font using the standard Windows system font.

If you want to change the font for all the slides in your presentation, switch to Slide Master View and then change the font. Details on how to do so are covered in Chapter 12.

PowerPoint automatically moves the fonts you use the most to the head of the font list. This feature makes picking your favorite font even easier.

Don't overdo it with fonts! Just because you have many different font choices doesn't mean that you should try to use them all on the same slide. Don't mix more than two or three typefaces on a slide, and use fonts consistently throughout the presentation. The PowerPoint Assistant reminds you if you use too many fonts.

Replacing fonts

PowerPoint has a nifty Replace Fonts command that lets you replace all occurrences of one font with another font in one swift move. For example, suppose you decide that Garamond is ugly and you'd rather use Book Antiqua. No problem! Just choose the Format⇨Replace Fonts command to summon the Replace Fonts dialog box, shown in Figure 9-2. Select the font you want to get rid of in the Replace drop-down list, and select the font you want to use in its place in the With drop-down list; then click Replace.

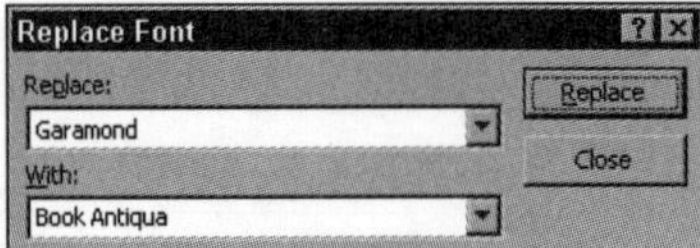

Figure 9-2: Replacing fonts all at once

Colorful metaphors

Color is an excellent way to draw attention to text in a slide if, of course, your slides print in color or you can display them on your computer monitor or using a projector, or if you plan to publish on the Web. Follow this procedure for changing text color:

1. **Highlight the text that is in the color you want to change.**

2. **Click the Font Color button (shown in the margin) on the Formatting toolbar.**

   A little box with color choices appears. Click the color you want to use.

To type new text in a different color, change the color and then begin typing. When you have had enough, change back to the original color and continue.

If you don't like any color that the Font Color button offers, click where it reads More Font Colors. A bigger dialog box with more color choices appears. If you still can't find the right shade of teal, click the Custom tab and have at it. Check out Chapter 11 if you need still more color help.

If you want to change the text color for your entire presentation, do so on the Slide Master (see Chapter 12 for details).

The shadow knows

Adding a shadow behind your text can make the text stand out against its background, which makes the entire slide easier to read. For that reason, many of the templates supplied with PowerPoint use shadows. These steps show you how to apply a text shadow:

1. **Highlight the text you want to shadow.**

2. **Click the Shadow button (shown in the margin).**

Embossed text

Embossed text looks like it has been chiseled in stone. PowerPoint achieves the embossed effect by adding a light shadow above the text rather than the dark shadow that appears below the text when you create Shadowed text. Note that you cannot create text that is both shadowed and embossed; you can use one or the other effect, but not both at the same time.

To create embossed text, follow these simple steps:

1. **Highlight the text you want to emboss.**

2. **Use the Format⇨Font command to pop up the Font dialog box.**

   Sorry — PowerPoint has no keyboard shortcut or toolbar button for embossing. You have to do it the hard way.

3. **Check the Emboss option.**
4. **Click the OK button.**

When you emboss text, PowerPoint changes the text color to the background color to enhance the embossed effect.

Embossed text is hard to read in smaller font sizes. This effect is best reserved for large titles.

Also, embossed text is nearly invisible with some color schemes. You may have to fiddle with the color scheme or switch templates to make the embossed text visible.

Biting the Bullet

Most presentations have at least some slides that include a bulleted list — a series of paragraphs accented by special characters lovingly known as *bullets*. In the old days, you had to add bullets one at a time. Nowadays, PowerPoint comes with a semiautomatic bullet shooter that is illegal in 27 states.

PowerPoint lets you create fancy bullets that are based on bitmap pictures rather than simple dots and checkmarks. Before you go crazy with picture bullets, take a look at the basic way to bite the bullet below.

To add bullets to a paragraph or series of paragraphs:

1. **Highlight the paragraphs to which you want to add bullets.**

   To add a bullet to just one paragraph, you don't have to highlight the entire paragraph. Just place the cursor anywhere in the paragraph.

2. **Click the Bullet button (shown in the margin).**

   PowerPoint adds a bullet to each paragraph that you select.

The Bullet button works like a toggle: Press it once to add bullets and press it again to remove bullets. To remove bullets from previously bulleted text, therefore, you select the text and click the Bullet button again.

If you don't like the appearance of the bullets that PowerPoint uses, you can choose a different bullet character, picture, or even a motion clip by using the Format⇨Bullet command. This command displays the Bullets and

Numbering dialog box, shown in Figure 9-3. From this dialog box, you can choose a different bullet character, change the bullet's color, or change its size relative to the text size.

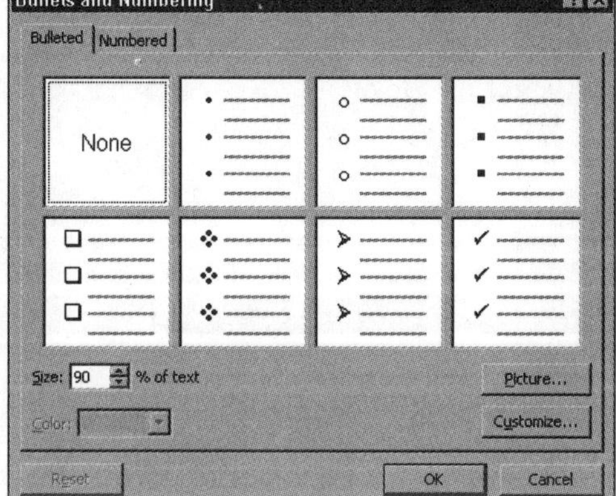

Figure 9-3: The Bullets and Numbering dialog box.

The following paragraphs point out some important tidbits to keep in mind when you use bullets.

- Several collections of characters are available for choosing bullet characters. If you don't like any of the bullet characters displayed for you in the dialog box, click Customize in the lower-right-hand corner of the dialog box. This brings up a dialog box that lists a variety of useful alternative bullet characters, such as pointing fingers, a skull and crossbones, and a time bomb. Pick the bullet you want to use, then click OK. If you can't find a bullet that suits your fancy, choose a different symbol font in the Font drop-down control.
- If the bullet characters don't seem large enough, increase the Size value in the Bullets and Numbering dialog box. The size is specified as a percentage of the text size.
- To change the bullet color, use the drop-down Color list box to choose the color you want to use. Colors from the current color scheme appear in the drop-down menu that appears when you use the Color list box. (For additional color choices, click More Colors to call forth a dialog box offering a complete range of color choices. For more information about using colors, see Chapter 11.)
- To use a picture bullet, click the Picture button located in the lower right of the Bullets and Numbering dialog box. This brings up the Picture Bullet dialog box, as shown in Figure 9-4. Choose the picture you want to use for your bullet, then click OK. (You can use the Import button on this dialog box to use your own bitmap file for a bullet.)

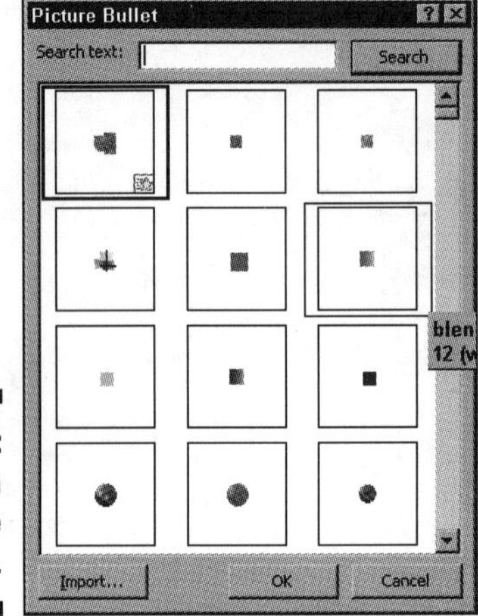

Figure 9-4: Using a picture bullet.

You can use certain bullet characters for good comic effect in your presentations. Be creative, but also be careful. A thumbs-down bullet next to the name of your boss may get a laugh, but it may also get you fired. One cool thing to do with bullets when you pitch a product or service is to use your logo as a bullet. It subliminally grinds your image in their brains until they submit to your will.

Lining Things Up

PowerPoint enables you to control the way your text lines up on the slide. You can center text, line it up flush left or flush right, or justify it. You can change these alignments by using the Format➪Alignment command, or you can use the convenient toolbar buttons and keyboard shortcuts.

Centering text

Centered text lines up right down the middle of the slide. (Actually, down the middle of the text object that contains the text; a text line appears centered on the slide only if the text object is centered on the slide.)

To center existing text, follow this procedure:

1. **Select the line or lines you want to center.**

2. **Click the Center button (shown in the margin) on the Formatting toolbar or press Ctrl+E.**

It's true that E doesn't stand for *center.* Ctrl+C was already taken (for Copy, remember?), so the Microsoft jocks decided to use Ctrl+E. They consider it to be some sort of demented practical joke.

3. **Admire your newly centered text.**

To type new centered text, skip Step 1; click the Center button or press Ctrl+E and begin typing.

Flush to the left

Centered text is sometimes hard to read. Align the text *flush left*, and the text lines up neatly along the left edge of the text object. All the bullets line up too. These steps show you how to make text flush left:

1. **Select the line or lines you want to scoot to the left.**

2. **Click the Align Left button (shown in the margin) on the Formatting toolbar or press Ctrl+L.**

   Hallelujah! The L in Ctrl+L stands for — you guessed it — *left.*

3. **Toast yourself for your cleverness.**

If you want to type new flush-left text, just click the Align Left button or press Ctrl+L and begin typing.

Other terms for flush left are *left justified* and *ragged right.* Just thought you may want to know.

Flush to the right

Yes, you can align text against the right edge, too. I don't know why you want to, but you can.

1. **Select the line or lines you want to shove to the right.**

2. **Click the Align Right button (shown in the margin) on the Formatting toolbar or press Ctrl+R.**

   R equals right — get it?

3. **Have a drink on me.**

If you want to type new flush-right text, just click the Align Right button or press Ctrl+R and continue.

Other terms for flush right are *right justified* and *ragged left*. With this extra cocktail party verbiage to add to your vocabulary, you'll be the hit at any nerd party.

Stand up, sit down, justify!

You also can tell PowerPoint to *justify* text: to line up both the left and right edges. The keyboard shortcut is Ctrl+J (J is for *justified*). And although there is no Justify button in the Formatting toolbar, you can add such a button via the Tools➪Customize command.

Messing with Tabs and Indents

PowerPoint enables you to set tab stops to control the placement of text within a text object. For most presentations, you don't have to fuss with tabs. Each paragraph is indented according to its level in the outline, and the template you use to create the presentation presets the amount of indentation for each outline level.

Although there's little need to, you can mess with the indent settings and tab stops if you're adventurous and have no real work to do today. Here's how you do it:

1. **Click the Slide button to switch to Normal View.**

   You can't mess with tabs or indents in Notes Pages or Slide Sorter

2. **If the Ruler is not visible, summon it by choosing the View➪Ruler command.**

   Rulers appear above and to the left of the presentation window and show the current tab and indentation settings. If your rulers are missing, you can get them back by choosing View➪Ruler.

3. **Select the text object whose tabs or indents you want to change.**

   Each text object has its own tabs and indents setting. After you click a text object, the ruler shows that object's tabs and indents.

4. **Click the ruler to add a tab stop.**

   Move the mouse pointer to the ruler location where you want to add a tab stop and then click. A tab stop appears.

5. **Grab the indentation doohickey and drag it to change the indentation.**

   Try dragging the different parts of the indentation doohickey to see what happens. Have fun. Good luck.

Tabs and indents can be pretty testy, but fortunately you don't have to mess with them for most presentations. If you're one of the unlucky ones, keep these pointers in mind:

- Each text object has its own tab settings. The tab settings for an object apply to all the paragraphs within the object, so you can't change tab settings for individual paragraphs within a text object. This is different from how Word works: In Word, each paragraph has its own tab settings.
- The ruler shows as many as five different indentation levels, one for each outline level. Only those levels used in the text object are shown, so if the object has only one outline level, only one indent is shown. To see additional indents, demote text within the object by pressing the Tab key.

Each text object is initially set up with default tab stops set at every inch. When you add a tab stop, any default tab stops to the left of the new tab stop disappear.

To remove a tab stop, use the mouse to drag the stop off the ruler (click the tab stop, drag it off the ruler, and then release the mouse button).

Spacing Things Out

Feeling a little spaced out? Try tightening the space between text lines. Feeling cramped? Space out the lines a little. These steps show you how to do it all:

1. **Highlight the paragraph or paragraphs whose line spacing you want to change.**
2. **Use the Format➪Line Spacing command.**

Don't even bother with this stuff about tab types

PowerPoint isn't limited to just boring left-aligned tabs. In all, it has four distinct types of tabs: left, right, center, and decimal. The square button at the far-left side of the ruler tells you which type of tab is added when you click the ruler. Click this button to cycle through the four types of tabs:

- **Standard left-aligned tab.** Press Tab to advance the text to the tab stop.
- **Right-aligned tab.** Text is aligned flush right with the tab stop.
- **Centered tab.** Text lines up centered over the tab stop.
- **Decimal tab.** Numbers line up with the decimal point centered over the tab stop.

Sorry, PowerPoint has no keyboard shortcut for this step. The Line Spacing dialog box suddenly appears, as shown in Figure 9-5.

3. **Change the dialog box settings to adjust the line spacing.**

   Line spacing refers to the space between the lines within a paragraph. Before Paragraph adds extra space before the paragraph, and After Paragraph adds extra space after the paragraph.

   You can specify spacing in terms of lines or points. The size of a line varies depending on the size of the text font. If you specify spacing in terms of points, PowerPoint uses the exact spacing you specify, regardless of the size of the text font.

4. **Click the OK button or press Enter.**

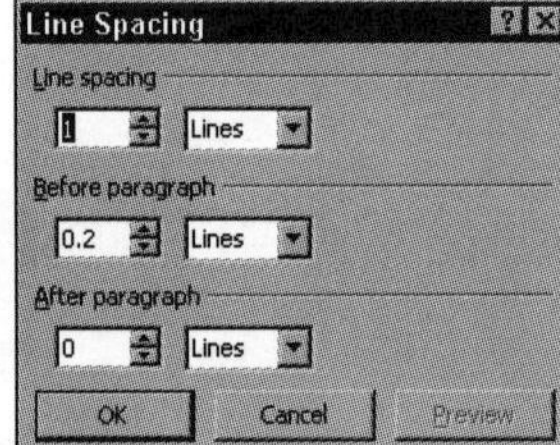

Figure 9-5: Changing the line spacing.

You can also increase or decrease the spacing between paragraphs by clicking the Increase Paragraph Spacing or Decrease Paragraph Spacing buttons found in the Formatting toolbar. If you can't find the buttons, remember to try the down arrow.

Chapter 10

Working with Pictures and Clip Art

In This Chapter

- Using free pictures
- Finding a picture you like
- Moving, sizing, and stretching pictures
- Adding a box, shaded background, or shadow to a picture
- Editing a clip art picture
- Inserting clips from the Internet

Face it: Most of us are not born with even an ounce of artistic ability. Some day, soon we hope, those genetic researchers combing through the billions and billions of genes strung out on those twisty DNA helixes will discover The Artist Gene. Then, in spite of protests from the DaVincis and Monets among us (who fear that their NEA grants will be threatened), doctors will splice the little bugger into our own DNA strands so that we all can be artists. Of course, this procedure will not be without its side effects: Some will develop an insatiable craving for croissants, and others will inexplicably develop French accents and whack off their ears. But artists we shall be.

Until then, we have to rely on clip art, pictures we've found on the Internet, or pictures we scanned into the computer using a scanner or took ourselves with a digital camera.

The Many Types of Pictures

The world is awash with many different formats by which pictures can be stored on your computer. Fortunately, PowerPoint works with almost all these formats.

The following sections describe the important details of the two basic types of pictures you work with in PowerPoint: bitmap pictures and vector drawings.

Bitmap pictures

A *bitmap picture* is a collection of small dots that make up an image. Bitmap pictures are most often used for scanned photographs and for icons and other buttons used on Web pages.

The dots that make up a bitmap picture are also called *pixels.* The number of pixels in a given picture depends on two factors: the picture's resolution and its size. *Resolution* refers to the number of pixels per inch. Most computer monitors (and projectors) display 72 pixels per inch. At this resolution, a 1" square picture requires 5,184 pixels (72 x 72). Photographs that are intended to be printed on an ink-jet or laser printer usually have a much higher resolution, perhaps 200 or 300 pixels per inch. At 300 pixels per inch, a 4" x 6" photograph requires more than two million pixels.

The amount of color information stored for the picture — also referred to as the picture's *color depth* — affects how many bytes of computer memory the picture requires. The color depth determines how many different colors the picture can contain. Most pictures have one of two color depths: 256 colors or 16.7 million colors. Most simple charts, diagrams, cartoons, and other types of clip art look fine at 256 colors. Only high-quality photographs need 16.7 million colors.

16.7 million color pictures are also known as *TrueColor* pictures or *24-bit color* pictures.

Our 4" x 6" photograph which has more than two million pixels requires about 2MB to store with 256 colors. With TrueColor, the size of the picture jumps to a whopping 6.4MB.

Fortunately, most bitmap file formats use compression methods to reduce the size of the picture. Depending on the actual contents of the picture, a 2MB picture may be reduced to 200KB without any noticeable loss in picture quality.

Bitmap picture files usually have filename extensions such as `.bmp`, `.gif`, `.jpg`, `.png`, or `.pcx`. Table 10-1 lists the bitmap file formats that PowerPoint supports.

Table 10-1 PowerPoint's Bitmap Picture File Formats

Format	*What It Is*
BMP	Garden variety Windows bitmap file, used by Windows Paint and many other programs
GIF	Graphics Interchange Format, a format commonly used for small Internet pictures

Format	What It Is
JPG	JPEG, a common format for photographs
PCD	Kodak Photo CD format
PCT	Macintosh PICT files
PCX	A variant type of bitmap file, also used by Windows Paint
PNG	Portable Network Graphics file, an image format designed for Internet graphics
TGA	Targa files
TIF	Tagged Image Format file, another bitmap program most often used for high-quality photographs

Victor, give me a vector

Besides bitmap pictures, the other category of picture files you can use with PowerPoint are vector drawings. A *vector drawing* is a picture file that contains detailed instructions for how to draw the basic shapes, such as lines, curves, rectangles, and so on, that make up drawn pictures. Vector drawings are usually created with high-powered drawing programs such as CorelDraw! or Adobe Illustrator.

PowerPoint supports all the most popular vector drawing formats, as described in Table 10-2.

Table 10-2 PowerPoint's Vector File Formats

Format	What It Is
CDR	CorelDRAW!, a popular, upper-crust drawing program
CGM	Computer Graphics Metafiles
DRW	Micrografx Designer or Micrografx Draw, two popular ooh-aah drawing programs
DXF	AutoCAD, a popular drafting program
EMF	An Enhanced Windows MetaFile picture
EPS	Encapsulated PostScript, a format used by some high-end drawing programs

(continued)

Table 10-2 *(continued)*

Format	*What It Is*
WMF	Windows MetaFile, a format that many programs recognize
WPG	A WordPerfect drawing

Using Clip Art

Are you sitting down? Whether you buy PowerPoint by itself or get it as a part of Microsoft Office, you also get a collection of thousands of pictures, sound, and motion clips that you can pop directly into your presentations. The PowerPoint clip art pictures are managed by a program called the Clip Organizer. This nifty little program keeps track of clip art, sound, and motion files spread out all over your hard disk and spares you the unpleasant chore of rummaging through your directories to look for that picture of Elvis you know that you have somewhere. Clip Organizer also takes the guesswork out of using clip art: Rather than choose a filename like ELVISFAT.PCX and hope that it's the one you remembered, you can see the clip art before you add it to your presentation.

Clip Organizer lets you search for clip art pictures using keywords. This makes it easy to search for the perfect clip art pictures for your slides.

The first time you access the clip art, PowerPoint launches the Clip Organizer, which offers to search your entire hard disk and create a catalog of all the pictures it contains. I suggest you accept this offer so that you can use it to access your own picture files in addition to the clip art files that come with PowerPoint.

Besides pictures, Clip Organizer works with sound and video clips as well. For more information about using sound and video, see Chapter 18.

Don't overdo the special effects. One surefire way to guarantee an amateurish look to your presentation is to load it down with three clip art pictures on every slide that all chime or go "zip" or "boing." Judicious use is much more effective.

Dropping In Some Clip Art

These steps show you how to drop clip art into your presentation:

1. Move to the slide on which you want to plaster the clip art.

If you want the same clip art picture to appear on every slide, move to Slide Master View by using the View⇨Master⇨Slide Master command (or Shift+click the Slide View button).

2. **Choose the Insert⇨Picture⇨Clip Art command.**

Sorry, PowerPoint offers no shortcut key for this command. If you like the mouse, though, you can click the Insert Clip Art button instead (shown in the margin).

Where you place the cursor before you choose the Insert⇨Picture⇨Clip Art command doesn't matter. PowerPoint sticks the clip art picture right smack dab in the middle of the slide anyway. The picture is probably way too big, so you have to move and shrink it.

3. **Behold the Insert Clip Art Task Pane in all its splendor.**

After a brief moment's hesitation, the Insert Clip Art Task Pane pops up, as shown in Figure 10-1.

4. **Type a keyword in the Search Text box, then click the Search button.**

For example, to search for pictures of trombones, type "Trombone" in the Search Text box, and then click Search.

PowerPoint searches through the Clip Organizer to locate the clip art you're looking for. Figure 10-2 shows how the Insert Clip Art Task Pane appears after PowerPoint has found some pictures of trombones.

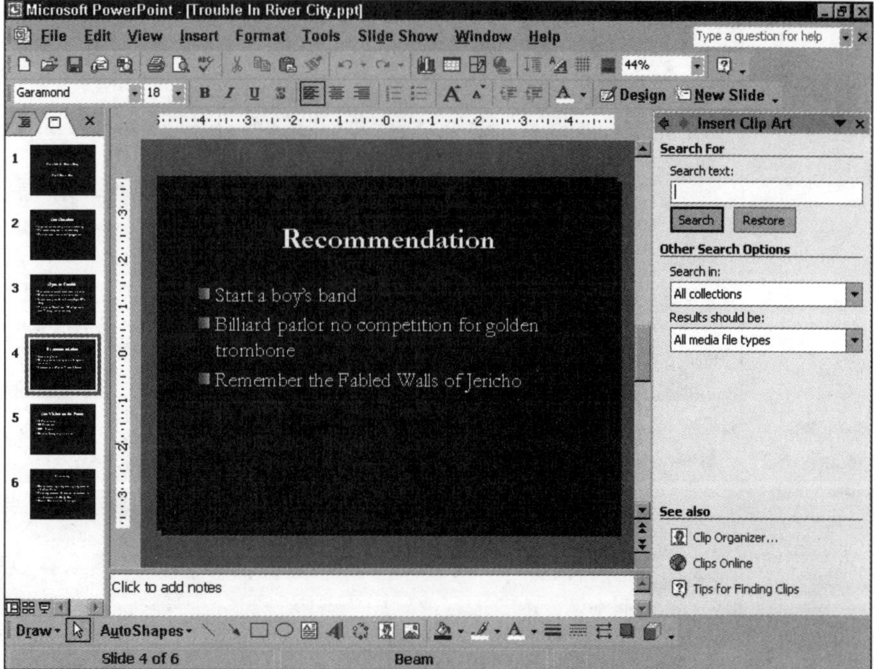

Figure 10-1: The Insert Clip Art Task Pane.

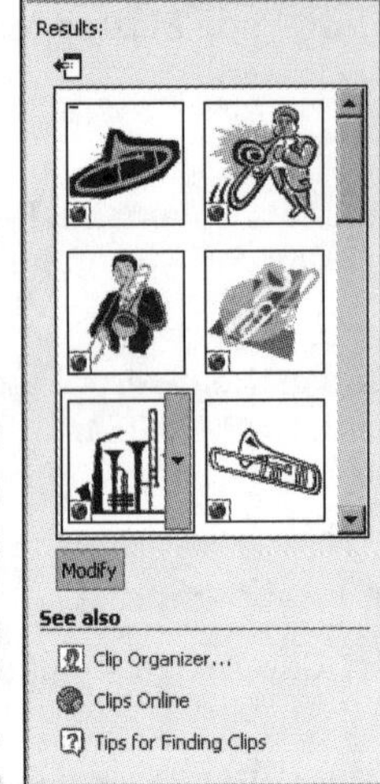

Figure 10-2: PowerPoint found nearly 76 pictures of trombones.

5. **Click the picture you want to use.**

   The picture is inserted on the current slide, as shown in Figure 10-3.

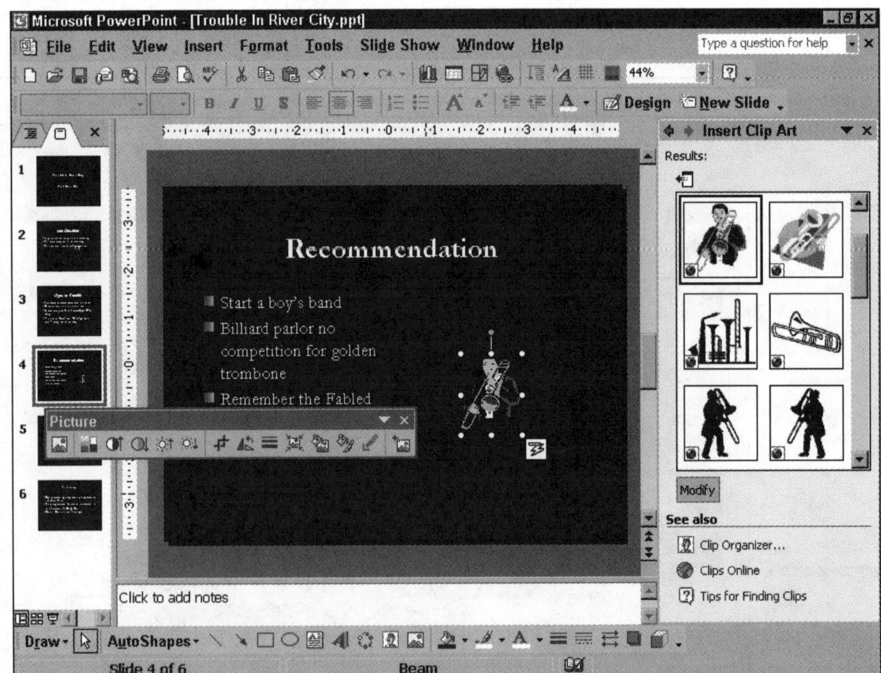

Figure 10-3: PowerPoint inserts the picture on the slide.

6. **If you're finished inserting pictures, click the Insert Clip Art Task Pane's close button (the X in the upper right corner of the task bar).**

   The Task Pane vanishes.

You'll probably want to move the picture and change its size. To find out how, see the section "Moving, Sizing, and Stretching Clip Art" later in this chapter.

If you find a clip art picture you like, you can find other pictures that are drawn in a similar style by right-clicking the picture in the Insert Clip Art Task Pane (or by clicking the down-arrow on the right side of the picture) and then choosing Find Similar Style.

Notice the Other Search Options section of the Insert Clip Art Task Pane. The controls in this section of the task bar let you choose which clip art collections to search and limit your search to clip art, pictures, sounds, or videos.

Moving, Sizing, and Stretching Clip Art

Because PowerPoint chooses an arbitrary position on the slide to insert clip art, you undoubtedly want to move the clip art to a more convenient location. You probably also want to change its size if it is too big or too small.

Follow these steps to force your inserted clip art into full compliance:

1. **Click the picture and drag it wherever you want.**

   You don't have to worry about clicking exactly the edge of the picture or one of its lines; just click anywhere in the picture and drag it around.

2. **Notice the eight handles. Drag one of them to resize the picture.**

   You can click and drag any of these handles to adjust the size of the picture. When you click one of the corner handles, the proportion of the picture stays the same as you change its size. When you drag one of the edge handles (top, bottom, left, or right) to change the size of the picture in just one dimension, you distort the picture's outlook as you go.

When you resize a picture, the picture changes its position on the slide. As a result, you can count on moving it after you resize it. If you hold down the Ctrl key while dragging a handle, however, the picture becomes anchored at its center point as you resize it. Therefore, its position is unchanged, and you probably don't have to move it.

Stretching a clip art picture by dragging one of the edge handles can dramatically change the picture's appearance. To illustrate, Figure 10-4 shows how the same clip art picture can resemble both Arnold Schwarzenegger *and* Danny DeVito. I just stretched one copy of the picture vertically to make it tall and stretched the other copy horizontally to make it, er, stout.

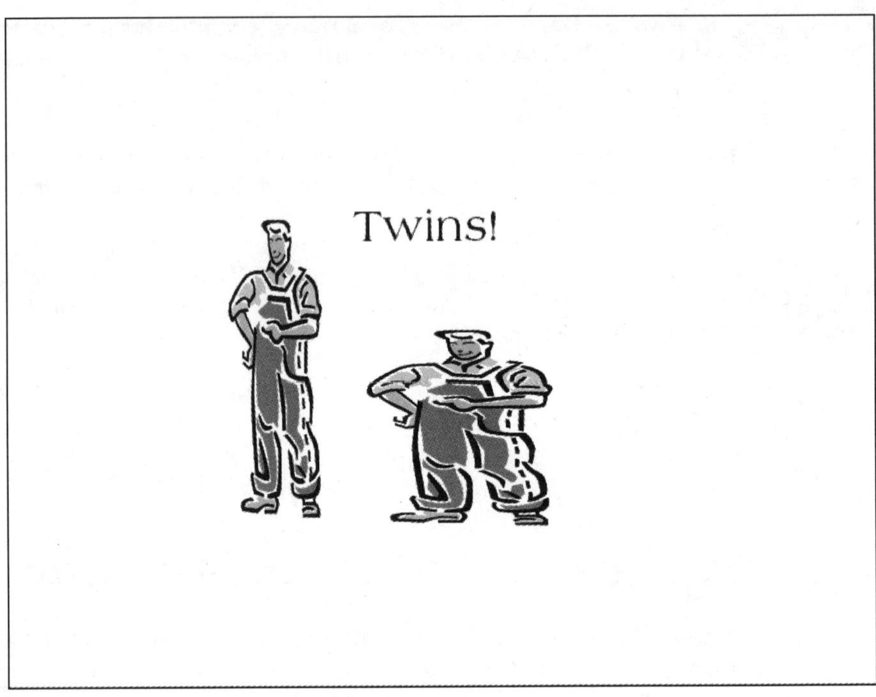

Figure 10-4: Twins.

Boxing, Shading, and Shadowing a Picture

PowerPoint enables you to draw attention to a clip art picture by drawing a box around it, shading its background, or adding a shadow. Figure 10-5 shows what these embellishments can look like.

The following steps show you how to use these features:

1. **Click the picture you want to encase.**

   The Picture toolbar appears when you select the picture.

2. **Click the Format Picture button (shown in the margin) in the Picture toolbar.**

   This summons the Format Picture dialog box shown in Figure 10-6.

3. **Use the Format Picture dialog box controls to draw a box around the picture or to shade its background.**

   Flip over to the Colors and Lines tab (if you're not already there) and choose a fill color from the Fill Color drop-down list box to give the picture a background color. Then choose a color from the Line Color drop-down list box to draw a line around the picture. You also can choose the line style and set up dashed lines. Click OK to draw the box.

4. **To add a shadow, click the Shadow button in the Drawing toolbar and select a shadow style.**

   Clicking the Shadow button brings up a menu of shadow styles, as shown in Figure 10-7. Pick the style you want by clicking the style in this menu.

Figure 10-5: Boxing in a picture.

Figure 10-6: The Format Picture dialog box.

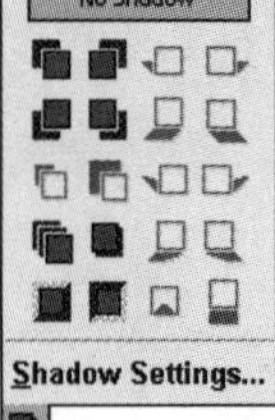

Figure 10-7: The Shadow menu.

If you apply a shadow to a picture to which you have not applied a fill color, the shadow is applied to the picture itself, as shown in the woman on the left in Figure 10-8. In this slide, both clip art pictures have a shadow. The one on the right also has a fill color and border, but the one on the left does not.

You can also apply a shadow by choosing Shadow Settings from the Shadow menu that appears when you click the Shadow button. This brings up a Shadow toolbar that lets you control the size, position, and color of the shadow.

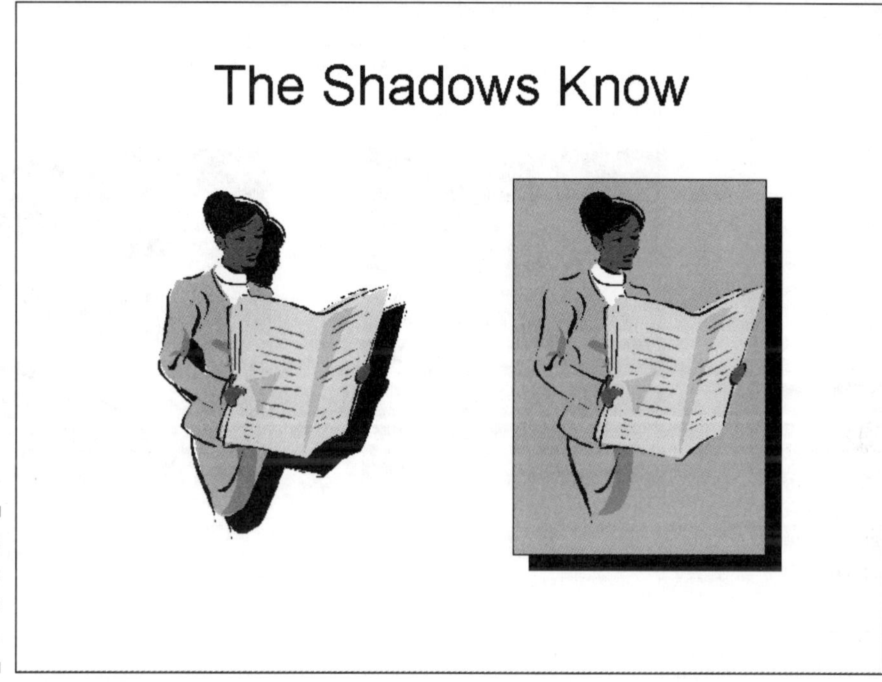

Figure 10-8: The Shadows know.

Editing a Clip Art Picture

Sometimes one of the clip art pictures supplied with PowerPoint is close but not exactly what you want. In that case, you can insert the picture and then edit it to make whatever changes are needed. For example, Figure 10-9 shows two versions of the same clip art picture. One has been edited to show the effects of an earthquake on a famous Seattle landmark.

You can't directly edit a clip art picture. Instead, you must first convert the picture to an equivalent bunch of PowerPoint shape objects. Then you can individually select and edit the objects using the shape-editing tools described in Chapter 14.

These steps tell how to edit a clip art picture:

1. **Click the picture you want to edit, then click the Draw button on the drawing toolbar and choose Ungroup command.**

   PowerPoint displays the warning message shown in Figure 10-10, indicating that you are about to convert a clip art picture to a PowerPoint drawing so that you can edit it.

Seattle Skew

Figure 10-9: You can edit a picture to change its appearance.

2. **Click Yes to convert the picture.**

   The picture is converted and will now obey your editing commands.

3. **Now ungroup the picture again.**

   Don't ask me why, but PowerPoint isn't smart enough to remember that, before it displayed the warning dialog box, you were trying to ungroup the picture. Because PowerPoint forgot to ungroup the picture, you have to do it again. This time it will work.

4. **Now edit the picture.**

   The clip art picture is converted to an equivalent group of PowerPoint shape objects, so you can use the PowerPoint shape-editing tools to change their appearance. You can drag any of the control handles to reshape an object, or you can change colors or add new stuff to the picture. See Chapter 14 for the details on editing PowerPoint shape objects.

After you've ungrouped and edited a picture, you may want to regroup it. You're much less likely to pull the nose off someone's face if the face is a group rather than a bunch of ungrouped ellipse objects.

When you convert a picture to PowerPoint objects, you're actually placing a copy of the clip art picture in your presentation. Any changes that you make to the picture are reflected only in your presentation; the original version of the clip art picture is unaffected.

Don't read this groupie stuff

What is all this talk of grouping and ungrouping? These common drawing terms are explained in more detail in Chapter 14. For now, consider how you can draw a simple picture of a face. You may start with a circle for the head and then add ellipses for the eyes, nose, and mouth. By the time you finish, you have five ellipses objects.

The only problem is, suppose that you want to move the face you just drew to the other side of the slide. If you just clicked and dragged it, odds are that you would move only the nose or one of the eyes. To move the whole thing, you have to select all five ellipses.

Wouldn't it be great if you could treat all five ellipses as a single object? That's what grouping is all about. When you group objects, they are treated as if they were a single object. When you click any one of the grouped objects, you click them all. Move one, and they all move. Delete one, and they all vanish.

Here are some other groupie thoughts to ponder:

- What happens if, after grouping the five face ellipses, you discover that you made the nose too big? You have to ungroup them so that they become five separate objects again. Then you can select and resize just the nose.
- PowerPoint has a regroup command that puts an ungrouped object back together without requiring that you first select all the original object's pieces.
- Most complex drawings use grouping. PowerPoint clip art pictures are no exception. That's why you have to ungroup them before you can edit them. Clip art pictures have the added characteristic that when you ungroup a clip art picture, you sever its connection to the Clip Organizer. The picture is no longer a Clip Organizer object but is now merely a bunch of PowerPoint rectangles, ellipses, and free-form shapes.
- Oops, this is way too much stuff about grouping for the clip art chapter. Maybe you should skip ahead to Chapter 14 if you're really this interested.

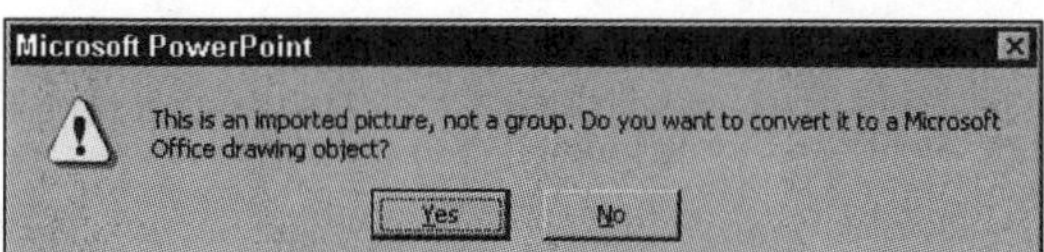

Figure 10-10: Pay no attention to this pathetic little warning.

Colorizing a Clip Art Picture

After inserting a clip art picture into your presentation, you may find that the colors used in the clip art clash with the colors you've chosen for the presentation's color scheme. Never fear! PowerPoint allows you to selectively change the colors used in a clip art picture. Just follow these steps:

1. **Select the picture you want to colorize and then click the Recolor Picture button (shown in the margin) from the Picture toolbar.**

   The Recolor Picture dialog box appears, as shown in Figure 10-11.

Figure 10-11: Colorizing your pictures.

2. **In the list of Original colors, click the original color you want to change.**
3. **From the drop-down list adjacent to the original color you chose, select a new color to replace the chosen color.**

   The drop-down list displays a standard color menu, with the colors from the color scheme and an Other Color command that brings up a dialog box that allows you to choose a custom color.

   If you want to change the fill color but leave the line color unchanged, click the Fills option button.

4. **Repeat Steps 2 and 3 for any other colors you want to change.**
5. **Click OK when you're finished.**

Getting Clip Art from the Internet

As if the vast collection of clip art that comes with Office and PowerPoint isn't enough, Microsoft also maintains a clip library on the Internet that you can use. If you have access to the Internet, clip art automatically searches

Microsoft's Design Gallery Live Web site, which features thousands of clips on just about every imaginable subject.

The beauty of Design Gallery Live is that it's integrated with Clip Organizer. The only difference between getting clip art from your hard disk or from Design Gallery Live is that the speed of your Internet connection becomes apparent as PowerPoint hesitates while it waits for pictures to arrive from Microsoft's Web site.

Inserting Pictures without Using Clip Organizer

PowerPoint also enables you to insert pictures directly into your document without using Clip Organizer. Use this technique to insert pictures that aren't a part of the clip art collection that comes with PowerPoint, or if you know the location of the file and you want to bypass Clip Organizer and go straight to the source. These steps show you how:

1. **Move to the slide on which you want to splash a picture.**

   If you want the clip art to show up on every slide, conjure up Slide Master View with the View⇨Master⇨Slide Master command (or Shift+click the Slide View button).

2. **Choose the Insert⇨Picture⇨From File command.**

   If you prefer, click the Insert Picture button (shown in the margin). Either way, you are rewarded with the Insert Picture dialog box, shown in Figure 10-12.

Figure 10-12: The Insert Picture dialog box.

3. **Dig through the bottom of your disk drive until you find the file you want.**

   The picture you want can be anywhere. Fortunately, the Insert Picture dialog box has all the controls you need to search high and low until you find the file. Just click the icons at the left-hand side of the box or click the Look In text box, and you are halfway there.

4. **Click the file and then click Insert.**

   You're done!

You also can paste a picture directly into PowerPoint by way of the Clipboard. Anything you can copy to the Clipboard you can paste into PowerPoint. For example, you can doodle a sketch in Paintbrush, copy it, and then zap over to PowerPoint and paste it. Voilà — instant picture!

If you want to narrow your search to files of a particular type, use the Files of Type drop-down list box, then choose the type of file you want to look for.

Chapter 11

When I Am Old, I Shall Make My Slides Purple

In This Chapter

- Using color schemes
- Changing the colors in a color scheme
- Creating new colors
- Shading the slide background
- Coloring objects and text
- Copying colors from other objects

Welcome to the Wonderful World of Color. Here is your opportunity to unleash the repressed artist hidden deep within you. Take up your palette, grasp your brush firmly, and prepare to attack the empty canvas of your barren slides.

PowerPoint enables you to use more than 16 million colors, but you shouldn't feel obligated to use them all right away. Pace yourself. Now would be a good time to grow a goatee or to cut off your ear. (Just kidding.)

Using Color Schemes

The PowerPoint templates come with built-in color schemes, which are coordinated sets of colors chosen by color professionals. Microsoft paid these people enormous sums of money to debate the merits of using mauve text on a teal background. You can use these professionally designed color schemes, or you can create your own if you think that you have a better eye than the Microsoft-hired color guns.

As far as I'm concerned, the PowerPoint color schemes are the best thing to come along since Peanut M&Ms. Without color schemes, people like me are free to pick and choose from among the 16 million or so colors that PowerPoint lets you incorporate into your slides. The resulting slides can easily appear next to Cher and Roseanne in *People* magazine's annual "Worst Dressed of the Year" issue.

Each color scheme has eight colors, with each color designated for a particular use, as shown in this list:

- **Background color:** Used for the slide background.
- **Text-and-lines color:** Used for any text or drawn lines that appear on the slide, with the exception of the title text (described in this list). It is usually a color that contrasts with the background color. If the background color is dark, the text-and-lines color is generally light, and vice versa.
- **Shadows color:** Used to produce shadow effects for objects drawn on the slide. It is usually a darker version of the background color.
- **Title text color:** Used for the slide's title text. Like the text-and-lines color, the title text color contrasts with the background color so that the text is readable. The title text usually complements the text-and-lines color to provide an evenly balanced effect. (That sounds like something an artist would say, doesn't it?)
- **Fills color:** When you create an object, such as a rectangle or an ellipse, this color is the default fill color to color the object.
- **Accent colors:** The last three colors in the color scheme. They are used for odds and ends that you add to your slide. They may be used to color the bars in a bar chart, for example, or the slices in a pie chart. Two of these accent colors are also used to indicate hyperlinks.

Each slide in your presentation can have its own color scheme. The Slide Master also has a color scheme, used for all slides that don't specify their own deviant color scheme. To ensure that your slides have a uniform look, simply allow them to pick up the color scheme from the Slide Master. If you want one slide to stand out from the other slides in your presentation, assign it a different color scheme.

PowerPoint picks up the initial color scheme for a presentation from the template on which the presentation is based as a part of the template's Slide Master. But each template also includes several alternate color schemes, which are designed to complement the main color scheme for the template. You can change the Master scheme later, but if you apply a new template, the new template's scheme overrides any change you made to the original template's color scheme.

Metaphor alert!

If you want, you can think of the color scheme as an artist's magic palette. The artist squeezes out eight little dabs of paint to use for various elements of a painting: one for the sky, another for the mountains, and still another for the trees. Then the artist paints the picture. So far, nothing special. But here's what makes this palette magic: If the artist sets it down and picks up a different palette (with eight different little dabs of color squeezed out), the entire painting is instantly transformed to the new colors, as though the artist used the second palette all along.

This magic palette enables the artist to make subtle changes to the painting's appearance with little effort. The artist can change the painting from midday to dusk, for example, simply by switching to a palette that has a darker blue for the sky color. Or the artist can change the scene from spring to fall by switching to a palette that has yellow or orange paint rather than green paint for the trees. Or maybe switch to a winter scene by changing the mountain color to white.

PowerPoint color schemes work just like this magic palette. The color scheme gives you eight colors to work with, with each color assigned to a different slide element. If you change the color scheme, the entire presentation changes as well.

If you find a template you like but aren't happy with any of its color schemes, you can create your own. The easiest way is to choose a scheme that's close to the colors you want and then modify the scheme's colors. I present the procedure to do so later in this chapter.

You can override the Master color scheme for an individual slide. You also can change the color for any object to any color in the scheme, or to any other color known to science. You can find step-by-step instructions later in this chapter.

Don't get all in a tizzy about color schemes if you plan to print overhead slides on a black-and-white laser printer. The slides look dazzling on-screen, but all those stunning colors are printed in boring shades of gray.

Using a different color scheme

If you don't like your presentation's color scheme, change it! Here's a simple way:

1. **Switch to Normal View if you aren't already there.**

   Click the Normal View button (shown in the margin) or choose View➪Normal.

2. **Choose the Format➪Slide Design command.**

   The Slide Design Task Pane appears to the right of the slide.

3. **Click Color Schemes at the top of the Slide Design Task Pane.**

   The Color Schemes Task Pane appears, as shown in Figure 11-1. As you can see, the Color Scheme Task Pane shows the color schemes that are available for your presentation.

4. **Click the color scheme you want to use.**

   You're done!

For most presentations, you'll want to use the same color scheme for all the slides in the presentation. However, in some cases you may want to use two or more color schemes to draw attention to certain slides in your presentation or to give your audience an immediate visual clue to your slide's contents. For example, if a market-analysis presentation frequently shifts back and forth between current data and last year's data, consider using a different color scheme for the slides that depict last year's data. That way, the audience is less likely to become confused.

You can change the color scheme for two or more slides by selecting the slides you want to recolor in the thumbnail view at the left side of the PowerPoint window and then applying the color scheme you want to use.

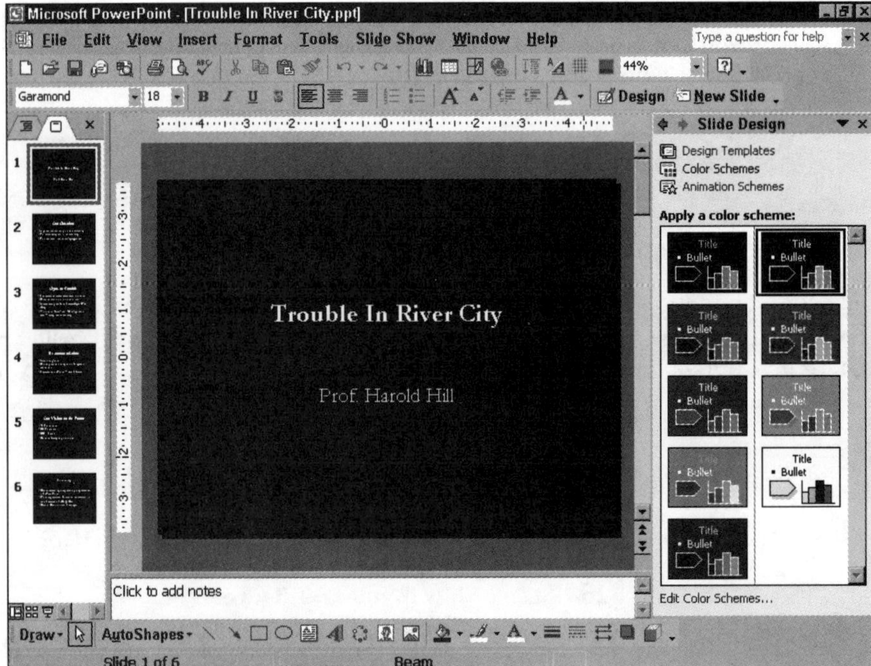

Figure 11-1: Changing a slide's color scheme.

When you change the color scheme for the entire presentation by clicking Apply to All, any slides to which you have applied a custom color scheme are changed as well. For example, suppose you create a presentation using a color scheme that has a deep blue background, and you highlight certain slides by applying an alternate (light blue) color scheme for those slides. You then decide that you'd rather use a maroon background for the bulk of the slides, so you call up the Format➪Slide Color Scheme command, select the new color scheme, and click Apply to All. After you do so, you discover that all slides are changed to the maroon background — even the ones that you had highlighted with the light blue color scheme.

Changing colors in a color scheme

To change one or more of the colors in the current color scheme, follow these steps:

1. **Select the slide whose color scheme you want to change.**
2. **Choose the Format➪Slide Design command; then click Color Scheme.**

   The Color Scheme Task Pane appears. Refer to Figure 11-1 if you've forgotten what it looks like.
3. **Click Edit Color Schemes at the bottom of the Color Scheme Task Pane.**

   The Edit Color Scheme dialog box appears, as shown in Figure 11-2.

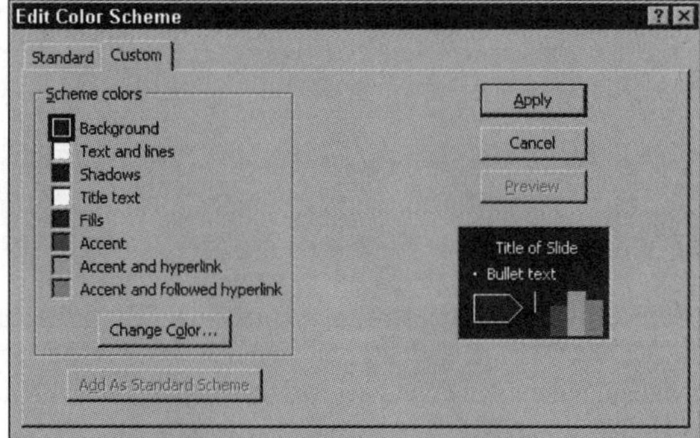

Figure 11-2: Editing a color scheme.

4. **Click the color box you want to change.**

   To change the background color, for example, click the Background color box.
5. **Click the Change Color button.**

   A dialog box similar to the one in Figure 11-3 appears. As you can see, PowerPoint displays what looks like a tie-dyed version of Chinese Checkers.

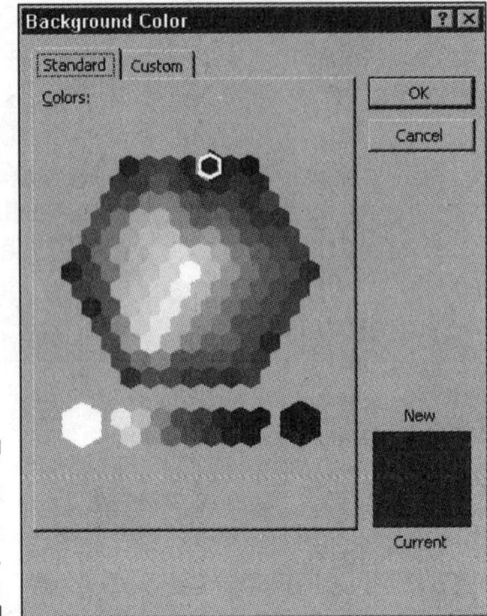

Figure 11-3: Changing a color

6. **Click the color you want and click OK.**

   If you want white or black or a shade of gray, click one of the color hexagons at the bottom of the dialog box. Otherwise, click one of the colored hexagons. After you click OK, you zip back to the Color Scheme dialog box (refer to Figure 11-2).

7. **Choose Apply.**

   The change is applied to the color scheme.

Be warned that after you deviate from the preselected color scheme combinations, you better have some color sense. If you can't tell chartreuse from lime, you better leave this stuff to the pros.

The color choice dialog box in Figure 11-3 shows 127 popular colors, plus white, black, and shades of gray. If you want to use a color that doesn't appear in the dialog box, click the Custom tab. This step draws forth the custom color controls, shown in Figure 11-4. From this dialog box, you can construct any of the 16 million colors that are theoretically possible with PowerPoint. You need a Ph.D. in physics to figure out how to adjust the Red, Green, and Blue controls, though. Mess around with this stuff if you want, but you're on your own.

Shading the Slide Background

You may have noticed that the slide background used in many of the PowerPoint templates is not a solid color. Instead, the color is gradually shaded from top to bottom. This type of shading — called a *gradient fill* —

creates an interesting visual effect. For example, look at the slide in Figure 11-5. This slide was based on the templates supplied with PowerPoint, but I modified the color scheme and the background shading to achieve the effect that I wanted.

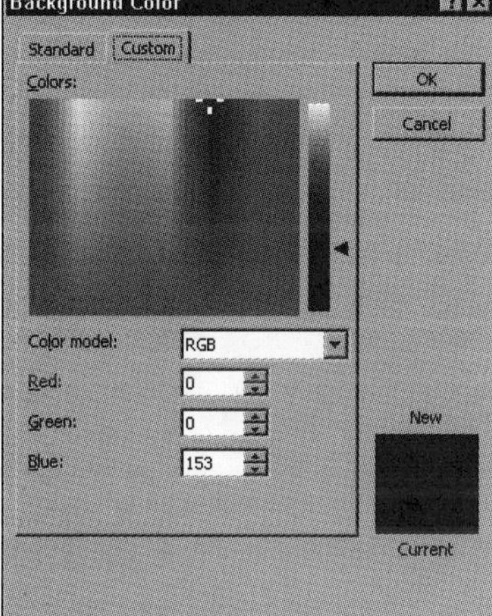

Figure 11-4: PowerPoint offers billions and billions of colors to choose from.

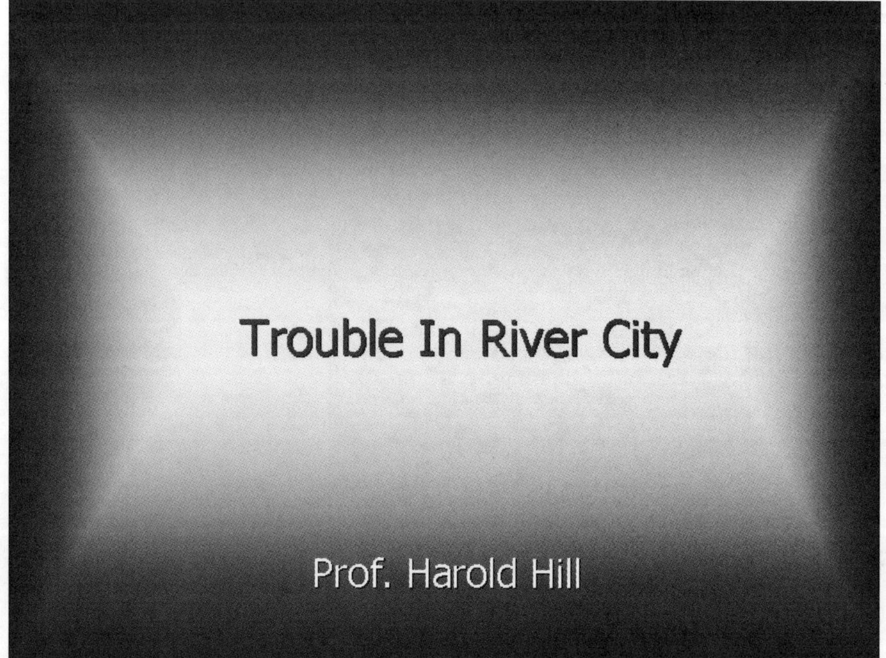

Figure 11-5: Using a gradient fill to create an interesting background.

Shading for the slide background works much like the color scheme. If you apply it to all slides, the Slide Master is affected as well so that any new slides pick up the new shading. Alternatively, you can apply shading to an individual slide. These steps show you how to shade the slide background:

1. **Choose the slide you want to shade.**

   This step isn't necessary if you want to apply the shading to all slides in the presentation.

2. **Summon the Format⇨Background command.**

   The Background dialog box appears. This dialog box includes a drop-down list under the Background fill, as shown in Figure 11-6.

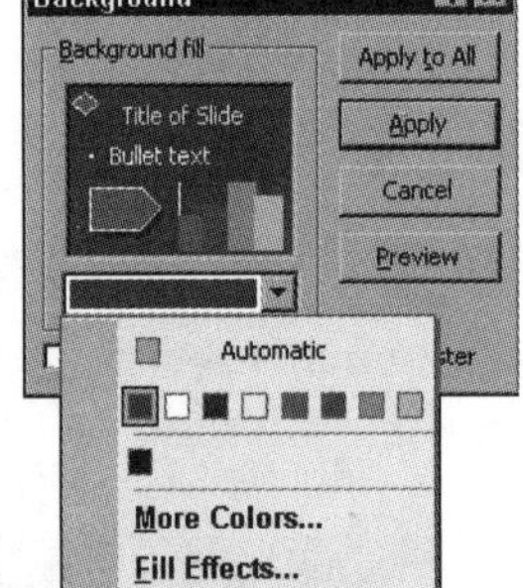

Figure 11-6: The Background dialog box.

3. **Select Fill Effects from the drop-down list.**

   The Fill Effects dialog box appears, as shown in Figure 11-7.

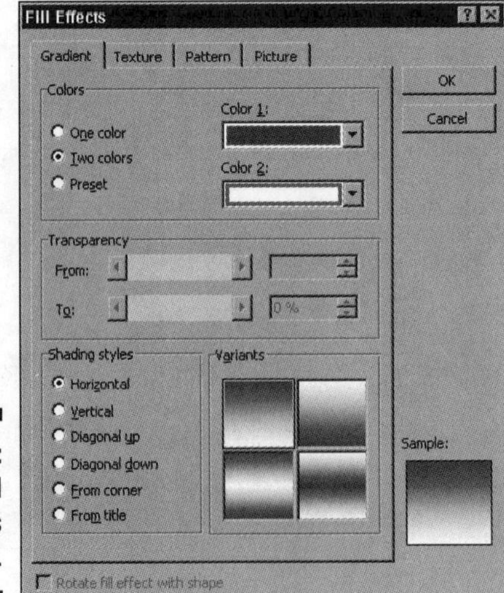

Figure 11-7: The Fill Effects dialog box.

4. **On the Gradient tab page, choose the shade style you want.**

   Start by selecting a one-color shade, in which a single color fades to white or black, or a two-color shade, in which one color fades into another. Then select the Shading Style — Horizontal, Vertical, Diagonal up, and so on. Finally, select one of the variants in the Variants area.

   Alternatively, you can select one of several preset shadings by picking the Preset option. The preset shading options include Early Sunset, Nightfall, Rainbow, and several other interesting effects.

5. **Click OK to return to the Background dialog box and then click Apply or Apply to all.**

   Clicking the Apply button applies the shading to just the slide or slides you chose (in Step 1). Clicking Apply to all applies the shading to all slides.

   You're done! Admire your work. Play with it some more if you don't like it.

When you apply a template, any background shading specified for the template's Masters is applied along with the color scheme.

Using Other Background Effects

Besides gradient fills, the Format⇨Background command provides several other types of interesting background effects. All these effects — Texture, Pattern, and Picture — are accessed via the tabs in the Fill Effects dialog box, which was shown in Figure 11-7.

If you select the Texture tab, the dialog box shown in Figure 11-8 appears. Here you can choose one of several textures to give your presentation that polished Formica look.

If you select the Pattern tab, you get another dialog box from which you can choose from any of 48 different patterns using your choice of foreground and background colors.

If you click the Picture tab and then click the Select Picture button, a dialog box appears that allows you to select a picture to be used as a background for your slides. You may have to do some searching to find the image you want.

Coloring Text and Objects

Normally, the color scheme you choose for a slide determines the color of the various objects on the slide. If the text color is yellow, for example, all text on the slide is yellow (except the title text, which is controlled by the color scheme's Title Text color). Similarly, if the fill color is orange, any filled objects on the slide are orange.

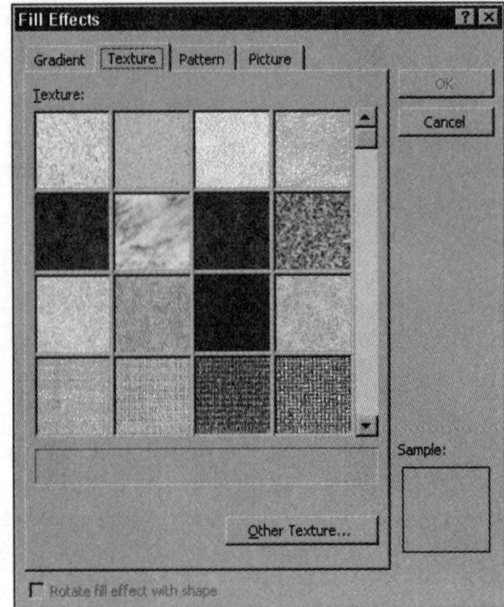

Figure 11-8: Creating a textured background.

If you change the colors in the color scheme, all the objects on the slide that follow the scheme are affected. But what if you want to change the color of just one object without changing the scheme or affecting other similar objects on the slide? No problemo. PowerPoint enables you to override the scheme color for any object on a slide. The following sections explain how.

Applying color to text

To change the color of a text object, follow these steps:

1. **Highlight the text whose color you want to change.**
2. **Summon the Format⇨Font command.**

   The Font dialog box appears. Click the Color control, and a cute little Color menu appears (see Figure 11-9).

   Alternatively, click the down arrow next to the Font Color button on the Drawing toolbar (shown in the margin). The same cute little Color menu appears directly under the button.
3. **Click the color you like from the cute little Color menu.**

   The eight colors in the top row of the Color menu are the colors from the slide's color scheme. The next row shows colors that mysteriously seem to coordinate with any clip art or other colorful elements in your presentation. Choose one of these colors if you want a warm fuzzy feeling that the colors coordinate. If you're bold and trust your color sense, continue to Step 4.

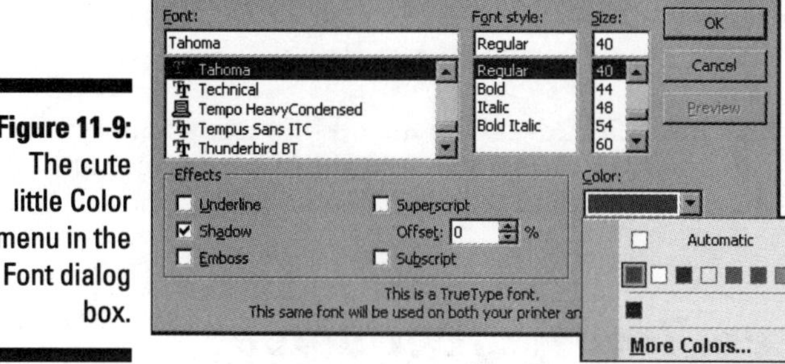

Figure 11-9: The cute little Color menu in the Font dialog box.

4. **Click More Colors and choose a color you like.**

   The same dialog box you used to handpick colors for the color scheme appears (refer to Figure 11-3). You can choose one of the many sensible colors displayed therein, or you can toss caution to the wind, put on your painting clothes, and click the Custom tab to build your own color by setting the Red, Blue, and Green values (refer to Figure 11-4).

5. **OK yourself back home.**

   You may have to click OK several times to fully unwind yourself.

Good news! If you use the More Colors option to assign a color, PowerPoint automatically adds to the Color menu the color you choose. You can distinguish your colors from the color scheme colors because your custom colors are always in the bottom line of eight complementary colors.

Changing an object's fill or line color

When you draw an object such as a rectangle or an ellipse, PowerPoint fills in the object with the color scheme's fill color and draws the object's outline using the color scheme's line color. You can change either of these colors by using the Fill Color and Line Color buttons on the Drawing toolbar. Just follow these steps:

1. **Select the object whose fill color you want to change.**

2. **To change the object's fill color, click the down arrow next to the Fill Color button and choose a color from the menu that appears.**

3. **To change the object's line color, click the down arrow next to the Line Color button and choose a color from the menu that appears.**

   That's all!

To create a transparent object — that is, an object that has no fill color — click the Fill Color button and choose No Fill. To create an object that has no outline, click the Line Color button and choose No Line.

The Fill Color button includes a Fill Effects command that lets you apply gradient fills, patterns, textures, or pictures to any object. The selections for these features are the same as shown in Figures 11-7 and 11-8.

Creating a semitransparent object

You can create a ghostly semitransparent fill by following these steps:

1. **Choose the object that you want to give a ghostly appearance.**
2. **Choose the Format➪Colors and Lines command.**

   The Format AutoShape dialog box appears, as shown in Figure 11-10.

Figure 11-10: The Format AutoShape dialog box.

3. **Slide the Transparency slider to make the object as transparent as you want.**

   With the Transparency slider all the way to the left (0%), the object will be a solid color. Increasing the Transparency value from 0% lets more and more of whatever lies behind the object show through. If you move the slider all the way to the right (100%), the object will be completely transparent, so the object's fill color won't show at all.
4. **Click OK.**

Note that this dialog box also lets you control the fill options for the object, plus it lets you set the line style for the border that's drawn around the object (if any).

Copying color from an existing object

If you want to force one object to adopt the color of another object, you can use a fancy tool called the Format Painter. It sucks up the formatting of one object and then spits it out onto another object at your command. It's a bit messy, but it gets the job done. (You should see it eat.)

To use the Format Painter, follow these steps:

1. **Choose the object whose color you like.**

   You can select a bit of text or an entire object.

2. **Click the Format Painter button (shown in the margin) on the Standard toolbar.**

   This step sucks up the good color.

3. **Click the object whose color you don't like.**

   This step spits out the desirable color onto the object.

In addition to the fill color, the Format Painter also picks up other object attributes, such as shading, textures, optional trim package, and aluminum alloy hubcaps.

If you want to apply one object's format to several objects, select the object whose color you like and then double-click the Format Painter. Now you can click as many objects as you want to apply the first object's format to. When you're done, press the Esc key.

Chapter 12

Yes, Master! (Igor's Favorite Chapter)

In This Chapter

- Finding out the stuff about Masters you have to know
- Changing Masters
- Using Masters
- Working with headers and footers
- Using more than one master
- Finding lost placeholders

Want to add a bit of text to every slide in your presentation? Or maybe add your name and phone number at the bottom of your audience handouts? Or place a picture of Rush Limbaugh at the extreme right side of each page of your speaker notes?

Masters is the surefire way to add something to every slide. No need to toil separately at each slide. Add something to the Master and it automatically shows up on every slide. Remove it from the Master and — poof! — it disappears from every slide. Very convenient.

Masters govern all aspects of a slide's appearance: its background color, objects that appear on every slide, text that appears on all slides, and more.

Working with Masters

In PowerPoint, a Master governs the appearance of all the slides or pages in a presentation. Each presentation has four Masters:

- **Slide Master:** Dictates the format of your slides. You work with this Master most often as you tweak your slides to cosmetic perfection.
- **Title Master:** Prescribes the layout of the presentation's title slide. This Master allows you to give your title slides a different look from the other slides in your presentation.
- **Handout Master:** Controls the look of printed handouts.
- **Notes Master:** Determines the characteristics of printed speaker notes.

Each Master specifies the appearance of text (font, size, and color, for example), the slide's background color, the layout of placeholders on the slide, and any additional text or other objects you want to appear on each slide or page.

Masters are not optional. Every presentation has them. You can, however, override the formatting of objects contained in the Master for a particular slide. This capability enables you to vary the appearance of slides when it's necessary.

One of the best new features of PowerPoint 2002 is its ability to let you create more than one Slide or Title Master in a single presentation, which allows you to mix two or more slide designs in your presentations. But you can still have only one Handout or Notes Master in each presentation.

A quick way to call up Slide Master View is to hold down the shift key while you click the Normal View button. You can also call up the Handout master by holding down the shift key while clicking the Slide Sorter View button. For Notes Master, you have to do it the old-fashion way: View⇨Master⇨Notes Master.

Modifying the Slide Master

If you don't like the layout of your slides, call up the Slide Master and do something about it, as shown in these steps:

1. **Choose the View⇨Master⇨Slide Master command or hold down the Shift key while clicking the Slide View button.**

   If you use the View⇨Master command, a submenu appears listing the three masters (Slide, Handout, and Notes). Choose Slide Master to call up the Slide Master.

2. **Behold the Slide Master in all its splendor.**

   Figure 12-1 shows a typical Slide Master. You can see the placeholders for the slide title and body text in addition to other background objects. Note also that the Slide Master includes placeholders for three objects that appear at the bottom of each slide: the Date Area, Footer Area, and

Number Area. These special areas are used by the View➪Header and Footer command and are described later in this chapter, under the heading "Using Headers and Footers."

A thumbnail of all the Slide and Title Masters in your presentation is shown on the left side of the screen. In most cases, you'll see just two thumbnails here: one for the Slide Master and one for the Title Master. If your presentation has more than one Slide Master, you'll see additional thumbnails. For more information, see the section "Yes, You Can Serve Two Masters" later in this chapter.

If the Title slide was selected when you called up Slide Master View, you'll see the Title Master instead of the Slide Master. Do not fear! Just press the Page Up key to summon the Slide Master.

3. **Make any formatting changes you want.**

   Select the text you want to apply a new style to and make your formatting changes. If you want all the slide titles to be in italics, for example, select the title text and press Ctrl+I or click the Italic button on the Formatting toolbar.

   If you're not sure how to change text formats, consult Chapter 9.

4. **Click the Close Master View button on the Slide Master View toolbar to return to Normal View.**

   Alternatively, you can just click the Normal View button. Either way, you'll be whisked back to your slides. The effect of any changes you made to the Slide Master should be apparent immediately.

PowerPoint applies character formats such as bold, italics, font size, and font to entire paragraphs when you work in Slide Master View. You don't have to select the entire paragraph before you apply a format; just click anywhere in the paragraph.

Notice that the body object contains paragraphs for five outline levels formatted with different point sizes, indentations, and bullet styles. If you want to change the way an outline level is formatted, this is the place.

You can type all you want in the title or object area placeholders, but the text you type doesn't appear on the slides. The text that appears in these placeholders is provided only so that you can see the effect of the formatting changes you apply. (To insert text that appears on each slide, see the next section, "Adding recurring text.")

You can edit any of the other objects on the Master by clicking them. Unlike the title and object area placeholders, any text you type in other Slide Master objects appears exactly as you type it on each slide.

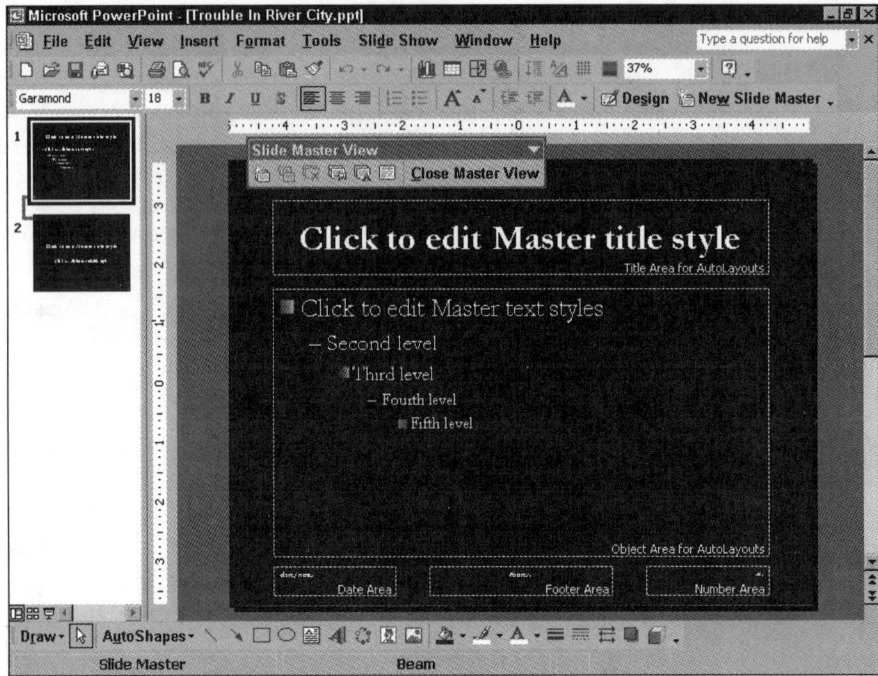

Figure 12-1: Slide Master View.

Adding recurring text

To add recurring text to each slide, follow this procedure:

1. **Call up the Slide Master if it's not displayed already.**

   The menu command is View➪Master➪Slide Master. Or you can Shift+click the Slide View button.

2. **Click the Text Box button (shown in the margin) on the Drawing toolbar.**

   This step highlights the Text Box button. The mouse cursor turns into an upside-down cross.

3. **Click where you want to add text.**

   PowerPoint places a text object at that location.

4. **Type the text that you want to appear on each slide.**

   For example: **Call 1-800-555-NERD today! Don't delay! Operators standing by!**

5. **Format the text however you want.**

   For example, if you want bold, press Ctrl+B.

6. **Click the Normal View button to return to your presentation.**

   Now's the time to gloat over your work. Lasso some coworkers and show 'em how proud you are.

You can add other types of objects to the Slide Master, too. You can click the Insert Clip Art button (shown in the margin) on the Drawing toolbar, for example, to insert any of the clip art pictures supplied with PowerPoint. Or you can use the Insert➪Movies and Sounds command to add a video or sound clip. (Clip art is described in detail in Chapter 10, and movies and sounds are covered in Chapter 18.) Anything you can add to an individual slide can be added to the Slide Master.

After you place an object on the Slide Master, you can grab it with the mouse and move it around or resize it any way you want. The object appears in the same location and size on each slide.

To delete an object from the Slide Master, click it and press the Delete key. To delete a text object, you must first click the object and then click again on the object frame. Then press Delete.

If you can't highlight the object no matter how many times you click it, you probably have returned to Slide View. Shift+click the Slide View button or choose the View➪Master➪Slide Master command again to call up the Slide Master.

Changing the Master color scheme

You can use the Slide Master to change the color scheme used for all slides in a presentation. To do that, follow these steps:

1. **Choose the View➪Master➪Slide Master command or Shift+click the Slide button to summon the Slide Master.**
2. **Choose the Format➪Slide Design to call up the Slide Design task pane. Then click Color Schemes and apply the color scheme you want to use.**

   Treat yourself to a bag of Doritos if it works the first time.

PowerPoint color schemes are hefty enough that I have devoted an entire chapter to them. Go to Chapter 11 if you forgot how they work.

If you don't have a color printer, don't waste your time messing with the color scheme unless you're going to make your presentation on-screen or with a projector. Mauve, teal, azure, and cerulean all look like gray when they're printed on a non-color laser printer.

Professionals who are colorblind in no more than one eye chose the PowerPoint color schemes. Stick to these schemes to avoid embarrassing color combinations! (I wish that my sock drawer came with a similar color-scheme feature.)

If you want to adjust the shading that's applied to the background slide color, choose the Format⇨Background command. Chapter 11 walks you through this feature.

Changing the Title Master

PowerPoint keeps a separate Master layout for title slides. That way, you can give your title slides a different layout than the other slides in your presentation. In Slide Master View, a thumbnail of the Title Master appears beneath the Slide Master thumbnail on the left side of the screen. Click the Title Master's thumbnail and the Title Master appears.

Figure 12-2 shows a Title Master. As you can see, it contains the same layout elements as the Slide Master, except that the "Object Area for AutoLayouts" is replaced with "Subtitle Area for AutoLayouts."

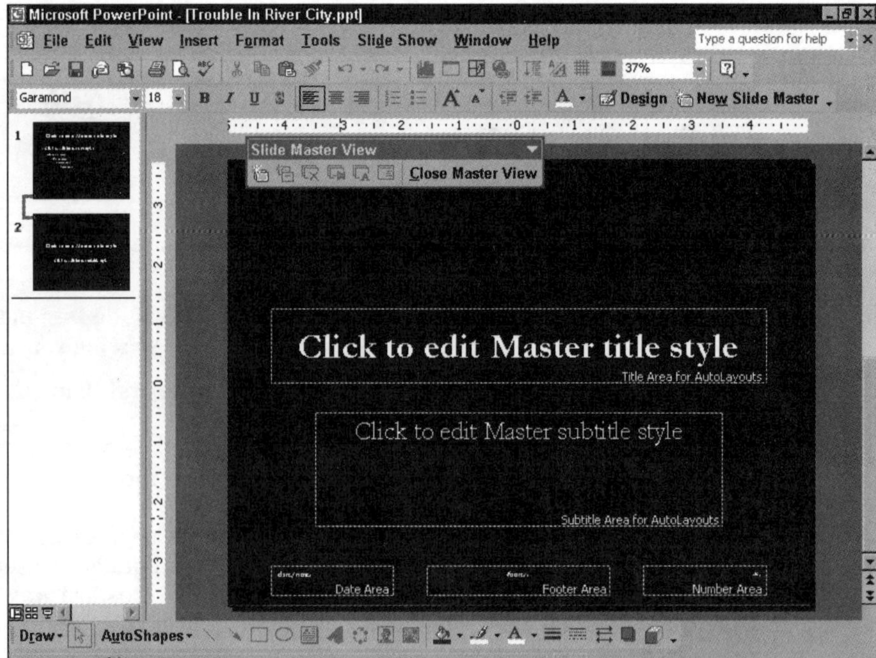

Figure 12-2: A Title Master.

Changing the Handout and Notes Masters

Like the Slide Master, the Handout and Notes Masters contain formatting information that's automatically applied to your presentation. This section tells you how you can modify these Masters.

Changing the Handout Master

Follow these simple steps to change the Handout Master:

1. **Choose the View⇨Master⇨Handout Master command or hold down the Shift key and click the Slide Sorter View button or the Outline View button.**

   The Handout Master rears its ugly head, as shown in Figure 12-3.

2. **Mess around with it.**

   The Handout Master shows the arrangement of handouts for slides printed two, three, four, six and nine per page, plus the arrangement for printing outlines. You can switch among these different handout layouts by clicking the buttons on the floating Handout Master toolbar. Unfortunately, you cannot move, resize, or delete the slide and outline placeholders that appear in the Handout Master. But you can add or change elements that you want to appear on each handout page, such as your name and phone number, a page number, and maybe a good lawyer joke.

3. **Click Close Master View in the Handout Master View toolbar.**

   You are returned to Normal View.

4. **Print a handout to see if your changes worked.**

   Handout Master elements are invisible until you print them, so you should print at least one handout page to check your work.

When you print handout pages, the slides themselves are formatted according to the Slide Master. You cannot change the appearance of the slides from the Handout Master.

Changing the Notes Master

Notes pages consist of a reduced image of the slide, plus notes you type to go along with the slide. For more information about creating and using notes pages, refer to Chapter 5.

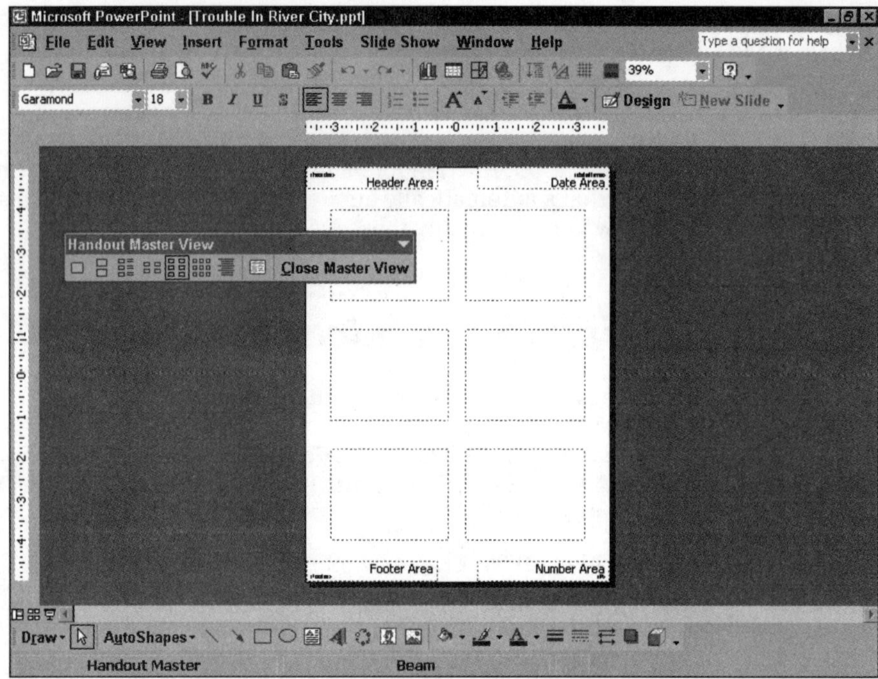

Figure 12-3: The Handout Master.

When printed, notes pages are formatted according to the Notes Master. To change the Notes Master, follow these steps:

1. **Choose the View➪Master➪Notes Master command.**

   The Notes Master comes to life, as shown in Figure 12-4.

2. **Indulge yourself.**

   The Notes Master contains two main placeholders; one for your notes text and the other for the slide. You can move or change the size of either of these objects, and you can change the format of the text in the notes placeholder. You also can add or change elements that you want to appear on each handout page. Also notice the convenient placement of the header, footer, date, and page number blocks.

3. **Click Close Master View in the Notes Master View toolbar.**

   You are returned to Normal View.

4. **Print your notes to see if your changes worked.**

   If you prefer, call up the File➪Print Preview command to check out your Notes pages without actually committing them to paper.

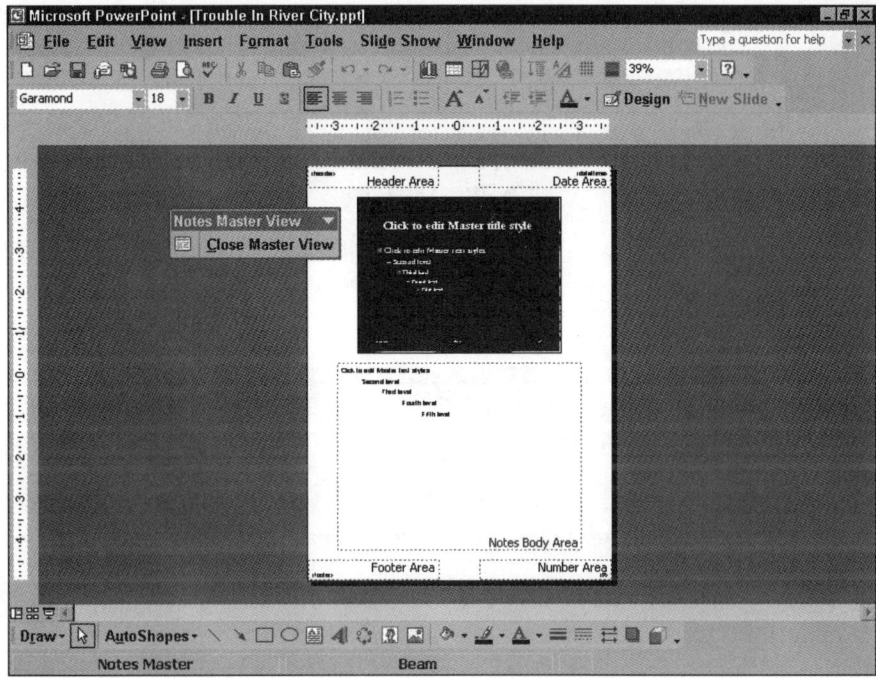

Figure 12-4: The Notes Master.

At the least, add page numbers to your speaker notes. If you drop a stack of notes pages without page numbers, you're up a creek without a paddle!

If public speaking gives you severe stomach cramps, add the text "Just picture them naked" to the Notes Master. It works every time for me.

Using Masters

You don't have to do anything special to apply the formats from a Master to your slide; all slides automatically pick up the Master format unless you specify otherwise. So this section really should be titled "Not Using Masters" because it talks about how to *not* use the formats provided by Masters.

Overriding the Master text style

To override the text style specified by a Slide or Title Master, simply format the text however you want while you're working in Normal View. The formatting changes you make apply only to the selected text. The Slide and Title Masters are not affected.

The only way to change one of the Masters is to do it directly by switching to the appropriate Master View. Thus, any formatting changes you make while in Slide View affect only that slide.

If you change the layout or formatting of text elements on a slide (for example, if you move the title placeholder or change the title font) and then decide that you liked it better the way it was, you can quickly reapply the text style from the Slide Master. Choose the Format⇨Slide Layout command to bring up the Slide Layout Task Pane. Then click the arrow to the right of the master you want to reapply and choose Reapply Layout from the menu that appears.

Hiding background objects

Slide and Title Masters enable you to add background objects that appear on every slide in your presentation. You can, however, hide the background objects for selected slides. You can also change the background color or effect used for an individual slide. These steps show you how:

1. **Display the slide you want to show with a plain background.**
2. **Choose Format⇨Background.**

   The Background dialog box appears, as shown in Figure 12-5. For notes, use Format⇨Notes Background. (The Notes Background dialog box looks much like the Background dialog box; the only difference is their titles.)
3. **Check the Omit Background Graphics from Master check box.**

   Check this box if you want to hide the Master background objects.
4. **Change the Background Fill if you want.**

   You can change to a different background color, or you can add an effect such as a pattern fill or a texture. These details are covered in Chapter 11.
5. **Click the Apply button or press Enter.**

   If you checked the Omit Background Graphics from master check box (Step 3), the background objects from the Slide Master vanish from the active slide. If you changed the background color or effect, you see that change, too.

Hiding background objects or changing the background color or effect applies only to the current slide. Other slides are unaffected.

If you want to remove some but not all the background objects from a single slide, try this trick:

1. **Follow the preceding Steps 1 through 5 to hide background objects for the slide.**
2. **Call up the Slide Master (View➪Master➪Slide Master).**
3. **Hold down the Shift key and click each object that you want to appear.**
4. **Press Ctrl+C to copy these objects to the Clipboard.**
5. **Return to Slide View.**
6. **Press Ctrl+V to paste the objects from the Clipboard.**
7. **Choose the Draw➪Order➪Send to Back command if the background objects obscure other slide objects or text. (The Draw menu is found on the Drawing toolbar.)**

Figure 12-5: The Background dialog box.

Using Headers and Footers

Headers and footers provide a convenient way to place repeating text at the top or bottom of each slide, handout, or notes page. You can add the time and date, slide number or page number, or any other information that you want to appear on each slide or page, such as your name or the title of your presentation.

The PowerPoint Slide and Title Masters include three placeholders for such information:

- The *date area* can be used to display a date and time.
- The *number area* can be used to display the slide number.
- The *footer area* can be used to display any text that you want to see on each slide.

In addition, Handout and Notes Masters include a fourth placeholder, the *header area,* which provides an additional area for text that you want to see on each page.

Although the date, number, and footer areas normally appear at the bottom of the slide in the Slide and Title Masters, you can move them to the top by switching to Slide or Title Master View and then dragging the placeholders to the top of the slide.

Adding a date, number, or footer to slides

To add a date, a slide number, or a footer to your slides, follow these steps:

1. **Choose the View⇨Header and Footer command.**

   The Header and Footer dialog box appears, as shown in Figure 12-6. (If necessary, click the Slide tab so that you see the slide footer options as shown in the figure.)

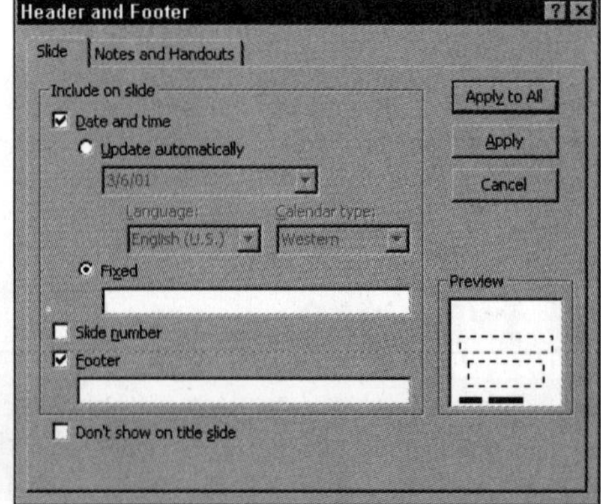

Figure 12-6: The Header and Footer dialog box.

2. **To display the date, check the Date and Time check box. Then select the date format you want in the list box beneath the Update Automatically option button.**

   Alternatively, you can type any text you want in the Fixed text box. The text you type appears in the Date Area of the Slide or Title Master.

   If you're the sort of bloke who begins a presentation with "G'day mates!" then you may want to change the Language and Calendar Type settings.

3. **To display slide numbers, check the Slide Number check box.**
4. **To display a footer on each slide, check the Footer check box and then type the text that you want to appear on each slide in the Footer text box.**

   For example, you may type your name, your company name, a subliminal message, or the name of your presentation.

5. **If you want the date, number, and footer to appear on every slide except the title slide, check the Don't Show on Title Slide check box.**

6. **Click Apply to All.**

If you're going to be giving a presentation on a certain date in the future (for example, at a sales conference or a trade show), type the date that you'll be giving the presentation directly into the Fixed text box. You can use the same technique to postdate presentations you never really gave but need to supply to your legal counsel to back up your alibi.

If you want to change the footer areas for just one slide, click Apply instead of Apply to All. This option comes in handy for those occasional slides that contain a graphic or a block of text that crowds up against the footer areas. You can easily suppress the footer information for that slide to make room for the large graphic or text.

Adding a header or footer to Notes or Handouts pages

To add header and footer information to Notes or Handouts pages, follow the steps described in the preceding section, "Adding a date, number, or footer to slides," except click the Notes and Handouts tab when the Header and Footer dialog box appears. Clicking this tab displays a dialog box that's similar to the Header and Footer dialog box for Slide, except that it gives you an additional option to add a header that appears at the top of each page. After you indicate how you want to print the date, header, number, and footer areas, click the Apply to All button.

Editing the header and footer placeholders directly

If you want, you can edit the text that appears in the header and footer placeholders directly. First, display the appropriate Master — Slide, Title, Handouts, or Notes. Then click on the date, number, footer, or header placeholder and start typing.

You may notice that the placeholders include special codes for the options you indicated in the Header and Footer dialog box. For example, the Date placeholder may contain the text *<date,time>* if you indicated that the date should be displayed. You can type text before or after these codes, but you should leave the codes themselves alone.

Yes, You Can Serve Two Masters

In spite of the Biblical edict, Microsoft's team of crack programmers decided to endow PowerPoint 2002 with the ability to have more than one Slide and Title Master. This feature, which is one that PowerPoint users have been requesting for years, lets you set up two or more Slide and Title Masters, then choose which master to use for each slide in your presentation.

Before I show you how to use this feature, I want to make sure you understand the relationship between Slide Masters and Title Masters. Every presentation has at least one Slide Master. Each Slide Master in a presentation may have a corresponding Title Master, but doesn't have to.

Suppose you create a new presentation that starts out with one Slide Master and one Title Master. Then, as you work with the presentation, you add two additional Slide Masters to create new slide designs. Now, the presentation has three Slide Masters but still only one Title Master.

If you want to add an additional Title Master, the new Title Master must be paired with an existing Slide Master that doesn't already have a Title Master. So, you can add a new Title Master to either of the two Slide Masters you created.

The following sections explain how to use the multiple masters feature.

Creating a new Slide Master

To add a new master to a presentation, follow these steps:

1. **Choose the View⇨Master⇨Slide Master command to switch to Slide Master View.**

   Or if you prefer, hold down the Shift key and click the Normal View button near the lower left corner of the screen.

2. **Click the Insert New Slide Master button (shown in the margin).**

   A new Slide Master appears, as shown in Figure 12-7. Notice that a thumbnail for the new Slide Master has been added to the list of thumbnails on the left side of the screen, and that the new Slide Master uses PowerPoint's default settings (white background, black text, and so on).

3. **Modify the new Slide Master to your liking.**

   You can make any formatting changes you want: Change the background color, text styles, add additional background objects, and so on.

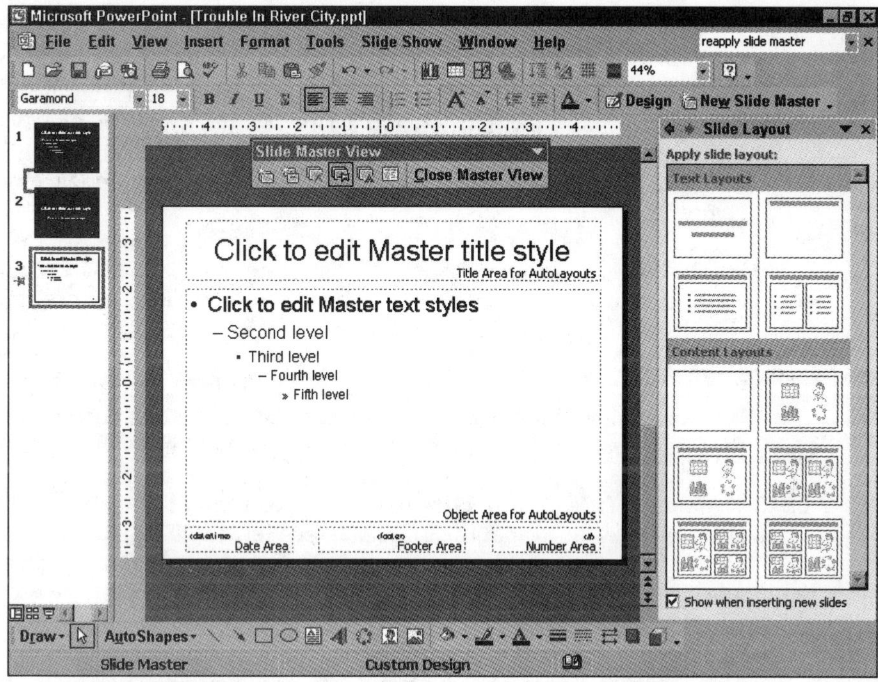

Figure 12-7: Creating a new Slide Master.

4. **Click Close Master View on the Slide Master View toolbar to return to Normal View.**

   You can now begin using the new master you created. (See "Applying masters" later in this chapter for more information.)

Another way to create a new Slide Master is to duplicate one of your presentation's existing Slide Masters. When you do that, the new Slide Master inherits the formatting of the original one. That can save you a lot of work, especially if you want to create a new Slide Master that varies from an existing one in only a minor way, such as having a different background color.

To duplicate a Slide Master, click the master you want to duplicate in the thumbnails on the left of the screen, then press Ctrl+D or choose Edit➪Duplicate.

To delete a Slide Master, click the master you want to delete and click the Delete Master button in the Slide Master View toolbar (shown in the margin), choose Edit➪Delete Master, or press the Delete key.

Creating a new Title Master

You can add a new Title Master to any Slide Master that does not yet have a Title Master paired with it. To add a Title Master, first select an available Slide Master by clicking its thumbnail on the left of the screen, then choose the Insert⇨New Title Master command. A new Title Master appears, as shown in Figure 12-8.

In Figure 12-8, you can see that the Title Master and Slide Master thumbnails are connected by a line to indicate that these Slide and Title Masters are paired.

When you create a Title Master, the Title Master inherits any formatting from its Slide Master. However, once created, the Title Master and Slide Master are formatted independently of one another. Thus, you can change the format of the Slide Master without affecting its Title Master, and vice versa.

To delete a Title Master, click the master you want to delete and click the Delete Master button in the Slide Master View toolbar (shown in the margin), choose Edit⇨Delete Master, or press the Delete key. If you delete a Slide Master that is paired with a Title Master, the Title Master is deleted as well.

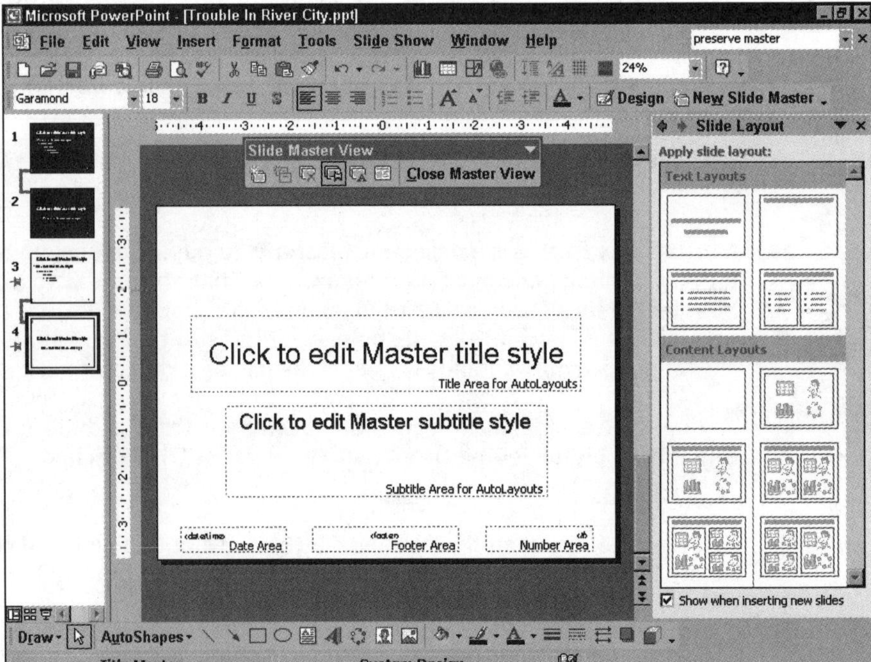

Figure 12-8: Creating a new Title Master.

Applying masters

If you have created multiple masters for a presentation, you can select which master to use for each slide in your presentation. To apply a master to one or more slides, follow these steps:

1. **Select the slide or slides you want to apply the alternate Slide Master to.**

   The easiest way to do this is to click the slide you want in the thumbnails on the left of the screen. To select more than one slide, hold down the Ctrl key and click each slide you want to select.

2. **Choose the Format⇨Slide Design command to bring up the Slide Design Task Pane.**

   Figure 12-9 shows the Slide Design Task Pane, with two slides selected in the thumbnail list.

   The Slide Design Task Pane shows a thumbnail list of Slide Masters and Design Templates you can apply to your slides. The first section of this list, labeled "Used in This Presentation," shows a thumbnail of each Slide Master in the presentation. (For more information about Design Templates, see Chapter 13.)

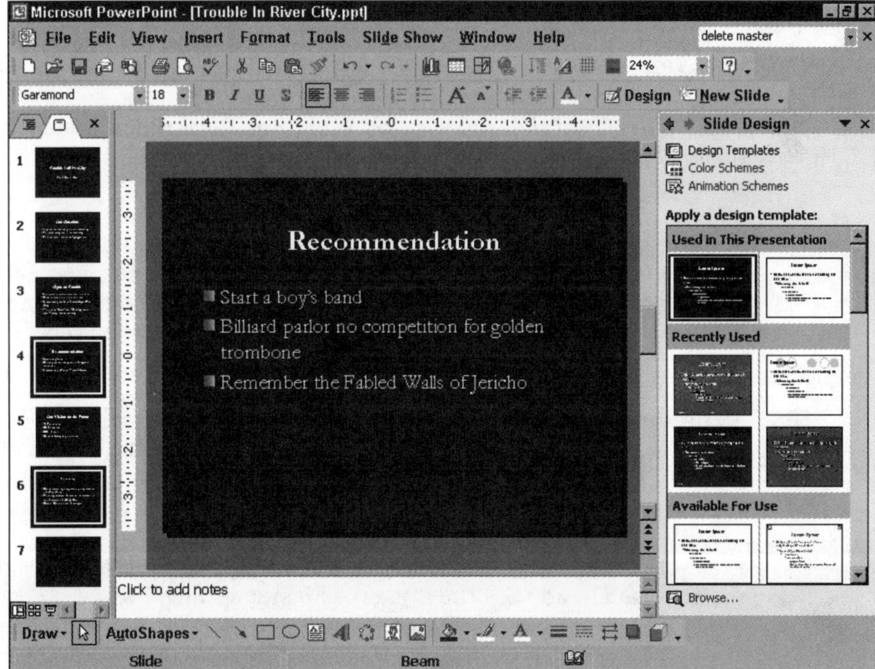

Figure 12-9: The Slide Design Task Pane lets you apply Slide Masters to your slides.

3. **Click the arrow next to the Slide Master you want to apply to the slides you've selected, then choose Apply to Selected Slides.**

   The Slide Master is applied to the selected slides.

Do not simply click the Slide Master you want to use in the Slide Design Task Pane or you may be surprised by the results. If you select two or more slides and then click a Slide Master, the Slide Master is applied to the slides you selected. But if you select only one slide and click a Slide Master, the Slide Master is applied to *all* the slides in the presentation, not just the one you selected! Worse yet, there's a good chance that PowerPoint will also delete the Slide Master that was applied to the other slides in the presentation. (This depends on whether the master has the Preserve setting, which you can find out about in the next section, "Pickling your Masters.")

To avoid this, I always click the arrow next to the Slide Master so I can select the Apply to Selected Slides command from the menu.

If you accidentally apply a Slide Master to all slides in your presentation and PowerPoint deletes the original Slide Master, just press Ctrl+Z or choose Edit⇨Undo to restore sanity to your presentation.

Pickling your Masters

PowerPoint has a bad habit of deleting Slide Masters when they are no longer used in your presentation. For example, if you create a new Slide Master, then apply it to all the slides in your presentation, PowerPoint assumes that you no longer need the original Slide Master. So the original is deleted. Poof! Your presentation is now one pickle short of a full jar.

You can prevent this from happening by using the Preserve Master option for your Slide Masters. Any new Slide Masters you create automatically get the Preserve Master option, so they won't be deleted. But the Slide and Title Masters your presentations start off with do not have the Preserve Master option, so you may want to set it yourself.

To preserve a master, first click the thumbnail for the master you want to preserve, then click the Preserve Master button in the Slide Master View toolbar (shown in the margin). A little pushpin icon will appear next to the master's thumbnail to show that the master will be preserved.

Don't click the Preserve Master button indiscriminately! If you click it for a master that already has the Preserve Master setting, Preserve Master is removed for that master. Then the master is subject to premature deletion.

Restoring Lost Placeholders

If you've played around with your masters too much, you may inadvertently delete a layout placeholder that you wish you could get back. For example, suppose you delete the footer placeholder from your Title Master and now you want it back. No problem! Just follow these steps:

1. **Choose View⇨Master⇨Slide Master to go to Slide Master View.**

   You can also shift-click the Normal View button near the bottom left of the screen.

2. **Call up the master with the missing placeholder.**

3. **Choose the Format⇨Master Layout command or click the Master Layout button in the Slide Master View toolbar (shown in the margin).**

   This calls up the Master Layout dialog box, shown in Figure 12-10.

Figure 12-10: The Master Layout dialog box.

The Master Layout dialog box is one of the strangest dialog boxes you'll encounter. If you summon it for a master that still has all its placeholders, all the check boxes on the Master Layout dialog box will be grayed out. So all you can do is look at the controls, grunt, scratch your head, and click OK to dismiss the seemingly useless dialog box. But if you *have* deleted one or more placeholders, the check boxes for the missing placeholders will be available. For example, the Footer checkbox is available in Figure 12-10.

4. **Click the checkboxes for the placeholders you want to restore.**

5. **Click OK.**

   The missing placeholders reappear.

Chapter 13

All About Templates

In This Chapter

- Understanding templates
- Using templates to create new presentations
- Switching your presentation to a different template
- Creating your own templates
- Creating a default template for blank presentations

If you had to create every presentation from scratch, starting with a blank slide and a plain Slide Master with basic black text on a basic white background, you probably would put PowerPoint back in its box and use it as a bookend. Creating a presentation is easy, but creating one that looks good is a different story. Making a good-looking presentation is tough even for the artistically inclined. For right-brain, nonartistic types like me, it's next to impossible.

Thank heavens for templates. A *template* is simply a PowerPoint presentation file with predefined Slide and Title Masters. When you create a presentation, PowerPoint gives you the option of stealing Masters from an existing template. Any PowerPoint presentation can serve as a template, including presentations you create yourself. But PowerPoint comes with more than 40 templates designed by professional artists who understand color combinations and balance and all that artsy stuff. Have a croissant and celebrate.

Because the templates that come with PowerPoint look good, any presentation you create by using one of them looks good, too. It's as simple as that. The template also supplies the color scheme for your presentation. You can override it, of course, but you do so at your own risk. The color police are everywhere, you know. You don't want to be taken in for Felony Color Clash.

Templates use the special file extension POT, but you can also use ordinary PowerPoint presentation files (PPT) as templates. You can, therefore, use any of your own presentations as a template. If you make extensive changes to a presentation's Masters, you can use that presentation as a template for other presentations you create. Or you can save the presentation as a template by using the POT file extension.

Some templates contain just Slide and Title masters. Because these templates affect the design of your presentations but don't offer any content of their own, they are called *Design Templates*. Other templates have, in addition to Slide and Title Masters, actual slides with sample content. These templates are known as *Content Templates* and are used primarily by the AutoContent Wizard (which I cover in Chapter 1).

Because a template is a presentation, you can open it and change it if you want.

Creating a Presentation Based on a Template

To create a new presentation based on a template, choose the File➪New command to summon the New Presentation Task Pane, then click From Design Template in the New section. The Slide Design Task Pane appears, as shown in Figure 13-1. Click the template you want to use and a new presentation will be created using it.

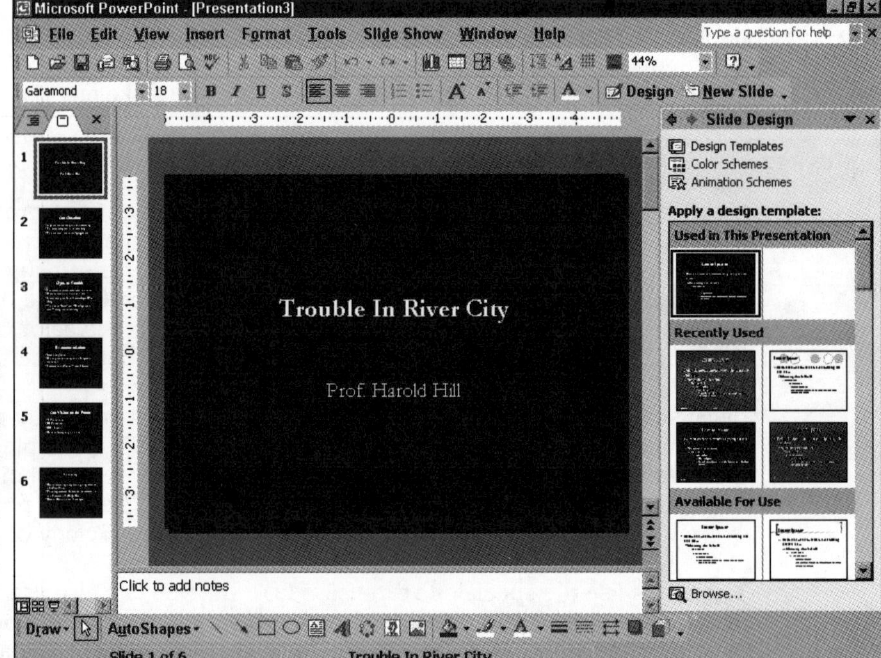

Figure 13-1: The Slide Design Task Pane lets you select a Design template for your presentation.

The most recent templates you use are listed directly in the New from Template section of the New Presentation Task Pane. If the template you want to use is listed, you can click it instead of clicking From Design Template. Then you won't have to deal with the Slide Design Task Pane.

Another way to create a new presentation using a template is to click General Templates in the New from Template section of the New Presentation Task Pane. This brings up the dialog box shown in Figure 13-2, which lets you choose the template you want to use. Notice the tabs across the top of this dialog box. Click these tabs to bring up several different categories of templates you can use. When you have selected the template you want to use, click OK.

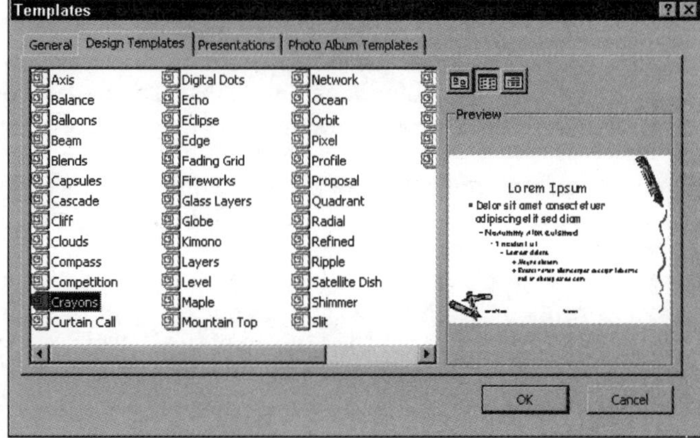

Figure 13-2: The Templates dialog box.

The New Presentation Task Pane also has links that let you look for templates on your own Web sites or on Microsoft's Web site.

Switching Templates

You're halfway through creating a new presentation when you realize that you can't stand the look of the slides. Oops — you picked the wrong template when you started the new presentation! Don't panic. PowerPoint enables you to assign a new presentation template at any time. These steps show you how:

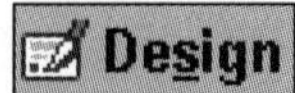

1. **Choose the Format➪Slide Design command or click the Design button in the Formatting toolbar (shown in the margin).**

   The Slide Design Task Pane appears (refer to Figure 13-1).

2. **Rummage around for a template you like better.**

   Scroll down the list to the Available for Use section, where you'll find the Design Templates that come with PowerPoint.

3. **Point the mouse at the template thumbnail you want to use, then click the arrow that appears next to the thumbnail and choose the Apply to All Slides command.**

   The Slide and Title masters in the template you chose is applied to your presentation.

You may still want to make minor adjustments to the Slide and Title Masters to make the slides look just right. Refer to Chapter 12 for the necessary instructions.

When you apply a new template, PowerPoint copies the Masters and the color scheme into your presentation. As a result, any changes you made to the presentation's Masters or color scheme are lost. Too bad. If you added background objects to the Slide Master, you have to add them again.

You don't have to worry about the new template undoing any formatting changes that you've made to individual slides. PowerPoint remembers these deviations from the Master format when it applies a new template.

Another way to bring up the Slide Design task bar is to double-click the name of the template in the status bar at the bottom of the PowerPoint window.

Creating a New Template

If none of the templates that come with PowerPoint appeals to you, you can easily create your own. All you have to do is create a presentation with the Masters and the color scheme set up just the way you want and then save it as a template. Here are a few points to remember about templates:

- The design templates that come with PowerPoint have no slides in them. To create a template without any slides, choose the New button, and then click the Cancel button when the Add New Slide dialog box appears. Then choose the View➪Master➪Slide Master command to switch to Slide Master View, then go to work on your template's design.
- If you want to make minor modifications to one of the supplied templates, open the template by using the File➪Open command and then immediately save it under a new name by using the File➪Save As command. Then change the Masters and the color scheme. Don't forget to save the file again when you're finished!
- Your templates are easily accessible if you store them in the \Windows\Application Data\Microsoft Office\Templates folder.

- You can also create your own presentation templates complete with skeleton slides. Just create the template as a normal presentation and add however many slides you want to include.
- When you are ready to save your template, use the Save As Type command. Set your type to Design Template (*.pot).

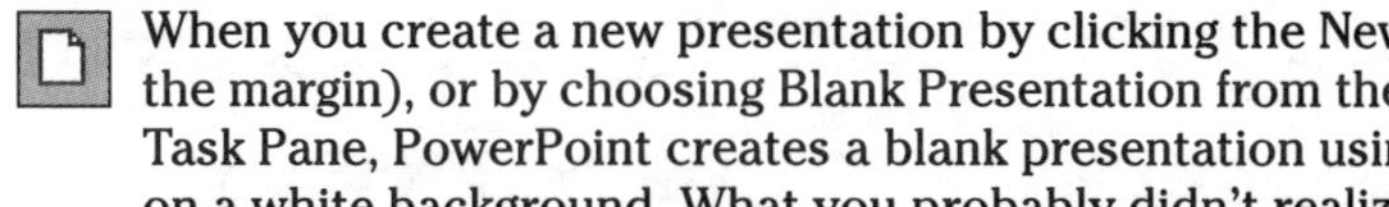

Creating a New Default Template

When you create a new presentation by clicking the New button (shown in the margin), or by choosing Blank Presentation from the New Presentation Task Pane, PowerPoint creates a blank presentation using default black text on a white background. What you probably didn't realize is that even blank presentations can use a template — a template named Blank.pot is automatically applied to new blank presentations.

If you want to create your own default template, all you have to do is save your template file by using the filename Blank.pot in the default folder for the Save As command (\Windows\Application Data\Microsoft\Templates). Then whenever you create a blank presentation, the Masters and the color scheme are copied from your new default template rather than from the bland default template that comes with PowerPoint.

To revert to the plain black-on-white blank template, just delete the Blank.pot file. If PowerPoint can't find the Blank.pot template, it uses the default black-on-white layout.

These steps show you how to create a new default template:

1. **Create a new presentation by clicking the New button or choosing Blank Presentation from the New Presentation Task Pane.**
2. **Choose View⇨Master⇨Slide Master to switch to Slide Master View.**
3. **Make any changes you want to the Slide and Title Masters.**

   For example, change the background color and the text fonts and colors.
4. **Click the Save button.**
5. **Change the Save as Type control to Design Template (*.pot).**
6. **Type Blank in the File Name field.**
7. **Click Save.**

Part III

Neat Things You Can Put on Your Slides

"NIFTY CHART, FRANK, BUT NOT ENTIRELY NECESSARY."

In this part . . .

You'll hear nothing but yawns from the back row if your presentation consists of slide after slide of text and bulleted lists with an occasional bit of clip art thrown in for good measure. Mercifully, PowerPoint is well equipped to add all sorts of embellishments to your slide — drawings, graphs, organizational charts, equations, animation, and more. You can even make your presentations belch on command.

Not that any of this is easy. That's why I devote an entire part to wrestling with these ornaments.

Chapter 14

Drawing on Your Slides

In This Chapter

- Using the PowerPoint drawing tools
- Drawing lines, rectangles, and circles
- Using predefined AutoShapes
- Drawing fancier shapes such as polygons or curved lines
- Changing colors and line types
- Creating 3-D objects
- Flipping and rotating objects
- Understanding layers and groups
- Lining things up and spacing them out

Chim-chiminey, chim-chiminey, chim-chim cheroo, I draws what I likes and I likes what I drew. . . .

Art time! Everybody get your crayons and glue and don an old paint shirt. You're going to cut out some simple shapes and paste them on your PowerPoint slides so that people think that you are a wonderful artist or scoff at you for not using clip art.

This chapter covers the drawing features of PowerPoint. One of the best things about PowerPoint is the cool drawing tools. Once upon a time, PowerPoint had but rudimentary drawing tools, the equivalent of a box of crayons. PowerPoint now has powerful drawing tools that are sufficient for all but the most sophisticated aspiring artists among us.

Some General Drawing Tips

Before getting into the specifics of using each PowerPoint drawing tool, this section describes a handful of general tips for drawing pictures.

Zoom in

When you work with the PowerPoint drawing tools, you may want to increase the zoom factor so that you can draw more accurately. I often work at 200, 300, or even 400 percent when I'm drawing. To change the zoom factor, click the down arrow next to the Zoom Control button (near the right side of the Standard toolbar) and choose a zoom factor from the list. Or you can click the zoom factor, type a new zoom percentage, and press Enter.

Before you change the zoom factor to edit an object, choose the object that you want to edit. That way, PowerPoint zooms in on that area of the slide. If you don't choose an object before you zoom in, you may need to scroll around to find the right location.

Also, get rid of the Task Pane when you're drawing. That makes more room on the screen for the slide.

Display the ruler

If you want to be precise about lining up objects on the slide, make sure the ruler is on. If you can't see the ruler on-screen, choose View⇨Ruler to display it. Figure 14-1 shows how PowerPoint looks when the ruler is activated.

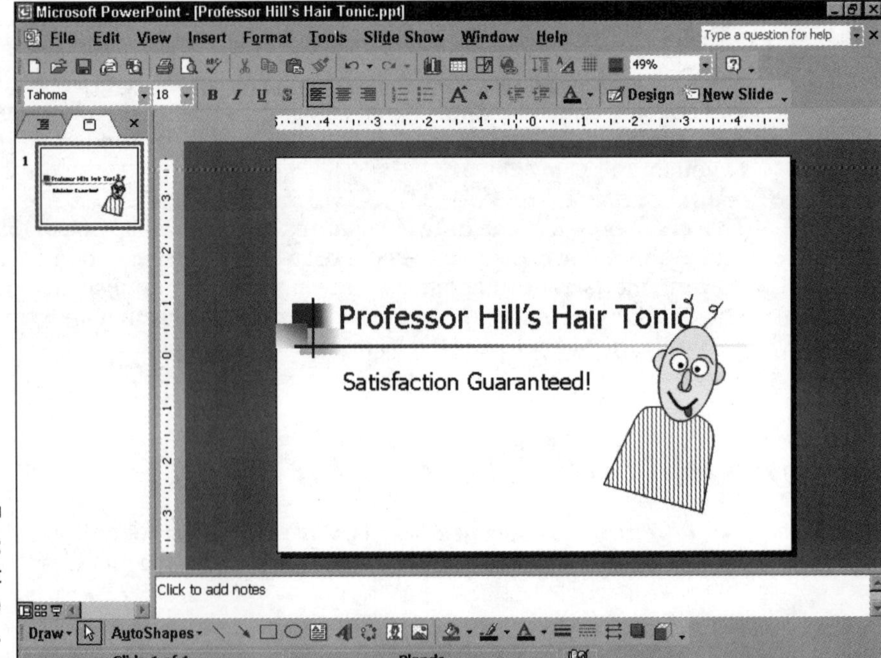

Figure 14-1: PowerPoint with the rulers on.

When you work with drawing objects, PowerPoint formats the ruler so that zero is at the middle of the slide. When you edit a text object, the ruler changes to a text ruler that measures from the margins and indicates tab positions.

Stick to the color scheme

You can assign individual colors to each object that you draw, but the point of the PowerPoint color schemes is to talk you out of doing that. If possible, let solid objects default to the color scheme's fill color. The beauty of doing this is that if you change the color scheme later on, the fill color for objects changes to reflect the new fill color. But after you change the fill color, the object ignores any change to the slide's color scheme.

If you must assign a separate color to an object, choose one of the eight colors that are a part of the color scheme. (If you decide to arbitrarily choose one of PowerPoint's 64 million colors for an object, a good lawyer may be able to get you off by using the "irresistible urge" defense.)

Save frequently

Drawing is tedious work. You don't want to spend two hours working on a particularly important drawing only to lose it all just because a comet strikes your building or an errant Scud lands in your backyard. You can prevent catastrophic loss from incidents such as these by pressing Ctrl+S or by frequently clicking the Save button with your mouse as you work. And always wear protective eyewear.

Don't forget Ctrl+Z

Ctrl+Z is the most important key in any Windows program, and PowerPoint is no exception. Always remember that you're never more than one keystroke away from erasing a boo-boo. If you do something silly — like forgetting to group a complex picture before trying to move it — you can always press Ctrl+Z to undo your last action. Ctrl+Z is my favorite and most frequently used PowerPoint key combination. (For left-handed mouse users, Alt+Backspace does the same thing.) And for those not ready to climb shrieking on a chair at the first sign of a mouse, try the handy Undo button on the Formatting toolbar.

The Drawing Toolbar

PowerPoint provides a whole row of drawing tools, located on the Drawing toolbar. If the Drawing toolbar has disappeared, you can make it appear again by choosing View⇨Toolbars and checking the Drawing check box.

Table 14-1 shows you what each drawing tool does.

Table 14-1 Buttons on the Drawing Toolbar

Drawing Tool	*What It's Called*	*What It Does*
	Select Objects button	Not really a drawing tool, but rather the generic mouse pointer used to choose objects.
AutoShapes ▾	AutoShapes button	Pops up the AutoShapes menu, which contains a bevy of shapes that you can draw, including fancy lines, arrows, crosses, flowchart symbols, stars, and more!
	Line button	Draws a line.
	Arrow button	Draws an arrow.
	Rectangle button	Draws a rectangle. To make a perfect square, hold down the Shift key while you draw.
	Oval button	Draws circles and ovals. To create a perfect circle, hold down the Shift key while you draw.
	Text box button	Adds a text object.
	Insert WordArt button	Summons forth WordArt, which lets you create all sorts of fancy text effects.
	Insert Diagram	Inserts a diagram or organization chart.
	Insert Clip Art button	Summons the Clip Gallery dialog box.
	Insert Picture	Inserts a picture.

Drawing Tool	What It's Called	What It Does
	Fill Color button	Sets the color used to fill solid objects such as circles and ellipses as well as AutoShapes.
	Line Color button	Sets the color used to draw lines, including lines around rectangles, ellipses, and AutoShapes.
	Font Color button	Sets the color used for text.
	Line Style	Sets the style used for lines.
	Dash Style	Creates dashed lines.
	Arrow Style	Creates arrowheads.
	Shadow Style	Creates shadows.
	3-D Style	Creates 3-D effects.

The good folks at Microsoft couldn't decide whether the Drawing toolbar should contain buttons or menus, so they threw in some of both. The Draw and AutoShapes buttons are actually menus that behave just like menus on a normal menu bar: Click them to reveal a menu of choices or use the Alt key shortcuts to activate them (Alt+R activates the Draw menu, and Alt+U activates the AutoShapes menu).

Drawing Simple Text Objects

To draw an object on a slide, just click the button that represents the object that you want to draw and then use the mouse to draw the object on the slide. Well, it's not always as simple as that. You find detailed instructions for drawing with the more important tools in the following sections. But first, I want to give you some pointers to keep in mind:

- Before you draw an object, move to the slide on which you want to draw the object. If you want the object to appear on every slide in the presentation, display the Slide Master by choosing View⇨Master⇨Slide Master or Shift+clicking the Normal View button on the status bar.
- PowerPoint has two types of objects: *shapes*, such as circles, rectangles, and crosses; *lines* and *arcs*. PowerPoint enables you to add text to any shape object, but you can't add text to a line or arc object.

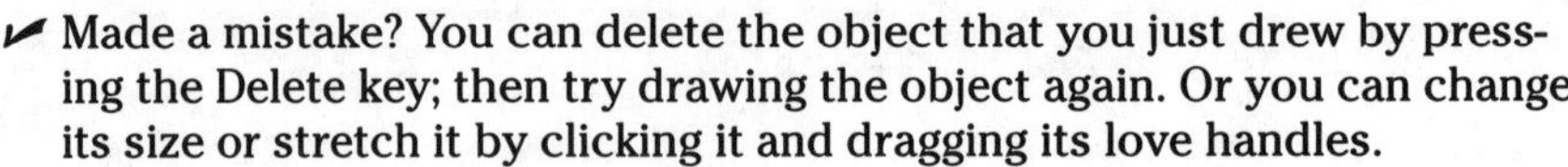

- Made a mistake? You can delete the object that you just drew by pressing the Delete key; then try drawing the object again. Or you can change its size or stretch it by clicking it and dragging its love handles.

- Table 14-2 summarizes some handy shortcuts that you can use while drawing. The last shortcut needs a bit of explanation. If you click a drawing tool button once (such as the rectangle or ellipse button), the mouse cursor reverts to an arrow after you draw an object. To draw another object, you must click a drawing tool button again. If you know in advance that you want to draw more than one object of the same type, double-click the drawing tool button. Then you can keep drawing objects of the selected type till who laid the rails. To stop drawing, click the Selection tool button (the arrow at the top of the Drawing toolbar).
- I have no idea what the expression "till who laid the rails" means. One of the residents of River City (the mayor, I believe) used it in *The Music Man,* and I've liked it ever since.

Table 14-2 Drawing Shortcuts

Shortcut	*What It Does*
Shift	Hold down the Shift key to force lines to be horizontal or vertical, to force arcs and ellipses to be true circles, to force rectangles to be squares, or to draw other regular shapes.
Ctrl	Hold down the Ctrl key to draw objects from the center rather than from end to end.
Ctrl+Shift	Hold down these two keys to draw from the center and to enforce squareness or circleness.
Double-click	Double-click any drawing button on the Drawing toolbar if you want to draw several objects of the same type.

Drawing straight lines

You use the Line button to draw straight lines on your slides. Here's the procedure:

1. **Click the Line button (shown in the margin).**
2. **Point to where you want the line to start.**
3. **Click and drag the mouse cursor to where you want the line to end.**
4. **Release the mouse button when you reach your destination.**

You can use the Format⇨Colors and Lines command to change the line color and other features (thickness, dashes, and arrowheads) for a line or arc object. Or you can click the Line Style button (in the margin) or Line Color button on the Drawing toolbar (see Table 14-1) to change these attributes.

After you've drawn a line, you can adjust it by clicking it and then dragging the handles that appear on each end of the line.

Remember that you can force a line to be perfectly horizontal or vertical by holding down the Shift key while you draw.

Drawing rectangles, squares, ovals, and circles

To draw a rectangle, follow these steps:

1. **Click the Rectangle button (shown in the margin).**
2. **Point to where you want one corner of the rectangle to be positioned.**
3. **Click the mouse button and drag to where you want the opposite corner of the rectangle to be positioned.**
4. **Release the mouse button.**

The steps for drawing an oval are the same as the steps for drawing a rectangle except that you click the Oval button (shown in the margin) rather than the Rectangle button. To draw a square or perfectly round circle, hold down the Shift key while you draw.

You can use the Format⇨Colors and Lines command to change the fill color or the line style for a rectangle or oval object. You also can use the Line Style button or the Fill Color button (shown in the margin) on the Drawing toolbar.

To apply a shadow, use the Shadow button. See the section "Applying a Shadow" later in this chapter for more information.

You can adjust the size or shape of a rectangle or circle by clicking it and dragging any of its love handles.

Using AutoShapes

Rectangles and circles aren't the only two shapes PowerPoint can draw automatically. When you click the AutoShapes button on the Drawing toolbar, a whole menu of AutoShapes appears. These AutoShapes make it easy to draw common shapes such as pentagons, stars, and flowchart symbols.

The AutoShapes menu organizes AutoShapes into the following categories:

- **Lines:** Straight lines, curved lines, lines with arrowheads, scribbly lines, and free-form shapes that can become polygons if you want. The free-form AutoShape is useful enough to merit its own section, "Drawing a Polygon or Free-form shape," which immediately follows this section.
- **Connectors:** Lines with various shapes and arrowheads with connecting dots on the ends.
- **Basic Shapes:** Squares, rectangles, triangles, crosses, happy faces, lightning bolts, and more.
- **Block Arrows:** Fat arrows pointing in various directions.
- **Flowchart:** Various flowcharting symbols.
- **Stars and Banner:** Shapes that add sparkle to your presentations.
- **Callouts:** Text boxes and speech bubbles like those used in comic strips.
- **Action Buttons:** Buttons that you can add to your slides and click during a slide show to go directly to another slide or to run a macro.
- **More AutoShapes:** In fact, 64 more. Some of these work great for your Web page presentation, and there is even one that looks like a Christmas tree.

These steps show you how to draw an AutoShape:

1. **Click the AutoShapes button on the Drawing toolbar.**

   The AutoShapes menu appears.

2. **Choose the AutoShape category you want.**

   A toolbar of AutoShapes appears. Figure 14-2 shows all the toolbars that you can access from the AutoShapes menu. Look this figure over to see what kind of AutoShapes are available. (Of course, when you actually use PowerPoint, only one of these toolbars is visible at a time.)

3. **Click the AutoShape that you want to draw.**
4. **Click the slide where you want the shape to appear and then drag the shape to the desired size.**

   When you release the mouse button, the AutoShape object takes on the current fill color and line style.

5. **Start typing if you want the shape to contain text.**

   Hold down the Shift key while drawing the AutoShape to create an undistorted shape.

To dismiss the AutoShapes toolbar, click its close button in the upper-right corner.

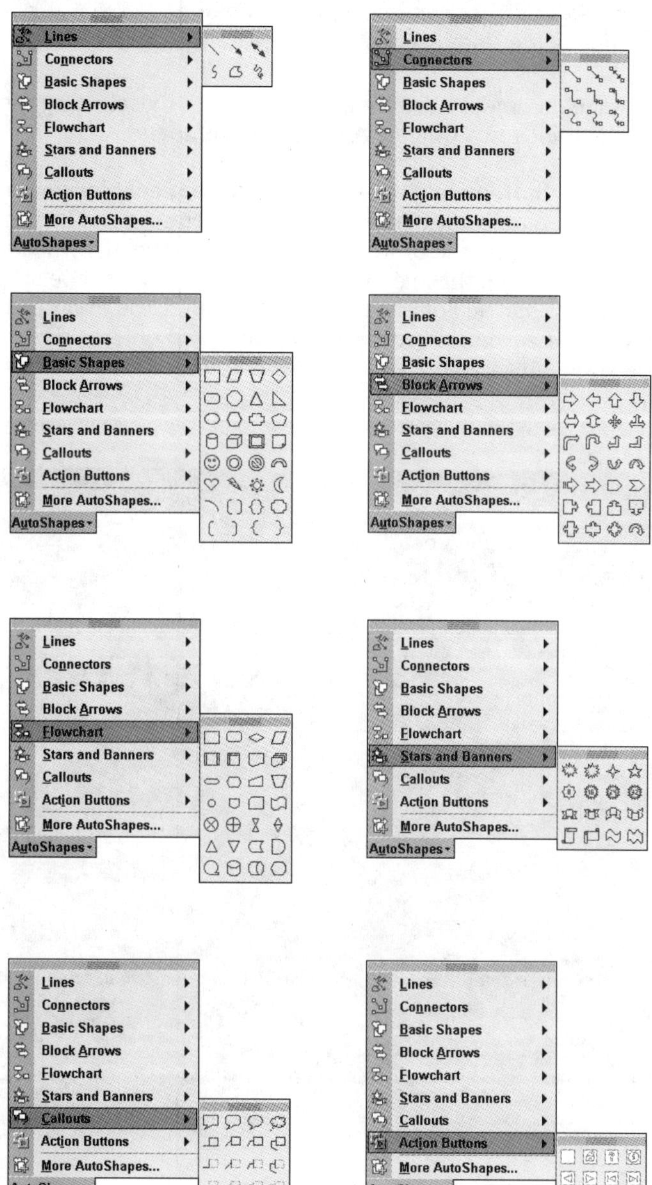

Figure 14-2: Basic shapes.

Some AutoShapes — especially the Stars and Banners — cry out for text. Figure 14-3 shows how you can use a star shape to add a jazzy burst to a slide.

You can change an object's AutoShape at any time by selecting the object and then choosing the Draw➪Change AutoShape command.

Many AutoShape buttons have an extra handle that enables you to adjust some aspect of the object's shape. For example, the arrows have a handle that enables you to increase or decrease the size of the arrowhead. Figure 14-4 shows how you can use these extra handles to vary the shapes produced by six different AutoShapes. For each of the six shapes, the first object shows how the AutoShape is initially drawn; the other two objects drawn with each AutoShape show how you can change the shape by dragging the extra handle.

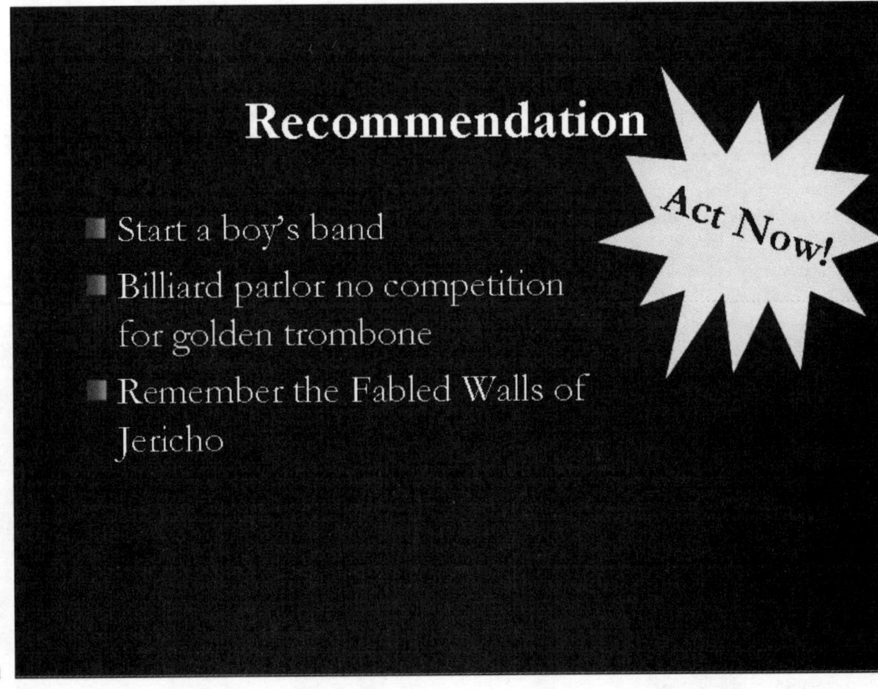

Figure 14-3: Use a star shape to make your presentation look like a late-night infomercial.

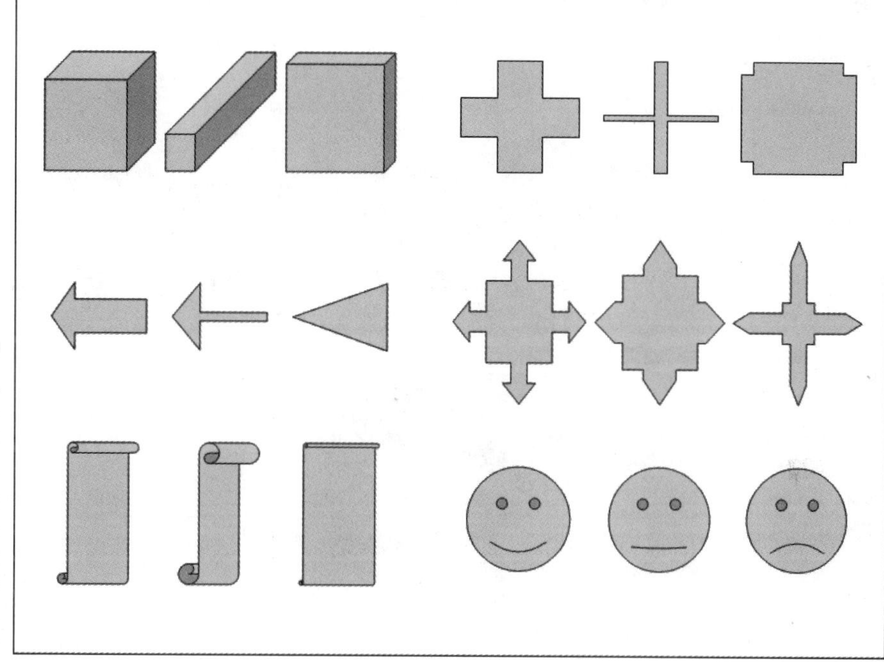

Figure 14-4: Interesting variations are possible by grabbing the extra handles on these AutoShapes.

Drawing a Polygon or Freeform Shape

Mr. Arnold, my seventh-grade math teacher, taught me that a *polygon* is a shape that has many sides and has nothing to do with having more than one spouse (one is certainly enough for most of us). Triangles, squares, and rectangles are polygons, but so are hexagons and pentagons, as are any unusual shapes whose sides all consist of straight lines. Politicians are continually inventing new polygons when they revise the boundaries of congressional districts.

One of the most useful AutoShapes is the Freeform tool. It's designed to create polygons, with a twist: Not all the sides have to be straight lines. The Freeform AutoShape tool lets you build a shape whose sides are a mixture of straight lines and freeform curves. Figure 14-5 shows three examples of shapes that I created with the Freeform AutoShape tool.

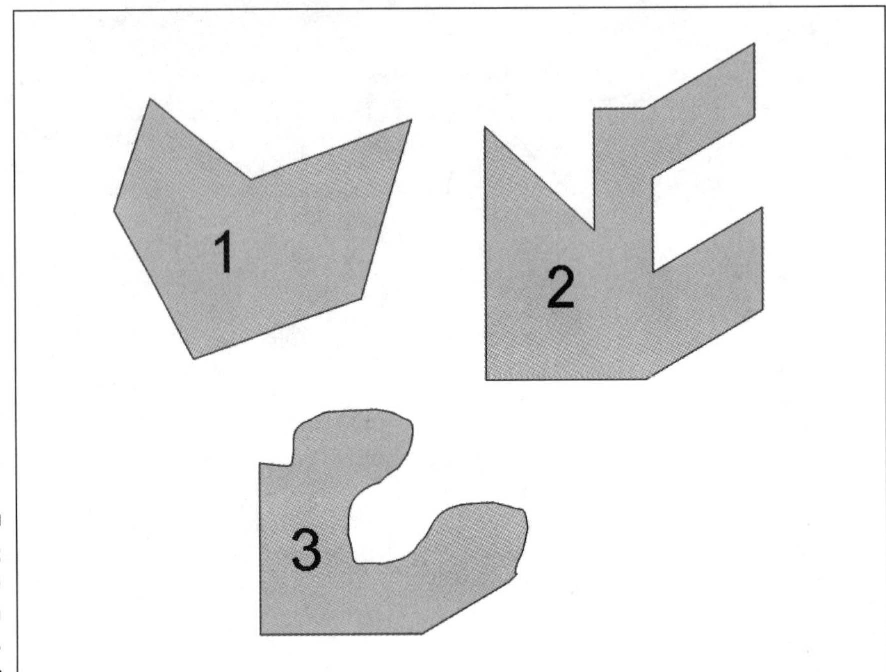

Figure 14-5: Three free-form shapes.

Follow these steps to create a polygon or free-form shape:

1. **Click the AutoShapes button and then choose Lines.**

   The Lines toolbar appears.

2. **Click the Freeform button (shown in the margin).**
3. **Click where you want to position the first corner of the object.**
4. **Click where you want to position the second corner of the object.**
5. **Keep clicking wherever you want to position a corner.**
6. **To finish the shape, click near the first corner, the one you created in Step 3.**

   You don't have to be exact: If you click anywhere near the first corner that you put down, PowerPoint assumes that the shape is finished.

You're finished! The object assumes the line and fill color from the slide's color scheme.

To draw a free-form side on the shape, hold down the mouse button when you click a corner and then draw the free-form shape with the mouse. When you get to the end of the free-form side, release the mouse button. Then you can click again to add more corners. Shape 3 in Figure 14-5 has one free-form side.

You can reshape a polygon or free-form shape by double-clicking it and then dragging any of the love handles that appear on the corners.

If you hold down the Shift key while you draw a polygon, the sides are constrained to 45-degree angles. Shape 2 in Figure 14-5 was drawn in this manner. How about a constitutional amendment requiring Congress to use the Shift key when it redraws congressional boundaries?

You also can use the Freeform AutoShape tool to draw a multisegmented line, called an *open shape.* To draw an open shape, you can follow the steps in this section, except that you skip Step 6. Instead, double-click or press the Esc key when the line is done.

Drawing a Curved Line or Shape

Another useful AutoShape tool is the Curve button, which lets you draw curved lines or shapes. Figure 14-6 shows several examples of curved lines and shapes drawn with the Curve AutoShape tool.

Here is the procedure for drawing a curved line or shape:

1. **Click the AutoShapes button and then choose Lines.**

   The Lines toolbar appears.

2. **Click the Curve button (shown in the margin).**
3. **Click where you want the curved line or shape to begin.**
4. **Click where you want the first turn in the curve to appear.**

   The straight line turns to a curved line, bent around the point where you clicked. As you move the mouse, the bend of the curve changes.

5. **Click to add additional turns to the curve.**

   Each time you click, a new bend is added to the line. Keep clicking until the line is as twisty as you want.

6. **To finish a line, double-click where you want the end of the curved line to appear. To create a closed shape, double-click over the starting point, where you clicked in Step 3.**

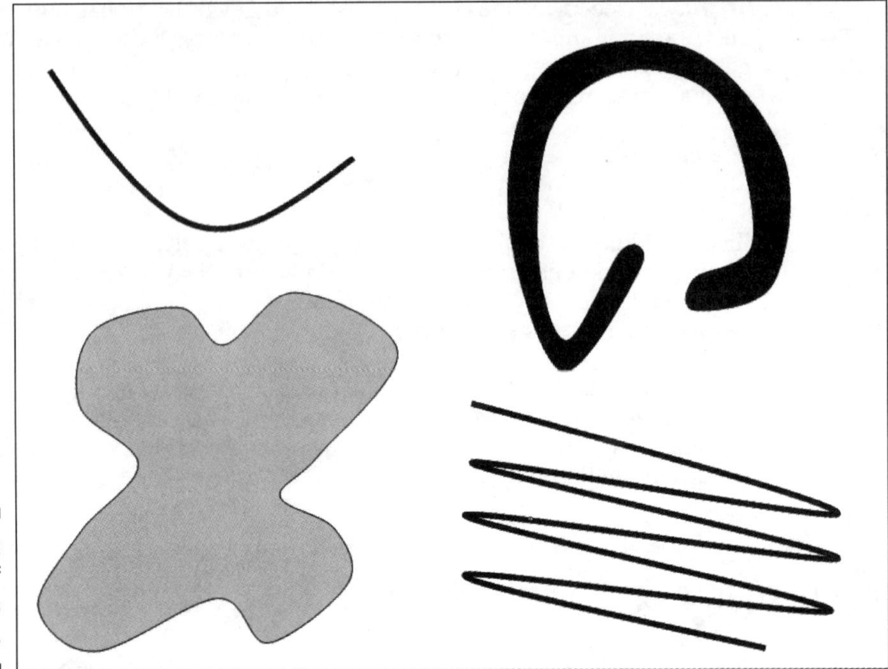

Figure 14-6: Examples of curved lines and shapes.

Drawing a Text Box

A text box is a special type of shape that is designed to place text on your slides. To draw a text box, click the text box button (shown in the margin); click where you want one corner of the text box to appear and drag to where you want the opposite corner, just like you're drawing a rectangle. When you release the mouse button, you can type text.

You can format the text you type in the text box by highlighting the text and using the text formatting controls on the Formatting toolbar. For more information about formatting text, refer to Chapter 9.

You can format the text box itself by using the Fill Color, Line Color, and Line Style buttons, described in the next section. By default, text boxes have no fill or line color so the box itself is invisible on the slide — only the text is visible.

Most AutoShapes also function as text boxes. If you want to add text to an AutoShape, just click the shape and start typing. The text appears centered over the shape. (The only AutoShapes that do not accept text are lines and connectors.)

Setting the Fill, Line, and Font Color

The three color controls that appear on the drawing toolbar let you set the fill color (that is, the color used to fill a solid object), the line color, and the color of an object's text. These buttons behave a little strangely, so they merit a bit of explanation.

Each of the color buttons actually consists of two parts: a button and an arrow. Click the button to assign the current fill, line, or text color to the selected object. Click the arrow to apply any color you want to the selected object.

When you click the arrow, a menu appears. For example, Figure 14-7 shows the Fill Color menu that appears when you click the arrow attached to the Fill Color button. As you can see, this menu includes a palette of colors that you can select. If you want to use a color that isn't visible on the menu, select More Fill Colors. This displays a dialog box that includes a color wheel from which you can select just about any color under the sun. Chapter 11 carefully explains this dialog box, so I won't review it here.

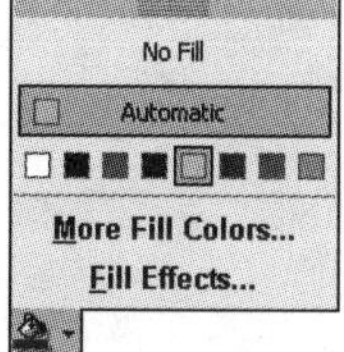

Figure 14-7: The Fill Color menu.

If you set the Fill Color, Line Color, or Font Color to Automatic, the fill color changes whenever you change the presentation's color scheme.

You can also apply a fill effect — such as gradient fill or a pattern — to an object by choosing the Fill Effects command from the Fill Color menu. This pops up the Fill Effects dialog box, which Chapter 11 describes in detail.

The Line Color and Font Color menus have similar commands. In addition, the Line Color menu includes a Patterned Lines command that lets you pick a pattern to apply to lines.

Setting the Line Style

Three buttons in the Drawing toolbar let you change the style of line objects:

- **Line Style:** The thickness of the lines that outline the object.

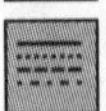

- **Dash Style:** The dashing pattern used for the lines that outline the object. The default uses a solid line, but different patterns are available to create dashed lines.

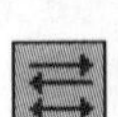

- **Arrow Style:** Lines can have an arrowhead at either or both ends. Arrowheads are used mostly on line and arc objects.

To change any of these object attributes, simply select the object or objects that you want to change and then click the appropriate button to change the style. A menu of style options appears.

The Line Style menu includes a More Lines command that summons the dialog box shown in Figure 14-8. From this dialog box, you can control all aspects of a line's style: its color, width, dash pattern, and end style (various arrowheads can be applied). The Arrow Style command includes a More Arrows command that summons the same dialog box.

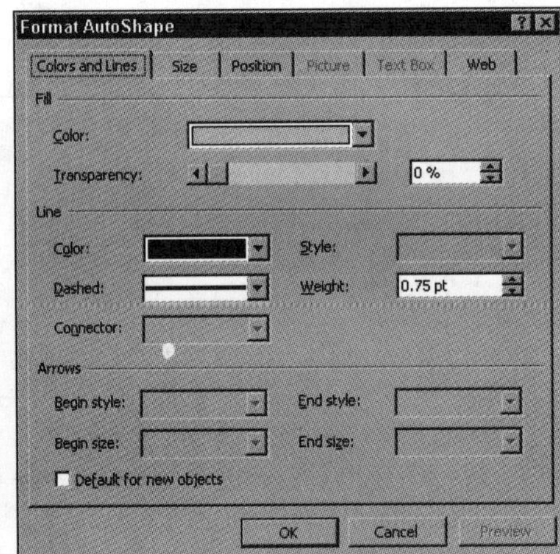

Figure 14-8: Setting the line style.

Applying a Shadow

To apply a shadow effect to an object, select the object and click the Shadow button. The Shadow menu shown in Figure 14-9 appears, offering several shadow styles. Click the shadow style that you want the object to assume.

Figure 14-9: The Shadow menu.

If you select the Shadow Settings command from the Shadow menu, the Shadow Settings toolbar shown in Figure 14-10 appears. The buttons on this toolbar allow you to nudge the shadow into exactly the right position and change the shadow color to create a custom shadow effect.

Figure 14-10: The Shadow Settings toolbar.

Adding 3-D Effects

The 3-D button is one of the coolest buttons on the Drawing toolbar. It lets you transform a dull and lifeless flat object into an exciting, breathtaking three-dimensional object. Figure 14-11 shows how you can use the 3-D button to transform several shapes into 3-D objects. In each case, the object on the left is a simple AutoShape, and the three objects to the right of the simple AutoShape are three-dimensional versions of the same shape.

To apply a 3-D effect to a shape, select the shape and click the 3-D button. The 3-D menu shown in Figure 14-12 appears. Click the effect that you want to apply. Or click No 3-D if you want to remove 3-D effects.

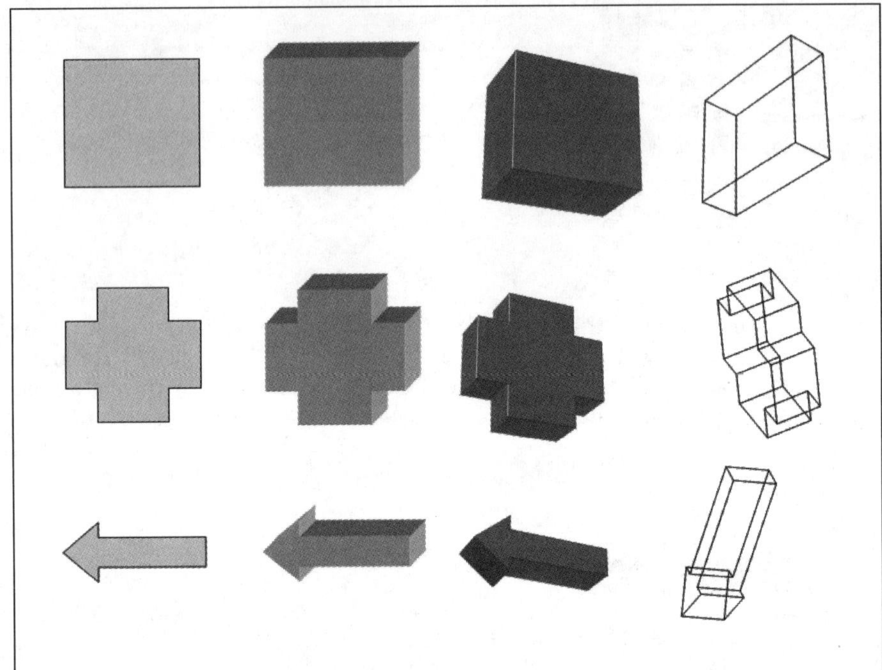

Figure 14-11: 3-D effects are cool.

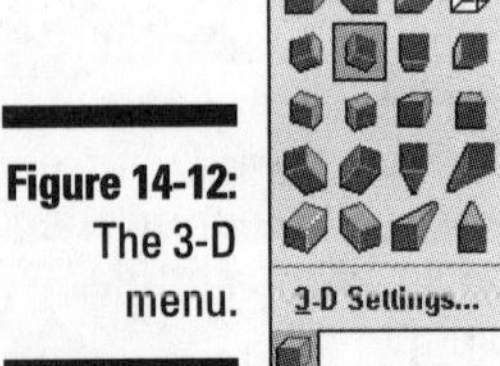

Figure 14-12: The 3-D menu.

If you select 3-D Settings from the 3-D menu, the toolbar shown in Figure 14-13 appears. You can use the controls on this toolbar to tweak the 3-D settings of the object to obtain just the right effect. You can tilt the object in any direction, set its depth, and apply lighting and surface textures.

Figure 14-13: The 3-D menu.

Flipping and Rotating Objects

To *flip* an object means to create a mirror image of it. To *rotate* an object means to turn it about its center. PowerPoint lets you flip objects horizontally or vertically, rotate objects in 90-degree increments, or freely rotate an object to any angle.

Rotation works for text boxes and AutoShape text. Thus, you can use rotation to create vertical text or text skewed to any angle you want. However, flipping an object does not affect the object's text.

Flipping an object

PowerPoint enables you to flip an object vertically or horizontally to create a mirror image of the object. To flip an object, follow these steps:

1. **Choose the object that you want to flip.**
2. **Click the Draw button to reveal the Draw menu, choose Rotate or Flip, and then choose Flip Horizontal or Flip Vertical.**

Rotating an object 90 degrees

You can rotate an object in 90-degree increments by following these steps:

1. **Choose the object that you want to rotate.**
2. **Click the Draw button to reveal the Draw menu, choose Rotate or Flip, and then choose Rotate Left or Rotate Right.**
3. **To rotate the object 180 degrees, click the appropriate Rotate button again.**

Using the rotate handle

Remember how all the bad guys' hideouts were slanted in the old *Batman* TV show? The rotation handle lets you give your drawings that same kind of slant. With the rotation handle, you can rotate an object to any arbitrary angle just by dragging it with the mouse.

The rotate handle is the green handle that appears above the object, connected to the object by a line as shown in Figure 14-14. You can rotate an object to any angle simply by dragging the rotate handle.

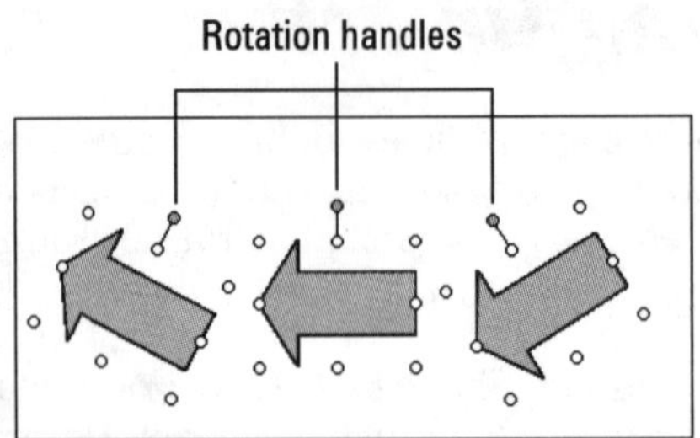

Figure 14-14: The rotation handle lets you rotate an object to any arbitrary angle.

The following steps show you how to use the rotate handle:

1. **Click the object that you want to rotate.**
2. **Drag the rotate handle in the direction you want to rotate the object.**

   As you drag, an outline of the object rotates around. When you get the object's outline to the angle you want, release the mouse button, and the object is redrawn at the new angle.

Another way to rotate an object is to select the object, click the Draw button, click Rotate or Flip, and then choose Free Rotate. Rotation handles then appear at all four corners of the object. You can rotate the object by dragging any of the four handles.

To restrict the rotation angle to 15-degree increments, hold the Shift key while dragging around the rotation handle.

When you hold down the Ctrl key while dragging a corner handle, the object rotates about the opposite corner handle rather than the center. This feature is very strange, but it's occasionally useful.

Drawing a Complicated Picture

When you add more than one object to a slide, several problems come up. What happens when the objects overlap? How do you line up objects so that they don't look like they were thrown at the slide from a moving car? And how do you keep together objects that belong together?

This section shows you how to use PowerPoint features to handle overlapped objects, align objects, and group objects. If you're interested in a description of how to use these PowerPoint features together to draw a picture, check out the sidebar titled "Don't let me tell you how I drew that funny face!" in this chapter.

Changing layers

Whenever you have more than one object on a slide, the potential exists for objects to overlap one another. Like most drawing programs, PowerPoint handles this problem by layering objects like a stack of plates. The first object that you draw is at the bottom of the stack; the second object is on top of the first; the third is atop the second; and so on. If two objects overlap, the one that's at the highest layer wins; objects below it are partially covered.

So far, so good — but what if you don't remember to draw the objects in the correct order? What if you draw a shape that you want to tuck behind a shape that you've already drawn, or what if you want to bring an existing shape to the top of the pecking order? No problem. PowerPoint enables you to change the stack order by moving objects toward the front or back so that they overlap just the way you want.

The Draw menu on the Drawing toolbar provides four commands for changing the stacking order, all grouped under the Order command:

- **Draw⇨Order⇨Bring to Front:** Brings the chosen object to the top of the stack.
- **Draw⇨Order⇨Send to Back:** Sends the chosen object to the back of the stack.
- **Draw⇨Order⇨Bring Forward:** Brings the chosen object one step closer to the front of the stack.
- **Draw⇨Order⇨Send Backward:** Sends the object one rung down the ladder.

Layering problems are most obvious when objects have a fill color. If an object has no fill color, objects behind it are allowed to show through. In this case, the layering doesn't matter much.

To bring an object to the top of another, you may have to use the Bring Forward command several times. The reason is that even though the two objects appear to be adjacent, other objects may occupy the layers between them.

Line 'em up

Nothing looks more amateurish than objects dropped randomly on a slide with no apparent concern for how they line up with one another. The Draw menu on the Drawing toolbar provides several alignment commands. To use them, first select the objects that you want to align. Then click the Draw button, click Align or Distribute, and then choose one of the following commands from the menu that appears:

- Align Left
- Align Center
- Align Right
- Align Top
- Align Middle
- Align Bottom

The first three of these commands align items horizontally; the last three align items vertically.

You can also distribute several items so that they are spaced evenly. Select the items that you want to distribute, click the Draw button, choose Align or Distribute, and then choose Distribute Horizontally or Distribute Vertically.

If you want objects to automatically adhere to an invisible grid when you draw them or move them about, click the Draw button, click Snap, and then choose To Grid. To turn the snap-to-grid feature off, choose the Draw⇨Snap⇨To Grid command again.

Using the grids and guides

To help you create well ordered slides, PowerPoint lets you display a grid of evenly spaced lines over the slide. These lines aren't actually a part of the slide, so your audience won't see them when you give your presentation. They exist simply to make the task of lining things up a bit easier.

In addition to the grid, PowerPoint also lets you use guides. The guides are two lines — one horizontal, the other vertical — that appear on-screen. While the gridlines are fixed in their location on your slides, you can move the guides around as you want. Any object that comes within a pixel's breath of one of these guidelines snaps to it. Like the grid, the guides don't show up when you give your presentation. They appear only when you're editing your slides. Guides are a great way to line up objects in a neat row.

To display the grid or guides, use the View⇨Grid and Guides command (the Grid and Guides command is also available on the Draw menu). This command summons the Grid and Guides dialog box, shown in Figure 14-15. (You can also summon this dialog box by pressing Ctrl+G.)

To activate the grid, check the Snap Objects to Grid checkbox, then adjust the grid spacing to whatever setting you want. If you want to actually see the grid on the screen, check the Display Grid on Screen checkbox.

To fire up the guides, check the Display Drawing Guides on Screen setting. Once the guides are visible, you can move them around the slide by dragging them with the mouse.

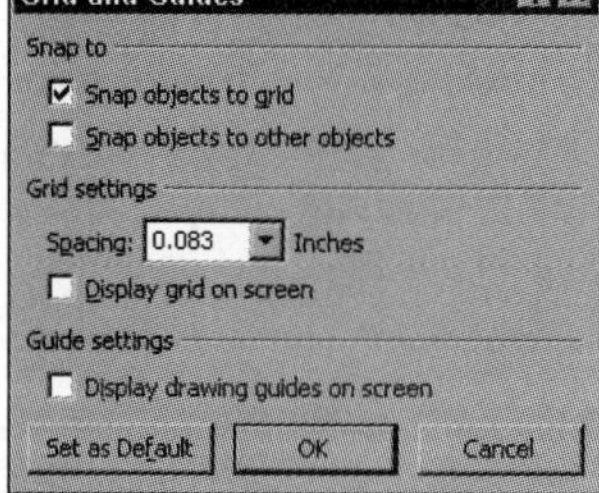

Figure 14-15: The Grid and Guides dialog box.

Group therapy

A *group* is a collection of objects that PowerPoint treats as though it were one object. Using groups properly is one key to putting simple shapes together to make complex pictures without becoming so frustrated that you have to join a therapy group. ("Hello, my name is Doug, and PowerPoint drives me crazy.")

To create a group, follow these steps:

1. **Choose all objects that you want to include in the group.**

   You can do this by holding down the Shift key and clicking each of the items, or by holding down the mouse button and dragging the resulting rectangle around all the items.

2. **Click Draw in the Drawing toolbar and then select the Group command.**

To take a group apart so that PowerPoint treats the objects as individuals again, follow these steps:

1. **Select the object group that you want to break up.**
2. **Choose the Draw⇨Ungroup command.**

If you create a group and then ungroup it so that you can work on its elements individually, you can easily regroup the objects. These steps show you how:

1. **Select at least one object that was in the original group.**

2. **Choose the Draw⇨Regroup command.**

   PowerPoint remembers which objects were in the group and automatically includes them.

PowerPoint enables you to create groups of groups. This capability is useful for complex pictures because it enables you to work on one part of the picture, group it, and then work on the next part of the picture without worrying about accidentally disturbing the part that you've already grouped. After you have several such groups, select them and group them. You can create groups of groups of groups and so on, ad nauseam.

Don't let me tell you how I drew that funny face!

In case you're interested, you can follow the bouncing ball to see how I created the goofy face in Figure 14-1. By studying this creature, you can get an idea of how you use layers, groups, and alignment to create complicated pictures, as shown in these steps:

1. **Draw the face shape using the Oval tool.**

   I filled the face with pale yellow.

2. **Draw the eyes using the Oval tool.**

   To draw the eyes, I started by using the Oval button to draw an oval for the left eye, which I filled with white. Next, I pressed Ctrl+D to make a duplicate of the oval. Then I dragged the duplicate eye to the right side of the face. Next, I used the oval again to draw a little pupil inside the left eye, which I filled with black. I then duplicated the pupil and dragged the duplicate over to the right eye. Finally, I used the Curve AutoShape to draw the eyebrows.

3. **Draw the ears using the Oval tool.**

   The only trick with the ears was using the Send to Back command to send the ears behind the face where they belonged.

4. **Draw the nose using the Oval tool.**

   The nose is actually three ovals. The first is the center part of the nose: It's a tall but narrow oval. The other two ovals are the nostrils, which are almost round. I used the Send Backward command on the nostrils to place them behind the first oval.

5. **Draw the mouth using the Curve AutoShape.**

6. **Draw the body using the Freeform AutoShape.**

   When the body is drawn, I used Send to Back to send it behind the face. Then, I used a pattern as the fill for the body to create a lovely striped shirt.

Oh, I almost forgot. The last step is to choose all the objects that make up the face (by dragging and clicking a dotted-line square around the entire picture) and group them using the Draw⇨Group command. That way, I don't have to worry about accidentally dismembering our little friend.

Chapter 15

Inserting a Diagram

In This Chapter

- Creating an organizational chart
- Creating fancy diagrams
- Embellishing charts and diagrams
- Using chart AutoFormats

One of the great new features of PowerPoint 2002 is the Diagram Gallery, which lets you add several different types of useful diagrams to your slides. With the Diagram Gallery, you can create Organization Charts, Cycle Diagrams, Radial Diagrams, Pyramid Diagrams, Venn Diagrams, and Target Diagrams.

Of the six types of diagrams you can create with the Diagram Gallery, all of them except the Organization Chart are variations on the same theme: showing simple relationships among the elements in a diagram. In fact, once you have created a diagram, you can easily change the diagram to a different type. Thus, if you start with a Radial Diagram but decide that a Pyramid Diagram would better make your point, you can change the diagram to a Pyramid Diagram. Organization Charts, however, show more complex relationships. So you can't change an Organization Chart to one of the other diagram types. (That's why the Organization Chart type is called a *chart*, but the other five types are called *diagrams*.)

Creating a Diagram

The easiest way to create a diagram is to insert a new slide using a slide layout that has a placeholder for a diagram. Just follow these steps:

1. **Choose Insert⇨New Slide or press Ctrl+M to insert a new slide.**

   A new slide is created and the Slide Layout Task Pane is summoned so that you can choose a layout for the slide.

2. **Choose the Title and Diagram or Organization Chart layout for the slide.**

   You'll have to scroll through the list of slide layouts to find the Title and Diagram or Organization Chart layout, since it's located near the end of the list. The thumbnail for this layout is shown in the margin.

3. **Double click the Diagram or Organization Chart placeholder.**

   This summons the Diagram Gallery dialog box, shown in Figure 15-1.

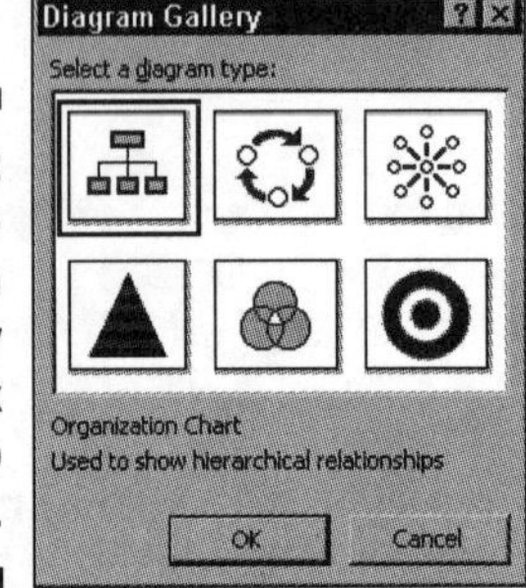

Figure 15-1: The Diagram Gallery dialog box comes to life.

4. **Choose the diagram type you want to create.**

   The Diagram Gallery lets you create six different types of diagrams. These diagram types are pictured and described in Table 15-1.

5. **Click OK.**

   The Chart is created. Figure 15-2 shows how an Organization Chart appears when you first create it. The other diagram types have a similar appearance.

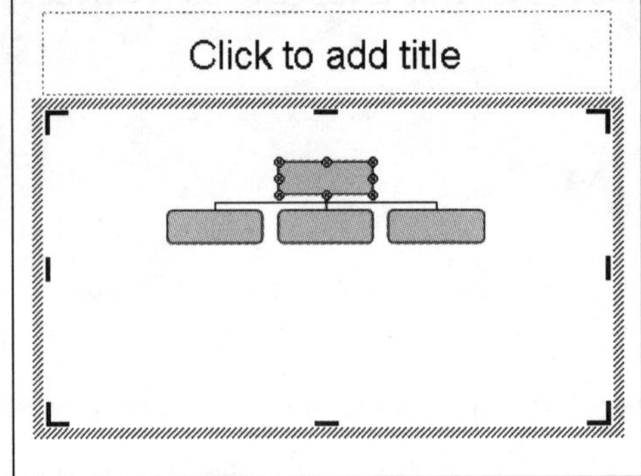

Figure 15-2: The Diagram Gallery dialog box comes to life.

6. **Modify the diagram however you see fit.**

   For more information on modifying diagrams, see the sections "Working with Organization Charts" and "Working with Other Diagrams" later in this chapter.

7. **You're done!**

   Well, you're never really done. You can keep tweaking your diagram until the end of time to get it perfect. But at some point, you have to say enough is enough and call it finished.

If you want to add a diagram to an existing slide without using the Title and Diagram or Organization Chart slide layout, click the Insert Diagram or Organization Chart button in the Drawing toolbar (shown in the margin). This brings up the Diagram Gallery dialog box. Choose the type of diagram you want to add, then click OK. The diagram is added to the slide.

Table 15-1 Types of Diagrams You Can Create

Icon	*Diagram Type*	*Description*
	Organization Chart	Used to show hierarchical relationships among elements.
	Cycle Diagram	Used to show a process that repeats a continuous cycle.
	Radial Diagram	Used to show how elements relate to a central element.
	Pyramid Diagram	Used to show how elements build upon one another to form a foundation.
	Venn Diagram	Used to show how different elements overlap one another.
	Target Diagram	Used to show elements that progress towards a goal.

Working with Organization Charts

Organization charts — you know, those box-and-line charts that show who reports to whom, where the buck stops, and who got the lateral arabesque — are an essential part of many presentations. You can draw organization charts by using the PowerPoint 2002 standard rectangle- and line-drawing tools, but that process is tedious at best. If Jones gets booted over to advertising, redrawing the chart can take hours.

Mercifully, the new Diagram Gallery feature is adept at drawing organization charts. You can create diagrams that show bosses, subordinates, coworkers, and assistants. You can easily rearrange the chain of command and add new boxes or delete boxes. Figure 15-3 shows a finished organization chart.

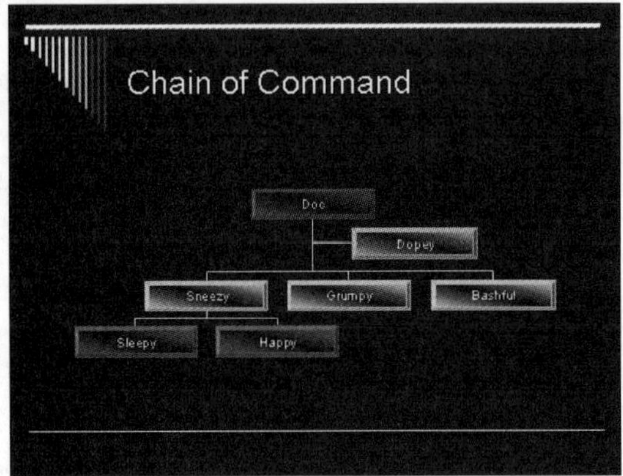

Figure 15-3: A finished organization chart.

Keep in mind that organization charts are useful for more than showing employee relationships. You also can use them to show any kind of hierarchical structure. For example, back when I wrote computer programs for a living, I used organization charts to plan the structure of my computer programs. They're also great for recording family genealogies, although they don't have any way to indicate that Aunt Milly hasn't spoken to Aunt Beatrice in 30 years.

Previous versions of PowerPoint used a clumsy program called Microsoft Organization Chart to handle organization charts. The new Diagram Gallery Organization Chart feature is easier to use, though it isn't as adept at creating complicated charts as the old program was.

Adding text to boxes

To add text to an organization chart box, click the box and start typing. If necessary, PowerPoint adjusts the size of the box to accommodate the text you type.

You can use any of PowerPoint's text formatting features to format text in your organization chart boxes. To keep the boxes small, avoid typing long names or job titles. To create two or more lines of text in a box, just press the Enter key whenever you want to start a new line.

OrgChart terms you can skip

OrgChart thrusts a bunch of specialized terminology in your face. This list explains some of the more important terms:

- **Manager**: A box that has subordinate boxes reporting to it.
- **Subordinate:** A box beneath a manager box that reports to that manager in a line relationship.
- **Co-worker:** Two or more boxes that report to the same manager.
- **Assistant**: A box that has a staff relationship to another box rather than a line relationship. Assistant boxes are drawn differently to indicate their different relationship to the chart.
- **Level**: All the boxes on the same level in a chart.
- **Branch**: A box and all the boxes that report directly and indirectly to it.
- **Connecting line**: A line that shows a relationship between two boxes.

Because of an annoying glitch in PowerPoint, the text in organization charts sometimes becomes too small to read. If that happens, click the top shape in the chart, then click the Select button in the Organization Chart toolbar and choose Branch. Then adjust the font size (using the Font Size control in the Formatting toolbar) to adjust the text to a more readable size.

Adding boxes to a chart

To add a new box to an organizational chart, follow these steps:

1. **Click the box you want the new box to be below or next to.**
2. **Click the arrow next to the Insert Shape button in the Organization Chart toolbar, then click one of the following buttons:**

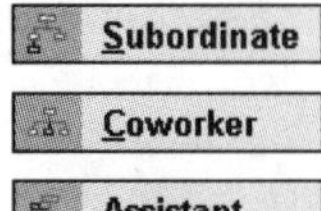

Inserts a new box beneath the selected box.

Inserts a new box at the same level as the selected box.

Inserts a new box beneath the selected box, but connected with a special elbow connector to indicate that the box is an assistant, not a subordinate.

3. **Click the new box, then type whatever text you want to appear in the box.**
4. **If necessary, drag the box to adjust its location.**

Deleting chart boxes

To delete a box from an organization chart, click the box to select it and press the Delete key. PowerPoint automatically adjusts the chart to compensate for the lost box.

When you delete a box from an organization chart, you should observe a moment of somber silence — or throw a party. It all depends on whose name was on the box, I suppose.

Moving a box

To move a box to a different position on the chart, drag the box with the mouse until it lands right on top of the box that you want it to be subordinate to. PowerPoint automatically rearranges the chart to accommodate the new arrangement. Dragging boxes can be a handy way to reorganize a chart that has gotten a little out of hand.

PowerPoint won't let you move a box that has subordinates unless you select all the subordinate boxes. You can do that easily by selecting the box you want to use, clicking the Select button in the Organization Chart toolbar, and clicking the Branch button. You can then move the entire branch.

Changing the chart layout

PowerPoint lets you choose from one of four methods of arranging subordinates in an organization chart branch:

- **Standard:** Subordinate shapes are placed at the same level beneath the superior shape.
- **Both Hanging:** Subordinates are placed two per level beneath the superior, with the connecting line between them.
- **Left Hanging:** Subordinates are stacked vertically beneath the superior, to the left of the connecting line.
- **Right Hanging:** Subordinates are stacked vertically beneath the superior, to the right of the connecting line.

Figure 15-4 shows an organization chart that uses all three of these layouts. The first layer of shapes beneath the top level uses the Standard layout. Beneath the first shape on this layer are two shapes with the Both Hanging layout. The other two shapes each have three subordinate shapes with the Left Hanging and Right Hanging layout.

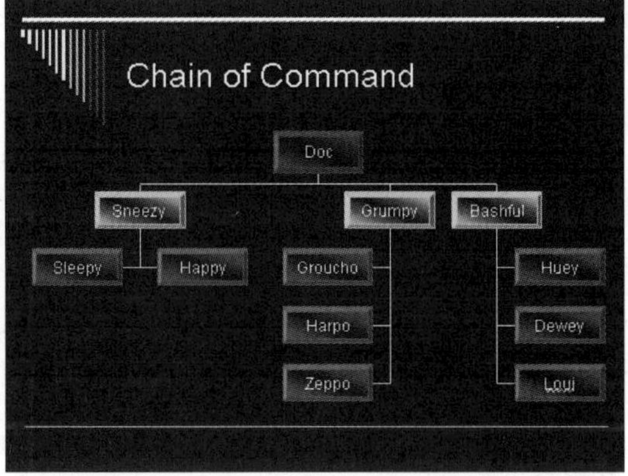

Figure 15-4: An organization chart that uses all four layout types.

To change the layout of a branch of your chart, first click the shape at the top of the branch. Then, click the Layout button in the Organization Chart toolbar and choose the layout type you want to use from the menu that appears.

Changing the chart style

You can fiddle for hours with the formatting for the boxes, lines, and text of an organization chart. But if you want to quickly apply a good-looking format to your chart, click the Autoformat button in the Organization Chart toolbar (shown in the margin). This summons the Organization Chart Style Gallery, shown in Figure 15-5. Select the style you want to apply to your chart, then click Apply.

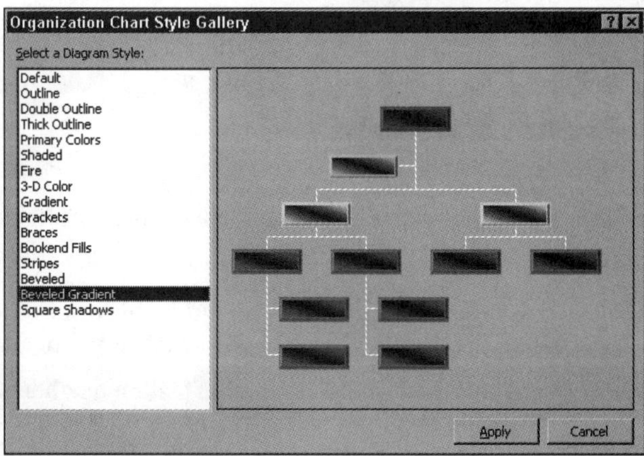

Figure 15-5: The Organization Chart Style Gallery lets you create a good-looking chart without much fuss.

Working with Other Diagrams

Cycle, Radial, Pyramid, Venn, and Target Diagrams are all useful in various situations to illustrate how different items relate to one another. For example, a Target Diagram can help your audience see how working through a series of steps or achieving a series of goals helps advance you toward your ultimate goal. And a Pyramid Diagram helps your audience see how one task or idea provides a foundation for other tasks or ideas.

You use similar toolbar controls and menus to create and format all five of these chart types. In fact, you can even switch a chart from one type to another. So if you decide that a Venn Diagram would be better than a Pyramid Diagram, you can simply switch types.

If you don't believe me, look at the two diagrams in Figure 15-6. Both present the same information, one as a Pyramid Diagram, the other as a Target Diagram. To create these diagrams, I first created the Pyramid Diagram, Then, I used the Edit⇨Duplicate command to duplicate the chart, then changed the chart type to Target Diagram.

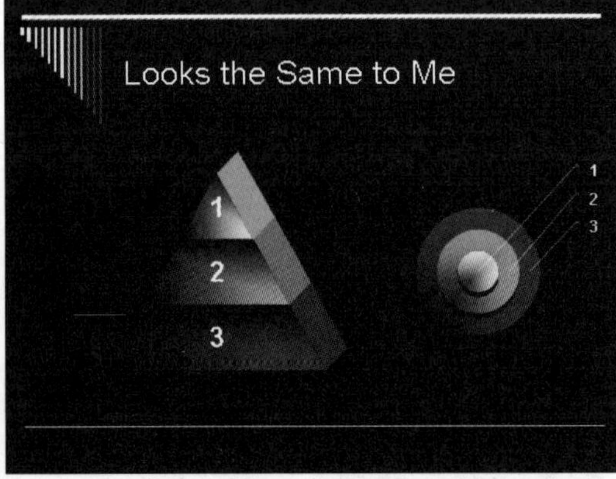

Figure 15-6: Two diagrams that present the same information in different ways.

The following paragraphs describe the basics of working with these types of diagrams:

- To change the diagram type, click the Change To button in the Diagram toolbar and choose the type of diagram you want to change to.

Any formatting changes you make to the chart, such as changing the colors of individual shapes or changing text fonts or size is lost if you change the diagram type. As a result, you should settle on a diagram type before you make extensive modifications to the diagram's formatting.

- To add text to a shape, click the shape and type. You can use PowerPoint's text formatting features to change the font, size, color, and style of your text.
- To add a shape to the diagram, click the Insert Shape button. PowerPoint adds a shape that is appropriate for your diagram type and automatically resizes and repositions the other shapes in the diagram to accommodate the new shape.
- To delete a shape, click the shape to select it and press the Delete key.

- You can reverse the order of shapes in the diagram by clicking the Reverse Diagram button (shown in the margin).
- To change the order of shapes in the diagram, click the shape you want to move, and then click the Move Shape Forward or Move Shape Backward button. (Each diagram type uses a different icon for these buttons, but they are always located next to the Reverse Diagram button.)

- To apply a built-in format to the diagram, click the AutoFormat button (shown in the margin). This brings up the Diagram Style Gallery dialog box, as shown in Figure 15-7. Select the diagram style you want, then click Apply.
- To change the color or style of an individual shape, click the shape to change it, then use buttons in the drawing toolbar to change the shape's fill or line color, line style, shadow style, or 3-D style. (If you've applied an AutoFormat to the diagram, you must first right-click the diagram and uncheck the Use AutoFormat command.)

- You can animate the individual elements of a diagram in clever ways. For more information, refer to Chapter 19.

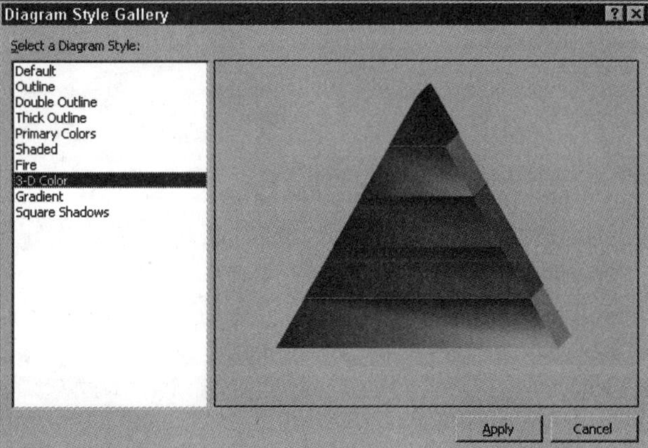

Figure 15-7: Choosing a style for your diagram.

Flowcharts, Anyone?

One type of diagram that people often want to create with PowerPoint is a flowchart. Although the Diagram Gallery doesn't have an option for creating flowcharts, you can easily create flowcharts using PowerPoint's AutoShapes. For example, here is a flowchart I created with just a few minutes work:

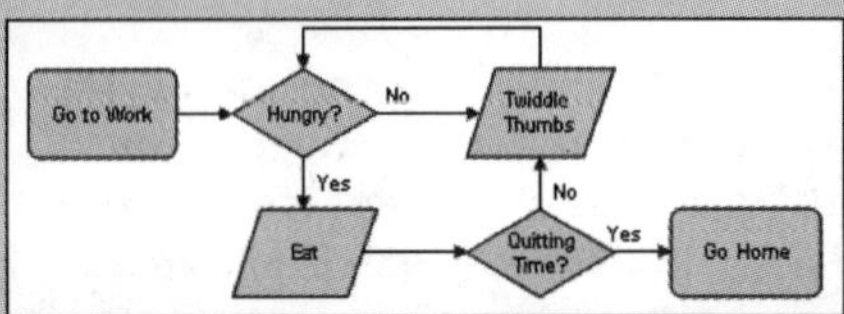

To create a flowchart like this, follow these basic steps:

1. Draw each flowchart shape by clicking AutoShapes in the Drawing toolbar, then choosing the shape you want to use from the Flowchart menu.
2. Type text into each flowchart shape by clicking the shape and typing. If necessary, adjust the text font and size.
3. Connect the flowchart shapes by using the Connectors AutoShapes. First choose the type of connector you want to use by clicking AutoShapes in the Drawing toolbar, then choosing the connector from the Connectors menu. Click the first shape you want the connector to attach to, then click the second shape. Notice that as you move the mouse around when you have selected a connector AutoShape, connection handles will appear on objects when you have moved within range. Slide the mouse over to one of these connection handles and click to snap the connector to the object.
4. Now adjust the alignment of your shapes. Here's where the flowcharting AutoShapes really shine: The connectors stay attached to the shapes even when you move the shapes around! Pretty slick, eh?

Chapter 16

Charting for Fun and Profit

In This Chapter

- Adding charts and graphs to PowerPoint
- Moving and resizing a chart
- Embellishing a chart with titles, legends, and other stuff

One of the best ways to prove a point is with numbers, and one of the best ways to present numbers is in a chart. With PowerPoint, adding a chart to your presentation is easy. And getting the chart to look the way you want is usually easy, too. It takes a little bit of pointing and clicking, but it works.

Adding Charts to PowerPoint Slides

If you've never attempted to add a chart to a slide before, it can be a little confusing. Microsoft Graph takes a series of numbers and renders it as a chart. You can supply the numbers yourself, or you can copy them from a separate file such as an Excel worksheet. You can create all kinds of different charts, ranging from simple bar charts and pie charts to exotic doughnut charts and radar charts. Very cool, but a little confusing to the uninitiated.

This list shows some of the jargon that you have to contend with when you're working with charts:

- **Graph or chart:** Same thing. These terms are used interchangeably. A graph or chart is nothing more than a bunch of numbers turned into a picture. After all, a picture is worth a thousand numbers.
- **Graph object:** A chart inserted on a slide. Charts are actually created by a separate program called Microsoft Graph. However, Microsoft Graph is so well integrated with PowerPoint that if I hadn't just told you, you probably wouldn't realize that it's a separate program from PowerPoint.

- **Chart type:** Microsoft Graph supports several chart types: bar charts, column charts, pie charts, line charts, scatter charts, area charts, radar charts, Dunkin' Donut charts, and others. Graph can even create cone charts that look like something that fell off a Fembot in an Austin Powers movie. Different types of charts are better suited to displaying different types of data.
- **3-D chart:** Some chart types have a 3-D effect that gives them a jazzier look. Nothing special here; the effect is mostly cosmetic.
- **Datasheet:** Supplies the underlying data for a chart. After all, a chart is nothing more than a bunch of numbers made into a picture. The numbers come from the datasheet, which works just like a spreadsheet program. So if you know how to use Excel or Lotus 1-2-3, finding out how to use the datasheet should take you about 30 seconds. The datasheet is part of the Graph object, but it doesn't appear on the slide. Instead, the datasheet appears only when you edit the Graph object.
- **Series:** A collection of related numbers. For example, a chart of quarterly sales by region may have a series for each region. Each series has four sales totals, one for each quarter. Each series is usually represented by a row on the datasheet, but you can change the datasheet so that each column represents a series. Most chart types can plot more than one series. Pie charts can chart only one series at a time, however.
- **Axes:** The lines on the edges of a chart. The *X-axis* is the line along the bottom of the chart; the *Y-axis* is the line along the left edge of the chart. The X-axis usually indicates categories. Actual data values are plotted along the Y-axis. Microsoft Graph automatically provides labels for the X and Y axes, but you can change them.
- **Legend:** A box used to identify the various series plotted on the chart. Microsoft Graph can create a legend automatically if you want one.

The Microsoft Graph that comes with PowerPoint is the same as the chart creating functions in Microsoft Excel. So if you know how to use Excel to create charts, you can pretty much skip this chapter: You already know everything you need to know.

When you create or edit a chart, Microsoft Graph comes to life. But rather than pop up in its own dialog box, Microsoft Graph sort of takes over the PowerPoint window and replaces the PowerPoint menus and toolbars with its own. So don't panic if the room seems to spin and your toolbar changes.

Microsoft Graph has its own Help system. To see Help information for Microsoft Graph, first call up Microsoft Graph by inserting a chart object or double-clicking an existing chart object. Then press F1 or click the Help button to summon the Assistant, or choose Help➪Contents and Index to access Graph help directly.

Creating a Chart

To add a chart to your presentation, you have two options:

- Create a new slide by using an AutoLayout that includes a chart object.
- Add a chart object to an existing slide.

Using an AutoLayout is the easier way to create a new slide because the AutoLayout positions other elements on the slide for you. If you add a chart to an existing slide, you probably have to adjust the size and position of existing objects to make room for the chart object.

Inserting a new slide with a chart

These steps show you how to insert a new slide that contains a chart:

1. **Move to the slide that you want the new slide to follow.**
2. **Choose Insert⇨New Slide to create a new slide and summon the Slide Layout Task Pane.**
3. **Click one of the slide layouts that includes a chart.**

   Several slide types include chart objects. Choose the one that you want and then click OK. PowerPoint adds a new slide of the chosen type. The chart object is simply a placeholder; you have to use Microsoft Graph to complete the chart.
4. **Double-click the chart object to conjure up Microsoft Graph.**

   PowerPoint awakens Microsoft Graph from its slumber, and the two programs spend a few moments exchanging news from home. Then Microsoft Graph takes over, creating a sample chart with make-believe data, as shown in Figure 16-1. Notice that your regular toolbar setup goes away to make room for the Graph toolbar buttons.

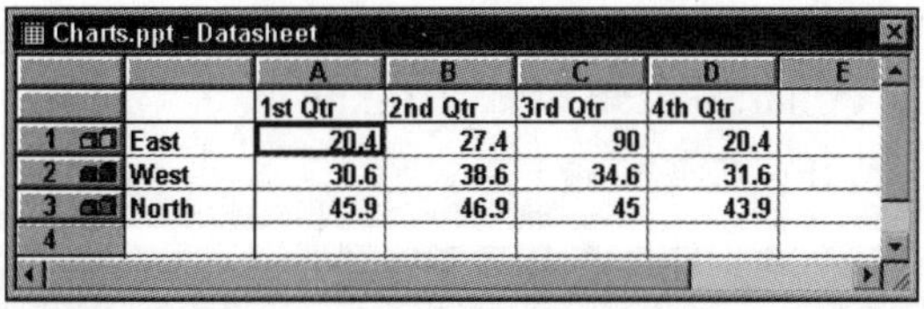

Charts.ppt - Datasheet

		A	B	C	D	E
		1st Qtr	2nd Qtr	3rd Qtr	4th Qtr	
1	East	20.4	27.4	90	20.4	
2	West	30.6	38.6	34.6	31.6	
3	North	45.9	46.9	45	43.9	
4						

Figure 16-1: Microsoft Graph takes over.

5. **Change the sample data to something more realistic.**

   The *datasheet,* visible in Figure 16-1, supplies the data on which the chart is based. The datasheet is in a separate window and is not a part of the slide. The datasheet works just like a spreadsheet program. For more information about using it, see the section "Working with the Datasheet" later in this chapter.

6. **Return to the slide.**

   Click anywhere on the slide outside the chart or the datasheet to leave Microsoft Graph and return to the slide. You can then see the chart with the new numbers, as shown in Figure 16-2.

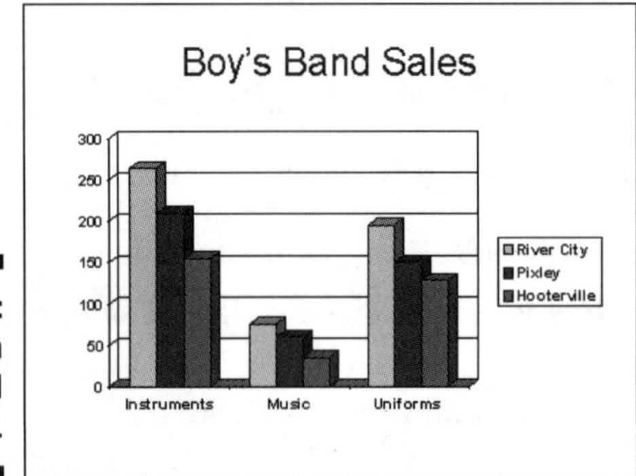

Figure 16-2: A slide with a finished chart.

Inserting a chart in an existing slide

Remember that this method is the more difficult of the two methods of adding charts to your slides. Use the preceding method unless you have already created your slide.

Follow these steps to add a chart to an existing slide:

1. **Move to the slide on which you want to place the chart.**
2. **Choose Insert⇨Chart.**

   Or click the Insert Chart button (shown in the margin).
3. **Type your data in the datasheet.**

   Replace the sample data with your numbers.
4. **Click outside the chart to return to the slide.**
5. **Rearrange everything.**

The chart undoubtedly falls on top of something else already on the slide. You probably need to resize and move the chart object and perhaps other objects on the slide to make room for the chart. Or you may want to delete any unnecessary text or clip art objects from the slide.

Working with the Datasheet

The datasheet contains the numbers plotted in your Microsoft Graph chart. The datasheet works like a simple spreadsheet program, with values stored in cells that are arranged in rows and columns. Like a spreadsheet, each column is assigned a letter, and each row is assigned a number. You can identify each cell in the datasheet, therefore, by combining the column letter and row number, as in A1 or B17. (Bingo!)

Ordinarily, each series of numbers is represented by a row in the spreadsheet. You can change this orientation so that each series is represented by a column by clicking the By Column button on the toolbar (shown in the margin) or by choosing Data⇨Series in Columns. The Data menu is a function of Microsoft Graph and like the toolbar, when your datasheet is complete, it vanishes.

The first row and column in the datasheet are used for headings and are not assigned a letter or number.

If you want to chart a large number of data values, you may want to increase the size of the datasheet window. Unfortunately, someone forgot to put the maximize button on the datasheet window, but you can still increase the size of the datasheet window by dragging any of its corners.

You can choose an entire column by clicking its column letter, or you can choose an entire row by clicking its row number. You also can choose the entire datasheet by clicking the blank box in the upper-left corner of the datasheet.

You can change the font used in the datasheet by choosing Format⇨Font. You also can change the numeric format by choosing Format⇨Number. Changing the font and number format for the datasheet affects not only the way the datasheet is displayed, but also the format of data value labels included in the chart.

Although the datasheet resembles a spreadsheet, you can't use formulas or functions in a datasheet. If you want to use formulas or functions to calculate the values to be plotted, use a spreadsheet program, such as Excel, to create the spreadsheet and then import it into Microsoft Graph. (Or create the chart in Excel rather than in PowerPoint. Then import the Excel chart into the PowerPoint presentation by choosing Insert⇨Object or copy the chart into PowerPoint by way of the Clipboard.)

To get rid of the datasheet, click the View Datasheet button on the toolbar (shown in the margin). To summon the datasheet back, click the View Datasheet button again.

Changing the Chart Type

Microsoft Graph enables you to create 14 basic types of charts. Each type conveys information with a different emphasis. Sales data plotted in a column chart may emphasize the relative performance of different regions, for example, and the same data plotted as a line chart may emphasize the increase or decrease in sales over time. The type of chart that's best for your data depends on the nature of the data and which aspects of it you want to emphasize.

Fortunately, PowerPoint doesn't force you to decide the final chart type up front. You can easily change the chart type at any time without changing the chart data. These steps show you how:

1. **Double-click the chart to activate Microsoft Graph.**
2. **Choose Chart⇨Chart Type.**

   Microsoft Graph displays the Chart Type dialog box. From this dialog box, you can choose the chart type that you want to use. The chart types are arranged in two groups: standard on the Standard Types tab and custom on the Custom Types tab. (To show the custom types, click the Custom Types tab at the top of the dialog box.)
3. **Click the chart type that you want.**
4. **To use a variant of the chart type, click the chart subtype that you want to use.**

   For example, the Column chart type has seven sub-types that enable you to use flat columns or three-dimensional columns and to change how the columns are positioned relative to one another.
5. **Click OK and you're done.**

Another way to summon the Chart Types dialog box is to double-click the chart object and then right-click the chart. When the quick menu appears, choose Chart Type. Make sure your arrow is on a series value when you double-click (one of those bars in the graph), or it won't work. The Chart area is very sensitive to random clicking, so be careful and proceed with patience.

You can change the chart type another way by using the Chart Type button on the Microsoft Graph toolbar. When you click the down arrow next to the button, a palette of chart types appears. The Chart Type button provides an assortment of 18 popular types of charts. If you want to use a chart type that isn't listed under the button, you have to use the Chart⇨Chart Type command.

If you choose one of the 3-D chart types, you can adjust the angle from which you view the chart by choosing Chart⇨3-D View. Experiment with this one; it's kind of fun.

Embellishing a Chart

Microsoft Graph enables you to embellish a chart in many ways: You can add titles, labels, legends, and who knows what else. You add these embellishments by choosing Chart⇨Chart Options, which summons a Chart Options dialog box that has several tabs from which you can control the appearance of the chart.

To add a chart embellishment, choose Chart⇨Chart Options, click the tab that relates to the embellishment that you want to add, fiddle with the settings, and click OK. The following paragraphs describe each of the Chart Options tabs in turn.

- **Chart titles:** You can add two types of titles to your chart: a *chart title,* which describes the chart's contents, and *axis titles,* which explain the meaning of each chart axis. Most charts use two axes: the *value axis* and the *category axis.* Some 3-D chart types use a third axis called the *series axis.*

  In most cases, the slide title serves as a chart title for a chart included on a PowerPoint slide. If that's the case, you don't need to use a chart title.

- **Axes:** Sometimes an ax is what you'd like to use to fix your computer. But in this case, *axes* refers to the X- and Y-axis on which chart data is plotted. The *x-axis* is the horizontal axis of the chart, and the *y-axis* is the vertical axis. For 3-D charts, a third axis — *Z* — is also used. The Axes tab of the Chart Options dialog box lets you show or hide the labels used for each chart axis.

- **Gridlines:** *Gridlines* are light lines drawn behind a chart to make it easier to judge the position of each dot, bar, or line plotted by the chart. You can turn gridlines on or off via the Gridlines tab,

- **Legends:** A *legend* explains the color scheme used in the chart. If you want a legend to appear in your chart, click the Legend tab of the Chart Options dialog box, Indicate where you want the legend to be placed (Bottom, Corner, Top, Right, or Left) and then click OK.

  Microsoft Graph enables you to create a legend, but you're on your own if you need a myth or fable.

- **Labels:** A *label* is the text that's attached to each data point plotted on the chart. You can tell Microsoft Graph to use the actual data value for the label, or you can use the category heading for the label. This setting is controlled by the Data Labels tab. For most slide types, data labels add unnecessary clutter without adding much useful information. Use labels only if you think that you must back up your chart with exact numbers.
- **Data tables:** A *data table* is a table that shows the data used to create a chart. The Data Table tab holds the controls that let you add a data table to your chart.

Chapter 17

Other Ways to Embellish Your Slides

In This Chapter

- WordArt
- Tables

Graphs and diagrams aren't the only ornaments that you can add to your presentations. For the typographers out there who would give their pica sticks to skew some text, there's WordArt. And for those who like to do everything decently and in order, there are tables that let you line up everything in nice, neat rows and columns. Both of these features are very useful — well, if you happen to need them. Otherwise, they just take up disk space.

Using WordArt

WordArt is a nifty little feature that takes a snippet of ordinary text and transforms it into something that looks like you paid an ad agency an arm and a leg to design. And the best part is that WordArt is free! Figure 17-1 is an example of what you can do with WordArt in about three minutes.

You're in luck if you already know how to use WordArt in Word. WordArt is the same in PowerPoint and Word.

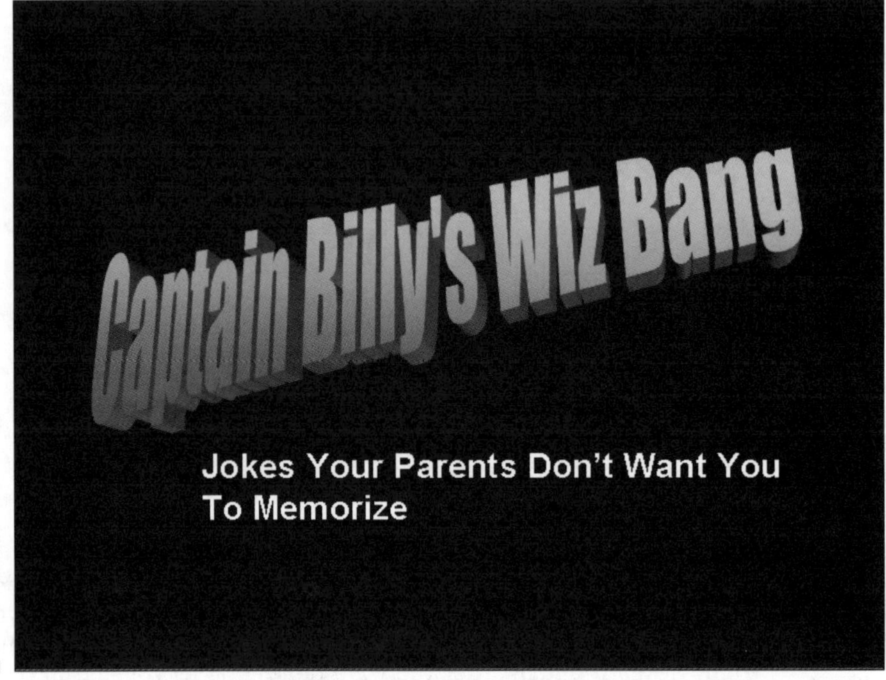

Figure 17-1: You, too, can create fancy text effects like this using WordArt.

Follow these steps to transform mundane text into something worth looking at:

1. **Choose Insert⇨Picture⇨WordArt.**

   The WordArt Gallery appears, as shown in Figure 17-2.

Figure 17-2: The WordArt Gallery offers a choice of WordArt styles.

2. **Click the WordArt style that most closely resembles the WordArt that you want to create and then click OK.**

   The Edit WordArt Text dialog box appears, as shown in Figure 17-3.

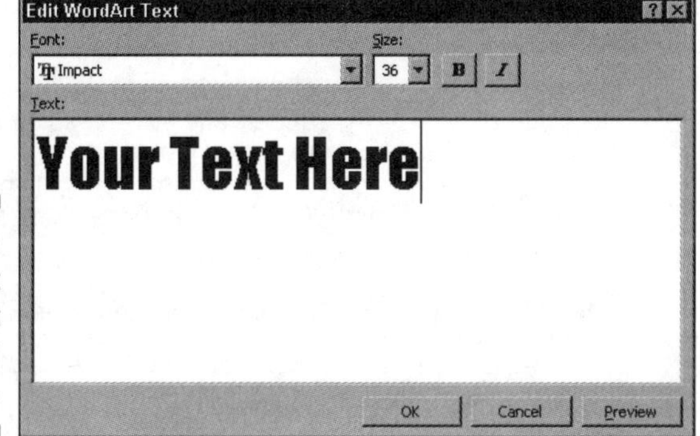

Figure 17-3: The Edit WordArt Text dialog box.

3. **Type the text that you want to use for your WordArt in the Edit WordArt Text dialog box and then click OK.**

   The WordArt object appears along with the WordArt toolbar.

4. **Fool around with other WordArt controls.**

   The various controls available on the WordArt toolbar are summarized in Table 17-1. Experiment as much as you want until you get the text to look just right.

5. **Click anywhere outside the WordArt frame to return to the slide.**

Table 17-1 WordArt Buttons

Button	*Name*	*What It Does*
	Insert WordArt	Creates another WordArt object.
Edit Text...	Edit Text	Opens the Edit WordArt Text dialog box so that you can change the text.
	WordArt Gallery	Opens the WordArt Gallery so that you can quickly apply a different format.
	Format WordArt	Calls up a dialog box that allows you to change the size and color of lines in the WordArt object and change other WordArt settings.

(continued)

Table 17-1 *(continued)*

Button	*Name*	*What It Does*
	WordArt Shape	Enables you to change the shape of the WordArt text.
	WordArt Same Letter Heights	Alternates between normal letters and same-height letters, in which upper- and lowercase letters are the same height.
	WordArt Vertical Text	Alternates between horizontal and vertical text.
	WordArt Alignment	Changes the alignment.
	WordArt Character Spacing	Changes the space between letters.

Don't forget that, in the eyes of PowerPoint, a WordArt object is not text. You can't edit it just by clicking it and typing. Instead, you have to double-click it to conjure up WordArt and then edit the text from within WordArt.

Using Tables

Tables are a great way to present lots of information in an orderly fashion. For example, if you want to create a slide that shows how many people like or hate various computer presentation programs, a table is the way to go. Or if you're considering purchasing some new computer equipment and want to list the prices for five different computer configurations from three different vendors, a table is the best way.

Basic tables are simple to create in PowerPoint. The easiest way to create a slide that contains a table is to use the Title and Table slide layout. Just follow these steps:

1. **Choose Insert⇨New Slide or press Ctrl+M.**

   A new slide is created, and the Slide Layout Task Pane appears.

2. **In the Slide Layout Task Pane, choose the Title and Table slide layout for the new slide.**

   You'll have to scroll down almost to the bottom of the list of slide layouts in the Slide Layout Task Pane to find the Title and Table layout.) Figure 17-4 shows how a slide with this layout initially appears.

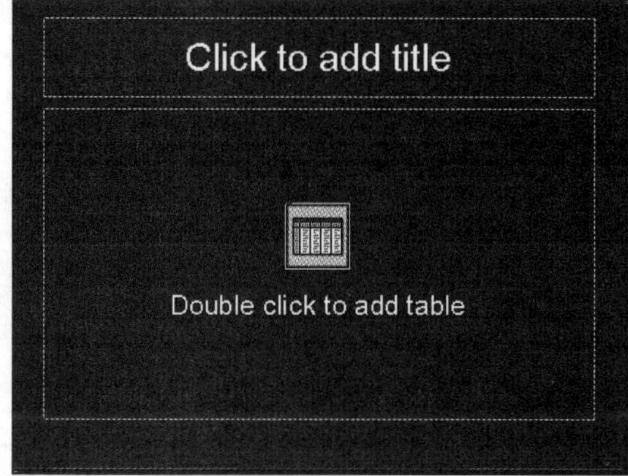

Figure 17-4: A slide that uses the Title and Table layout.

3. **Double-click the Table placeholder in the new slide.**

   The Insert Table dialog box appears, as shown in Figure 17-5.

Figure 17-5: The Insert Table dialog box.

4. **Set the number of rows and columns you want for the table, then click OK.**

   The table appears, as shown in Figure 17-6. Alongside the table is a Tables and Borders toolbar that contains buttons you can use to adjust the table's layout and formatting.

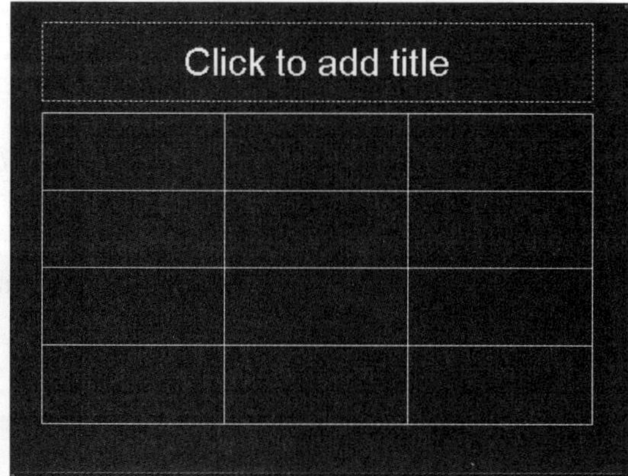

Figure 17-6: An empty table, waiting for data.

5. **Type information into the table's cells.**

   You can click any cell in the table and start typing. Or you can move from cell to cell by pressing the tab key or the arrow keys.

6. **Play with the formatting if you want.**

   You may want to change the format of the text in each cell. Or you may want to use the buttons in the floating Tables and Borders toolbar to adjust the borders around each table cell.

7. **Stop and smell the roses.**

   When you're done, you're done. Admire your work.

Figure 17-7 shows an example of a finished table. For this table, I used the Tables and Borders toolbar to erase all the table's borders, and I adjusted the height and width of the rows and columns to fit the text.

Three Popular Programs

	Love It	*Hate It*
PowerPoint 2002	93%	7%
Binford ShowStopper	48%	52%
Ronko Slide-a-Matic	35%	65%

Figure 17-7: A finished table.

If you want to add a table to an existing slide, you have two choices:

- Choose the Insert⇨Table command. This summons the Insert Table dialog box (see Figure 17-5). Indicate the number of rows and columns you want, then click OK.

- Click the Tables and Borders button (shown in the margin) in the Standard toolbar. This summons the Tables and Borders toolbar. You can then use the buttons on the Tables and Borders toolbar to draw a new table.

The Tables and Borders toolbar appears whenever you work in a table. The controls that appear in this toolbar are summarized in Table 17-2.

Table 17-2 Tables and Borders Toolbar Buttons

Button	Name	What It Does
	Draw Table	Creates a table by dragging a box where you want to put it. Use the same function to draw lines for rows and columns.
	Eraser	Removes lines and borders by dragging over the unwanted lines.
	Border Style	Choose the flavor of line you enjoy.
1 pt	Border Width	Determines border width — hey, that was easy!
	Border Color	Never miss an opportunity to make your presentation special.
	Outside Borders	Choose from 12 styles of cells and borders.
	Fill Color	Make your table stand out from the slide background. Includes gradients, textures, and patterns.
Table	Table	Brings up a healthy drop-down menu of its own. You can start a new table, completely rearrange/insert/delete the rows and columns, and maul your table beyond recognition with this toolset. Don't even mention the Borders and Fill option here. It brings up a dialog box that is completely redundant and also duplicates the functions already on the Tables and Borders toolbar. So there! I won't even mention it.
	Merge Cells	Removes cell dividers and combines the contents of multiple selected cells.

(continued)

Table 17-2 *(continued)*

Button	***Name***	***What It Does***
	Split Cell	Divides a cell into what PowerPoint thinks are logical breaking points. Get ready to edit. For fun try merging cells and splitting them. How often did it split the cells back to their original form? Don't mistake this for an Undo button.
	Align Top	Sets up the text near the top of the cell.
	Center Vertically	Vertically centers the text in the cell.
	Align Bottom	Plops the text close to the bottom of the barrel.
	Distribute Rows Evenly	Spreads out the rows so they are evenly spaced.
	Distribute Columns Evenly	Spreads out the columns so they are evenly spaced.

Part IV
The Special Effects Department

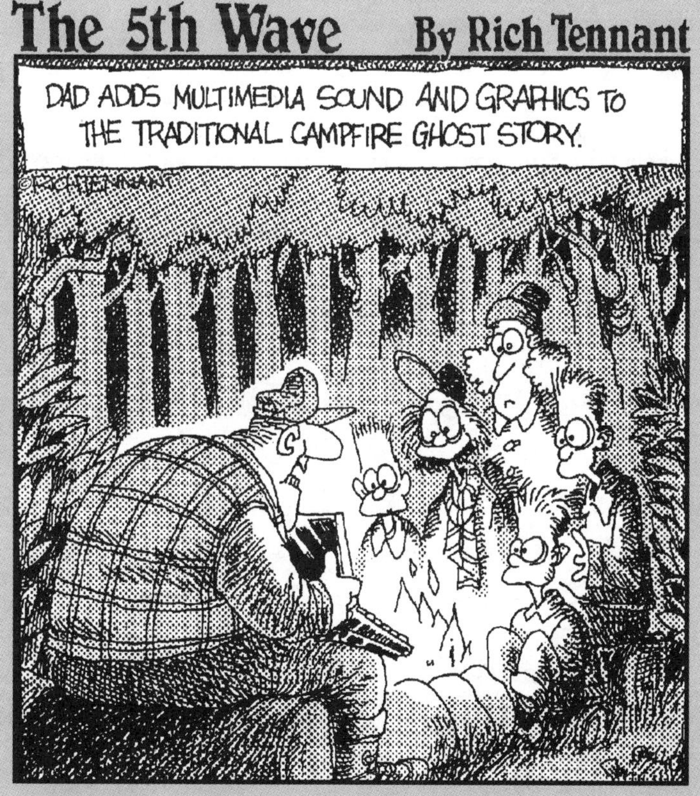

The 5th Wave
By Rich Tennant
DAD ADDS MULTIMEDIA SOUND AND GRAPHICS TO THE TRADITIONAL CAMPFIRE GHOST STORY.

In this part . . .

The two chapters in this part introduce you to some of PowerPoint's coolest features: multimedia and animation. With PowerPoint's multimedia features, you can add sound and video to your presentation, create a musical background, or even add a voice narration. And while the animation features aren't going to get you nominated for a *Best Animated Short* Oscar, they will dazzle your audience.

Chapter 18

Lights! Camera! Action! (Adding Sound and Video)

In This Chapter

- Adding burps, chortles, and gee-whizzes to your presentation
- Playing music from a CD with your presentation
- Narrating your presentations
- Fiddling with video

One of the cool things about PowerPoint is that it lets you create slides that contain not only text and pictures but also sounds and even movies. You can add sound effects such as screeching brakes or breaking glass to liven up dull presentations. You can even add your own applause, making your presentation like a TV sitcom or game show. Or you can add a musical background to your presentation.

You can also insert a film clip from *The African Queen* or a picture of the space shuttle launching if you think that will help keep people awake. This chapter shows you how to add those special effects.

This chapter is short because you can't do as much with sound and video in PowerPoint as you can with, say, a professional multimedia-authoring program such as Multimedia Director. Still, PowerPoint allows you to paste sound and video elements into your slide show, giving you the power to craft some impressive high-tech presentations.

Adding Sound to a Slide

A sterile *beep* used to be the only sound you could get from your computer. Nowadays, you can make your computer talk almost as well as the computers in the *Star Trek* movies, or you can give your computer a sophomoric sense of audible distaste. At last, the computer can be as obnoxious as the user!

There's a catch. Your computer must be equipped with a *sound card* to play these types of sounds. Chances are if you bought your computer since 1997, it already has a sound card. If you can't hear sounds from your computer, it's probably because the speakers aren't connected or the volume is turned down.

If you have an older computer that doesn't have sound capability, you can buy and install a sound card for under $50. However, any computer that is old enough to not have a sound card probably isn't capable of running PowerPoint 2002, at least not very well. Maybe it's about time you fork out the dough for a new computer.

All About Sound Files

Computer sounds are stored in *sound files,* which come in two basic varieties:

- **WAV files:** Contain digitized recordings of real sounds, such as Darth Vader saying, "I find your lack of faith disturbing" or DeForest Kelly (that's Dr. McCoy, for you non-Trekkers) saying, "I'm a doctor, not a bricklayer." If you have Windows installed as your operating system, you have access to many interesting sounds. Windows comes with a variety of WAV files; for example: Chimes.wav, Chord.wav, Ding.wav, and Tada.wav. Notice that these files all have names that end with .wav.
- **MIDI files:** Contain music stored in a form that the sound card's synthesizer can play. Windows comes with lots of these, including a Looney Tunes MIDI File. All MIDI files have names that end in MID. Why not try the file search again and see whatcha have?

Another popular format for sound files is MP3. For the lowdown on MP3 files, see the sidebar "What about MP3 and Napster?"

To insert a sound into a PowerPoint presentation, all you have to do is paste one of these sound files into a slide. Then when you run the presentation in Slide Show View, you can have the sounds play automatically during slide transitions, or you can play them manually by clicking the Sound button.

You're more likely to use WAV files than MIDI files in a PowerPoint presentation. MIDI files are great for playing music, but the WAV files enable you to add truly obnoxious sounds to a presentation.

Fortunately we have no national shortage of sound files. PowerPoint itself comes with a handful of useful sound files, including drum rolls, breaking glass, gunshots, and typewriter sounds. And Windows comes with some useful sounds, too. If you have access to the Web, you have a virtually unlimited supply of sounds at your disposal. Pop into any of the popular search services (such as `www.yahoo.com` or `www.google.com`) and perform a general search such as "wav file collection" or a specific search such as "Star Trek sounds."

Also, Windows includes a sound recorder in its Accessories folder that enables you to experiment with your own sounds if you dare. Move your computer into the living room some weekend, plug a microphone into the microphone jack on the back of your computer, and rent the following movies:

- *Star Wars* ("I find your lack of faith disturbing." and "Apology accepted.")
- *The Princess Bride* ("As you wish." and "He's been mostly dead all day.")
- Any of the *Saturday Night Live Best Of* tapes ("Live from New York!")
- Monty Python's *Holy Grail* ("It's just a flesh wound.")
- *2001: A Space Odyssey* ("I'm sorry Dave." and "Daisy, Daisy, Give me your answer do... .")

Have a ball, but remember not to violate any copyright laws with what you use. The copyright cops may be watching!

Sound files consume large amounts of disk space. Even just a few seconds of sound can take 100K or more. It doesn't seem like much space, but it adds up.

What about MP3 and Napster?

In the last few years, a new sound format has emerged: MP3. MP3 files are similar to WAV files but much smaller. For example, the Steppenwolf song, "Wild Thing," weighs in at just under 2.5MB in an MP3 file. The same file in WAV format requires a whopping 26MB — more than ten times the space.

The MP3 format was made popular by Napster, an online file exchange system that lets users trade MP3 files with one another (`www.napster.com`). Of course, this bothered the music industry, which sued because they said users were illegally trading copyrighted music without paying for it, which of course they were and we (oops, I mean they) all knew it.

At the time that I wrote this, the courts were cracking down on Napster by requiring it to block copyrighted music from being exchanged. During its heyday, Napster was a great source for all kinds of music files that you could use in your presentations. But because most (if not nearly all) of the files you could get from Napster were copyrighted, the legality of using them in your presentations was questionable.

So if you use hot MP3 files you got from Napster or some other online source, don't blame me if one day you wake up and find your house surrounded by Federal Agents and CNN news crews, who refer to you as a "dangerous copyright abuser" and your house as a "compound." They'll probably even interview your ninth grade English teacher, who will tell the nation that all you could talk about when you were a troubled teen was stealing Aerosmith music from the Internet and using it in illegal PowerPoint presentations.

Don't say I didn't warn you.

Inserting a Sound Object

If you have a sound file you want to add to a PowerPoint slide, follow these steps:

1. **Move to the slide to which you want to add the sound.**
2. **Choose the Insert⇨Movies and Sounds⇨Sound from File command.**

   The Insert Sound dialog box appears, as shown in Figure 18-1.

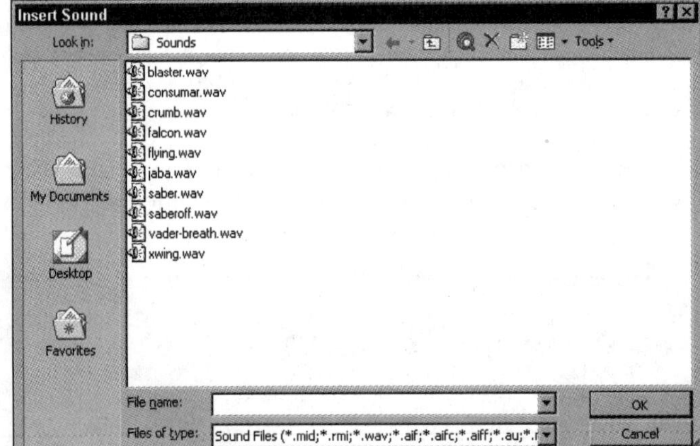

Figure 18-1: The Insert Sound dialog box.

3. **Select the sound file that you want to insert.**

   You may have to rummage about your disk drive to find the folder that contains your sound files.
4. **Click OK.**

   The dialog box shown in Figure 18-2 appears.

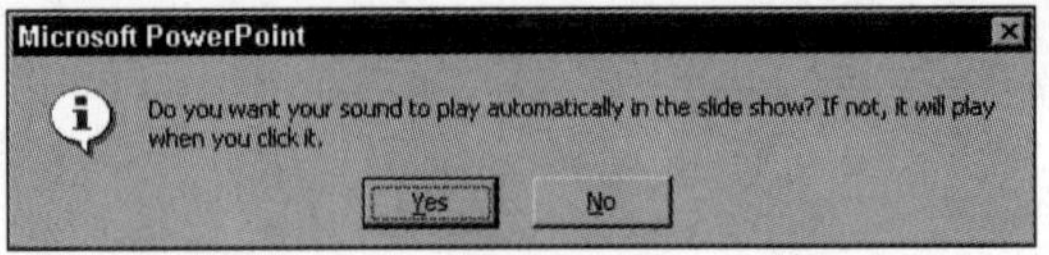

Figure 18-2: Choose wisely.

5. **Make an important choice: Do you want to have the sound byte play as you move to the slide automatically (Yes), or would you prefer to click on the sound icon (No)?**

   Either way, the sound clip is added to your slide and represented by a little speaker icon, shown in the margin.

6. **If you chose to have the sound played automatically and you don't want the sound icon to be visible on your slide, drag the icon off the slide.**

   The sound icon doesn't have to be visible on the slide for it to be played, so you can drag the icon just off the slide to hide the icon. However, if you answered No to the dialog box in Figure 18-2, you must leave the icon visible on the slide. Otherwise, you won't be able to click the icon to play the sound during your presentation.

You can also insert one of the many sounds that come with PowerPoint's Media Gallery or that are available online on the Microsoft Web site. To do so, choose the Insert⇨Movies and Sounds⇨Sound from Media Gallery command. This summons the Insert Clip Art Task Pane (see Figure 18-3) with a list of sound files that are available for your use. Scroll through the list to find the sound you want, then double-click the sound to add it to your file. (To hear a preview of the sound before you insert it, right-click the sound and choose the Preview/Properties command.)

Here are a few other random thoughts on adding sounds to your slides:

- To play a sound while working in Normal View, double-click the sound icon. However, to play the sound during a slide show, only one click is needed.

- If the sound file is smaller than 100KB, PowerPoint copies the sound file into your presentation file. However, if the sound file is larger than 100KB, PowerPoint just adds a link to the sound file so that your presentation won't become bloated with large sound files. If you use large sound files, then copy your presentation to another computer, be sure to copy the large sound files as well. (You can change the 100KB threshold by choosing Tools⇨Options to summon the Options dialog box and then changing the Link Sounds with File Size Greater Than setting under the General tab.)
- If you change your mind and decide you don't want any sounds, you can easily remove them. To remove a sound, click it and press the Delete key.
- You can also use sounds to embellish slide transitions and animations. This embellishing is covered in Chapter 19.
- If you want the sound to automatically loop, so that it keeps playing as long as the slide is displayed, right-click the sound icon and choose Edit Sound Object. The dialog box shown in Figure 18-4 appears. Check the Loop Until Stopped option, then click OK.
- Besides sound files, PowerPoint can also tell your CD player to play tracks from a regular audio CD. To use this feature, first insert the CD you want to play into your computer's CD drive, then call up the Insert⇨Movies and Sounds⇨Play CD Audio Track. A dialog box appears asking which track or tracks you want to play. Fill in the required information and click OK.

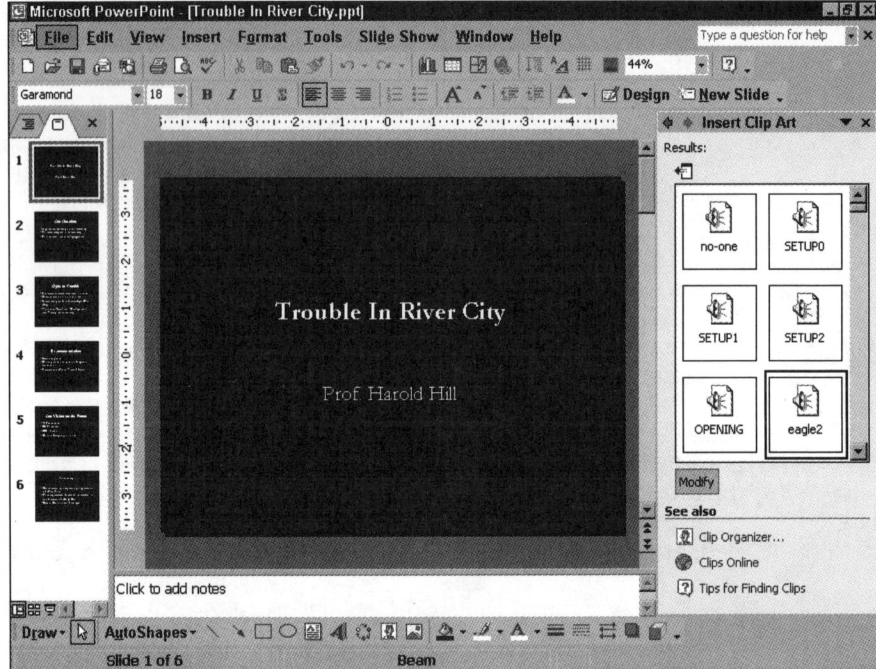

Figure 18-3: Inserting a sound from the Media Gallery.

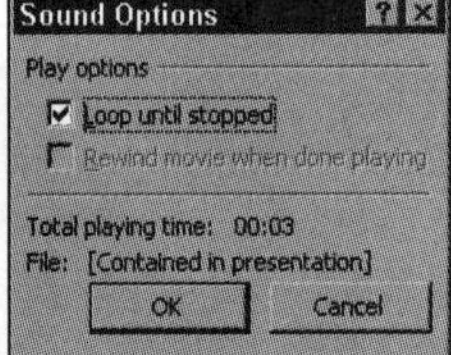

Figure 18-4: Setting a sound to loop.

Playing a Sound Over Several Slides

Sometimes, you have a sound file that you want to have played while you display several slides. You may even have a sound that you want to loop endlessly until your presentation ends. Unfortunately, PowerPoint has a nasty habit of stopping a sound when you move on to the next slide. But you can alter this behavior by following these steps:

1. **Right-click the sound icon, then choose Custom Animation from the menu that appears.**

   Yes, this is actually a Custom Animation feature and I know I'm not covering Custom Animation until Chapter 19, but this particular aspect of Custom Animation is more closely related to playing sound files, so here it is.

When you choose Custom Animation, the Custom Animation Task Pane appears to the right of the slide, as shown in Figure 18-5.

2. **Click the down arrow next to the sound item (labeled "Media 1" in Figure 18-5), then choose Effect Options from the menu that appears.**

   This action summons the Play Sound dialog box, shown in Figure 18-6.

3. **Click the After option button, then set the number of slides you want the sound to play for.**

   When you count the slides, start counting with the slide the sound is on. For example, suppose you have a presentation with 10 slides, and you insert a sound on slide 3 and you want the sound to play while slides 3, 4, 5, and 6 are displayed and to stop when slide 7 is displayed. In this case, you would set the number of slides to 4.

4. **Click OK.**

   That's it!

If the sound file is not long enough to last through all the slides you want it to play over, right-click the sound icon, choose Edit Sound Object to bring up the Sound Options dialog box, and then set the Loop Until Stopped option.

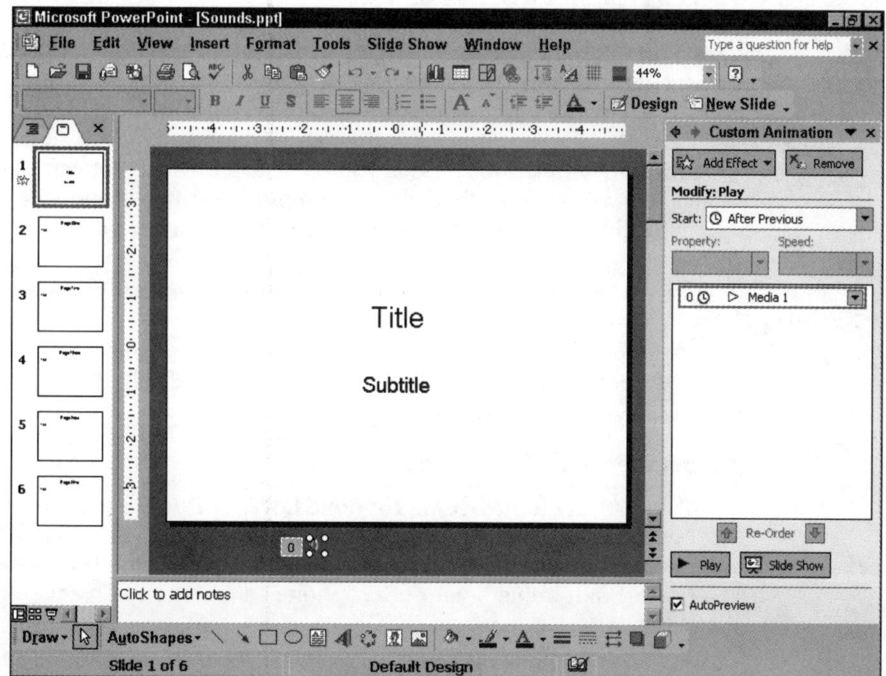

Figure 18-5: The Custom Animation Pane for a sound.

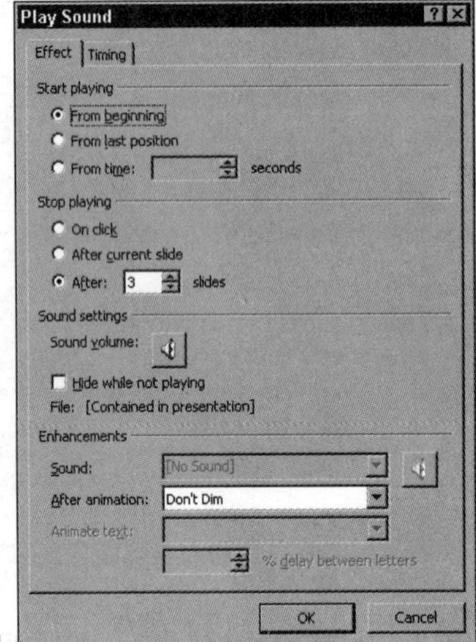

Figure 18-6: The Play Sound dialog box.

Recording a Narration

PowerPoint also includes a nifty feature that lets you record your own voice to use as a narration for the slide show. As you record your narration, PowerPoint stores the narration you record for each file separately so that when you play back your presentation with the narration, the slides are automatically synchronized with the narrations you recorded. PowerPoint can also store timings for each slide so that when you replay the presentation, PowerPoint automatically advances each slide along with the narration.

To record a narration, go to the first slide of your presentation; then follow these steps:

1. **Choose the Slide Show➪Record Narration command.**

   The dialog box shown in Figure 18-7 appears.

2. **Set the microphone level.**

   To do so, click the Set Microphone Level button. This brings up the Microphone Check dialog box, shown in Figure 18-8. Talk into the microphone, reading the text displayed in the dialog box. As you speak, PowerPoint adjusts your microphone sensitivity to an acceptable range. When you're finished, click OK.

3. **Click OK to begin the slide show.**

   The first slide of your presentation is displayed.

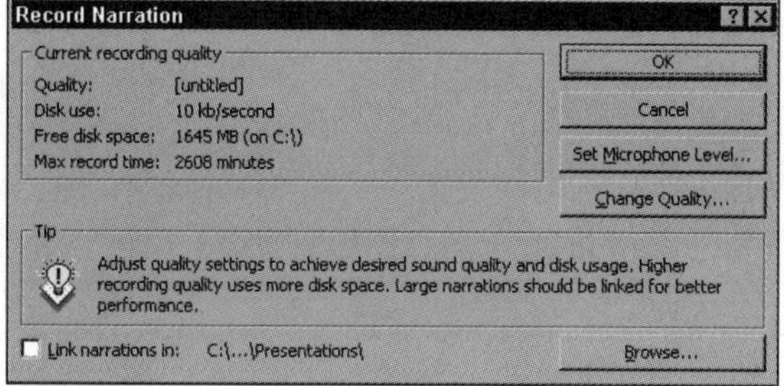

Figure 18-7: The Record Narration dialog box lets you record a narration for your slide show.

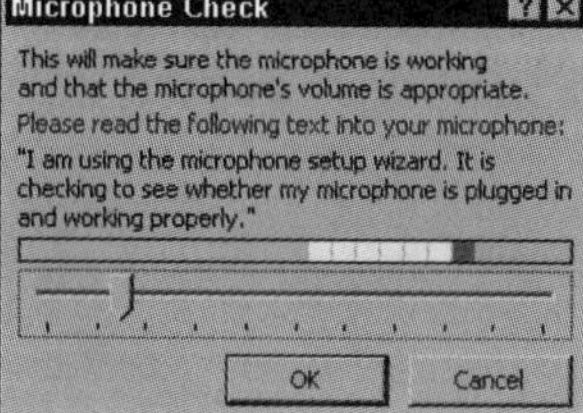

Figure 18-8: Setting the microphone level.

4. **Speak your narration into the microphone. Press Enter each time you want to advance to a new slide.**

   Or, if you have set up builds or other animations, press Enter to advance through the builds and animations.

   When you reach the end of the slide show, PowerPoint displays the dialog box shown in Figure 18-9.

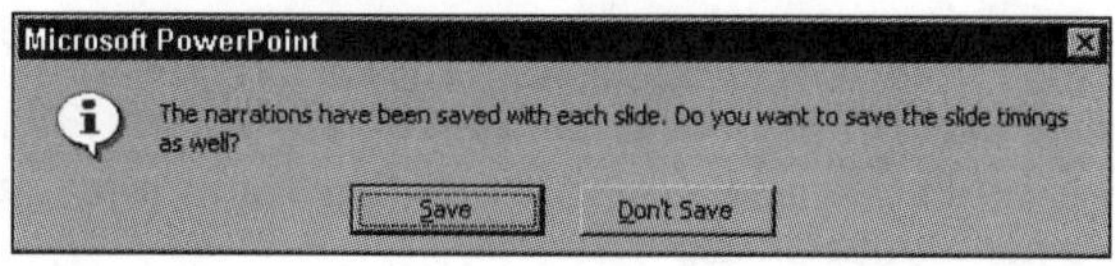

Figure 18-9: The narration is recorded. Do you want to save the slide timings?

5. **Click Save if you want PowerPoint to automatically advance your slides in sequence with your narration. To advance slides manually, click Don't Save.**

   You're taken to PowerPoint's Slide Sorter View, where the timing for each slide is displayed along with the slides.

6. **Press F5 or click the Slide Show button to begin the slide show so you can see if your narration works.**

   The slide show begins. You should hear your narration through your computer's speakers, and the slides should advance automatically along with the narration if you clicked Save in Step 5.

Here are some additional things to keep in mind about narrations:

- PowerPoint records the narration for each slide as a separate sound file, then attaches the sound to the slide. You'll see a speaker icon in the corner of your slides after you record a narration.
- The narration cancels out any other sounds you placed on the slides.

- If you want to show the presentation without the narration, call up the Slide Show⇨Set Up Show command, then check the Show Without Narration checkbox.

- You can record or rerecord a narration for just one slide by calling up that slide in Normal View, then choosing Slide Show⇨Record Narration. PowerPoint asks if you want to begin recording at the current slide or the first slide: Click the Current Slide button. When you're finished recording the slide's narration, press Esc to stop the show.
- To delete a narration, click the speaker icon in the corner of the slide and hit the Delete key. To delete the narration for an entire presentation, delete the speaker icon from every slide.

Working with Video

Welcome to the MTV era of computing. If your computer has the chutzpah, you can add small video clips to your presentations and play them at will. I'm not sure why you would want to, but hey, who needs a reason?

Adding a movie motion clip to a slide is similar to adding a sound clip. A crucial difference exists, however, between motion clips and sound bites: Video is meant to be *seen* (and sometimes *heard).* An inserted motion clip should be given ample space on your slide.

If you think sound files are big, wait till you see how big motion clips are. Ha! The whole multimedia revolution is really a conspiracy started by hard disk manufacturers.

These steps show you how to add a video clip to a slide:

1. **Find a good movie.**

   The hardest part about using video in a PowerPoint presentation is finding a video file that's worth showing. Many good sources offer video clips. PowerPoint comes with movies in the Media Gallery, and Microsoft has additional movies that you can download from the online Media Gallery. You can also find a wide variety of video clips available for download on the Web.

2. **Move to the slide on which you want to insert the movie.**

   Hopefully, you left a big blank space on the slide to put the movie in. If not, rearrange the existing slide objects to make room for the movie.

3. **Choose the Insert⇨Movies and Sounds⇨Movie from File command.**

   The Insert Movie dialog box appears.

4. **Select the movie that you want to insert.**

   You may need to scroll the list to find the movie you're looking for or navigate your way to a different folder.

5. **Click OK.**

   PowerPoint asks if you want to play the movie automatically when the slide come up or wait for you to click the movie before playing it. (The dialog box that appears to ask this question is the same as the one that was shown in Figure 18-2.)

6. **Click Yes to play the movie automatically or No to start the movie manually.**

   The movie is inserted on the slide, as shown in Figure 18-10.

6. **Resize the movie if you wish and drag it to a new location on the slide.**

   That's all there is to it! To play the movie while you're working on the presentation in Normal View, double-click the movie. During a Slide Show, a single click will do the trick.

You can also insert a movie by choosing Insert⇨Movies and Sounds⇨Movie from Clip Organizer. This calls up the Insert Clip Art Task Pane to display movies you can access from the Clip Organizer.

For technical reasons you probably don't really want to know, sometimes PowerPoint chokes on movies that you can easily play outside of PowerPoint using the Windows Media Player. If that happens, you can insert the movie as a Media Player object, which is a little more cumbersome than inserting a movie but still works. Choose the Insert⇨Object command to bring up the Object dialog box. Click the Create From File tab, click Browse, and select the movie file. Click Insert to return to the Object dialog box, then click OK to insert the movie.

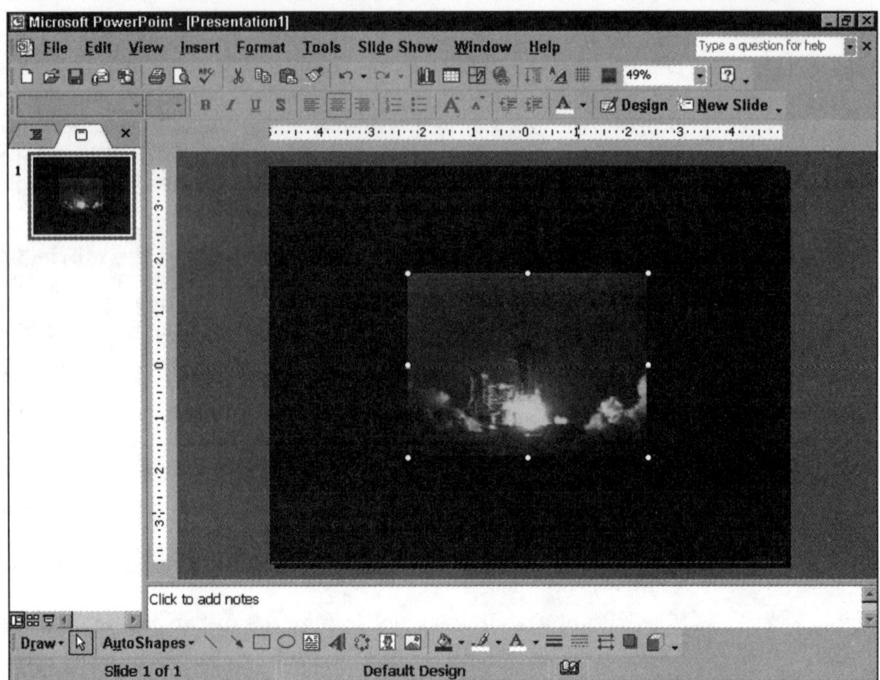

Figure 18-10: A movie inserted on a slide.

Chapter 19

Animation: It Ain't Disney, But It Sure Is Fun

In This Chapter

- Using slide transitions
- Applying animation schemes
- Working with the Custom Animation Task Pane
- Animating text
- Setting animation timings

If you plan to run your presentation on your computer's screen or on a computer projector, you can use or abuse a bagful of exciting on-screen PowerPoint animations. Your audience probably won't be fooled into thinking that you hired Disney to create your slides, but they'll be impressed all the same. Using animations is just one more example of how PowerPoint can make even the dullest content look spectacular.

This chapter begins with slide transitions, which are not technically animations because they don't involve movement of individual items on a slide. However, slide transitions are usually used in concert with animations to create presentations that are as much fun to watch as they are informative.

Using Slide Transitions

A transition is how PowerPoint gets from one slide to the next during an on-screen slide show. The normal way to segue from slide to slide is simply to cut to the new slide — effective, but boring. PowerPoint enables you to assign any of something in the neighborhood of 60 different special effects to each slide transition. For example, you can have the next slide scoot over the top of the current slide from any direction, or you can have the current slide scoot off the screen in any direction to reveal the next slide. You can have slides fade out, dissolve into each other, open up like Venetian blinds, or spin in like spokes on a wheel.

To use a slide transition, follow these steps:

1. **Move to the slide you want to apply the transition to.**

   If you want to apply the animation scheme to all your slides, you can skip this step as it won't matter which slide you start from.

   If you want to apply different transitions to different slides, you may prefer to work in Slide Sorter View, which allows you to see more slides at once. Slide Sorter View also has a few added bells and whistles for working with transitions, which I'll explain in a bit. But if you're going to use the same transition for all your slides, there's no benefit from switching to Slide Sorter View.

2. **Choose the Slide Show➪Slide Transition.**

   The Slide Transition Task Pane appears, as shown in Figure 19-1. (This figure shows PowerPoint in Slide Sorter View, but the Slide Transition Task Pane looks the same in Normal View.)

3. **Click the slide transition you want to use.**

   PowerPoint previews the transition by animating the current slide. If you want to see the preview again, just click the transition again.

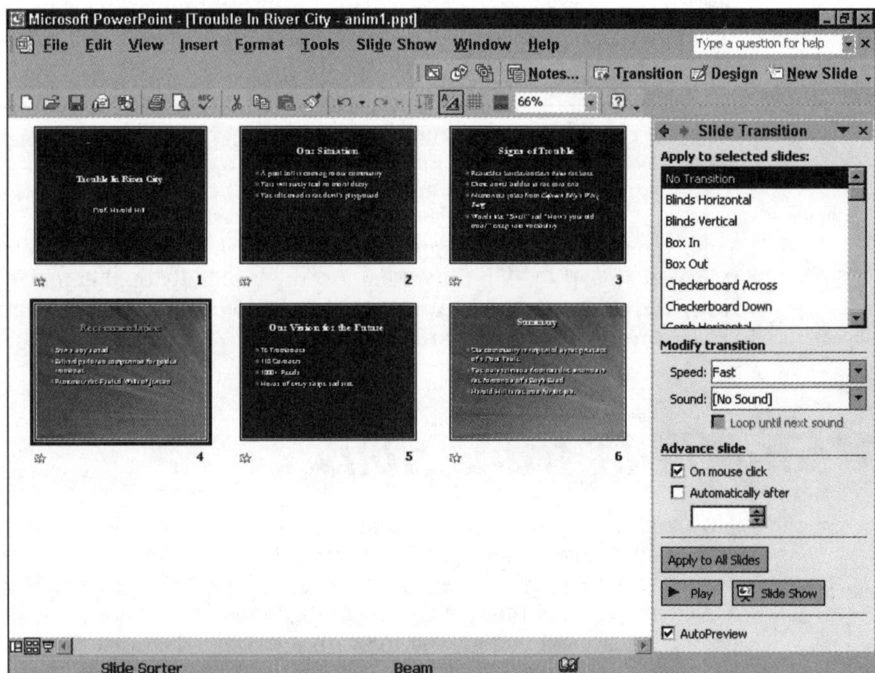

Figure 19-1: Setting a slide transition.

4. **Adjust the transition speed if you want.**

   You can choose from Slow, Medium, and Fast. Choose the setting that looks best on your computer.

5. **If you really want to be obnoxious, add a sound.**

   The Sound drop-down box lists a collection of standard transition sounds, such as applause, a cash register, and the standard "whoosh." You can also choose Other Sound to use your own .wav file.

6. **If you want the slide to advance automatically, check the Automatically check box and set the number of seconds.**

   If you leave this box unchecked, PowerPoint waits for you to click the mouse or press a key to advance to the next slide.

7. **If you want to apply the animation to the entire presentation, click Apply to All Slides.**

   This applies the animation to all the slides in the presentation.

Here are some additional points to keep in mind when using slide transitions:

- Transition effects look better on faster computers, which have more raw processing horsepower to implement the fancy pixel dexterity required to produce good-looking transitions. If your computer is a bit slow, change the speed setting to Fast so the transition won't drag.
- Some of the transition effects come in matched sets that apply the same effect from different directions. You can create a cohesive set of transitions by alternating among these related effects from slide to slide. For example, set up the first slide using Wipe Right, the second slide using Wipe Left, the third with Wipe Down, and so on.
- If you can't decide which transition effect to use, set all the slides to Random Transition by selecting all the slides and then choosing Random Transition from the toolbar. PowerPoint then randomly picks a transition effect for each slide.

- If the next slide has the same color scheme as the current slide, even the most bizarre transition effects, such as "Wheel Clockwise, 8 Spokes" or "Wedge" looks pretty tame. To maximize the impact of the transitions, use slides with contrasting color schemes.

- When you work in Slide Sorter View, you can click the little star icon beneath each slide (shown in the margin) to animate that slide. Also, the automatic slide timing is shown beneath the slide if you set the slide to advance automatically.

Using Animation Schemes

The easiest way to use transitions and builds is to use the predefined animation schemes that come with PowerPoint. Animation schemes are a new feature of PowerPoint 2002, so if you're upgrading from an earlier PowerPoint version, you'll appreciate how much animation schemes simplify the task of setting up animations.

An animation scheme is simply a predefined slide transition and a collection of animation effects applied to slide objects. One of the most basic animation schemes is called Appear, which sets up the body paragraphs so that they appear out of thin air one at a time. More complex animation schemes cause text to fly in, do back flips and somersaults, and spin around until it gets dizzy.

I suggest you take a few minutes someday to work your way through all the animation schemes to see how each one works. You can get a good idea about how each animation effect looks by using the previews in the Animation Scheme Task Pane. But to really see how the animation schemes work, you should set up a simple presentation with four or five slides with several paragraphs on each slide, and a couple of drawing objects here and there. Then, one at a time, apply each animation effect and run the slide show.

To apply an animation scheme to your slides, follow these steps:

1. **Move to the slide you want to apply the animation scheme to.**

   If you want to apply the animation scheme to all your slides, you can skip this step as it won't matter which slide you start from.

2. **Choose the Slide Show⇨Animation Schemes command.**

   The Animation Schemes Task Pane appears, as shown in Figure 19-2.

3. **Click the animation scheme you want to use.**

   PowerPoint gives you a preview of what the animation looks like by animating the current slide. If you want to see the preview again, just click the animation scheme again.

   The animation schemes are organized into three categories: Subtle, Moderate, and Exciting. At the very beginning of the list of animation schemes you'll find the five schemes you've most recently used. In addition, you'll find a category called "No Animation" with just one entry, "No Animation," (duh) which removes all animation from the slide.

   Clicking the animation scheme doesn't just preview the animation on the current slide, but actually assigns that scheme to the current slide. If you choose to retain the animation you had before, just press Ctrl+Z or choose Edit⇨Undo.

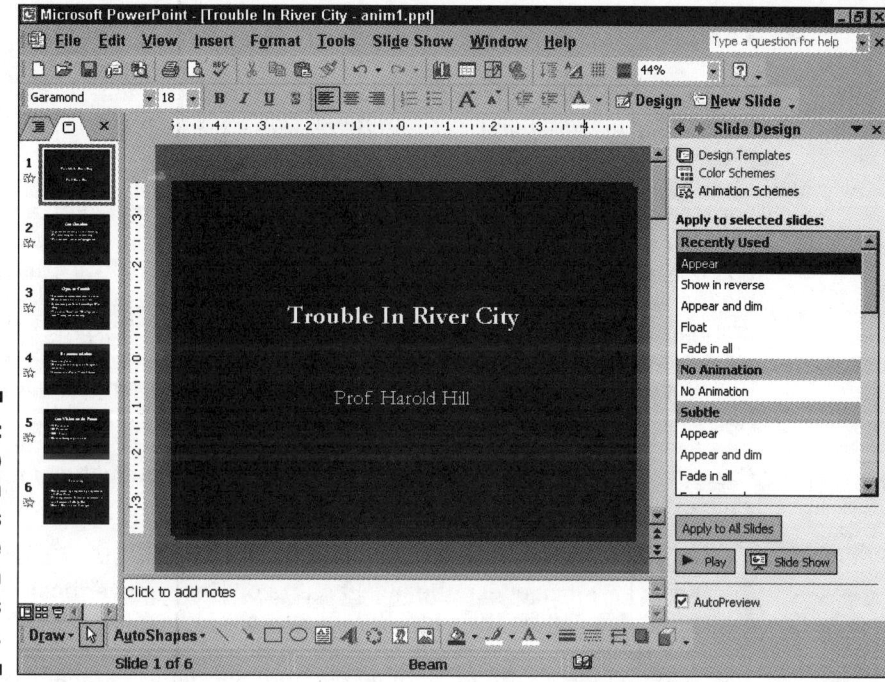

Figure 19-2: Setting up animation effects using the Animation Schemes Task Pane.

4. **If you want to apply the animation to the entire presentation, click Apply to All Slides.**
5. **Preview the entire show to make sure the animation works.**

   You can start the slide show by clicking the Slide Show button in the Animation Scheme Task Pane, or by choosing Slide Show➪View Show or pressing F5.

Custom Animation

Custom animation is the nitty-gritty of PowerPoint animation. Although you can create satisfactory animations using the predefined animation schemes, you can really dazzle your audience by using custom animation features. If you want, you can have objects moving all around your slides; some of them automatically, some of them when you click the mouse, two or more at a time, and with sound effects. Wow!

Understanding custom animation

Before I get into the details of setting up custom animation, there are some basic concepts you need to understand. Don't worry, this won't get too technical. But this is stuff you need to know.

For starters, you can apply custom animations to any object on a slide, whether it's a text placeholder, a drawing object such as an AutoShape or a text box, or a clip art picture. For text objects, you can specify that the animation should be applied to the text object as a whole, or to individual paragraphs within the object. You can also specify whether the effect should go all at once, word by word, or letter by letter. And you can indicate whether the effect should happen automatically or whether PowerPoint should wait for you to click the mouse or press Enter to initiate the animation.

Custom animation lets you create four basic types of animation effects for slide objects:

- **Entrance Effect:** This is how an object enters the slide. If you don't specify an entrance effect, the object starts out in whatever position you have placed it on the slide. But if you want to be more creative, you can have objects appear using any of 52 different effects, such as Appear, Blinds, Fade, Descend, Boomerang, Bounce, Sling, and many others.
- **Emphasis Effect:** This effect lets you draw attention to an object that is already on the slide. PowerPoint offers 31 different emphasis effects, including Change Fill Color, Change Font Size, Grow/Shrink, Spin, Teeter, Flicker, Color Blend, Blast, and many more.
- **Exit Effect:** This is how an object leaves the slide. Most objects don't have exit effects, but if you want an object to leave, you can apply one of 52 different effects which are similar to the entrance effects: Disappear, Blinds, Peek Out, Ease Out, Spiral Out, and so on.
- **Motion Path:** Motion paths are the most interesting types of custom animation. A motion path lets you create a track along which the object travels when animated. PowerPoint provides you with 64 predefined motion paths, such as circles, stars, teardrops, spirals, springs, and so on. If that's not enough, you can draw your own custom path to make an object travel anywhere on the slide you want it to go.

  If the motion path begins off the slide and ends somewhere on the slide, the motion path effect is similar to an entrance effect. If the path begins on the slide but ends off the slide, the motion path effect is like an exit effect. And if the path begins and ends on the slide, it is similar to an emphasis effect. You can also create a path that both begins and ends off the slide. In that case, when the animation starts, the object appears, travels along its path, then zips off the slide.

You can create more than one animation for a given object. For example, you can give an object an entrance effect, an emphasis effect, and an exit effect. That lets you bring the object onto the screen, draw attention to it, then have it leave. If you want, you can have several emphasis or motion path effects for a single object. You can also have more than one entrance and exit effect, but in most cases one will do.

Each effect you apply has one or more property settings you can tweak to customize the effect. All the effects have a speed setting that lets you set the speed for the animation. Some effects have an additional property setting that lets you control the range of an object's movement (for example, the Spin effect has an Amount setting that governs how far the object spins).

Adding an effect

To animate an object on a slide, follow these steps:

1. **In Normal View, call up the slide that contains the object you want to animate and click the object to select it.**
2. **Choose the Slide Show⇨Custom Animation command.**

   The Custom Animation Task Pane appears, as shown in Figure 19-3. In this example, I want to animate a smiley-face AutoShape.

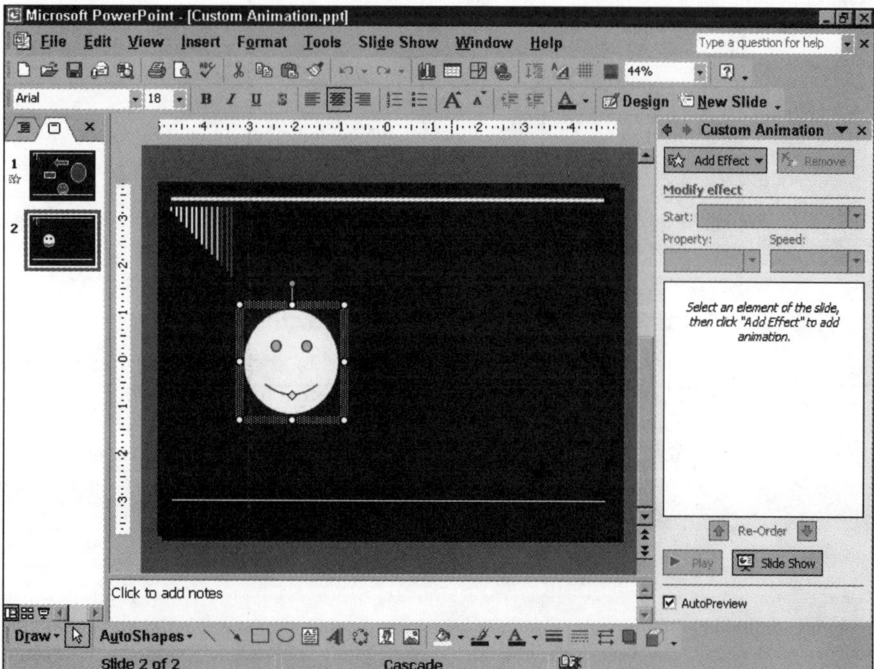

Figure 19-3: Animating an object.

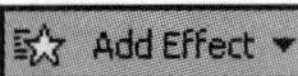

3. **Click the Add Effect button (shown in the margin), then select the type of effect you want to create from the menu that appears.**

   The menu lists the four types of effects: Entrance, Emphasis, Exit, and Motion Path. In this example, I'll choose Entrance so that I can create an entrance effect. A menu listing the effects appears.

4. **Choose the specific effect you want to apply. If the effect you want isn't on the menu, choose More Effects.**

   An Add Effect dialog box listing all the effects for the type you chose appears. For example, Figure 19-4 shows the Add Entrance Effect dialog box that appears if you choose Add Effect➪Entrance➪More Effects.

   The most commonly used effects for each type are listed right on the effect type menu. If the effect you want to use appears on the menu, you can select it without calling up the Add Effect dialog box.

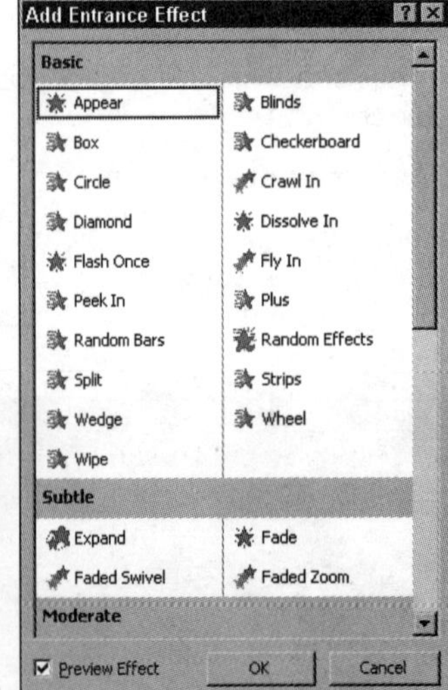

Figure 19-4: The Add Entrance Effect dialog box lists all the possible entrance effects.

5. **Choose the effect you want, then click OK.**

   The entrance effect you selected is added to the Custom Animation list Task Pane, as shown in Figure 19-5. The effect's number (in this case, 1) also appears on the slide next to the object the effect applies to. (Fear not; this number appears on the slide in Normal View only, and only when the Custom Animation Task Pane is active. Your audience won't see the number when you show your presentation.)

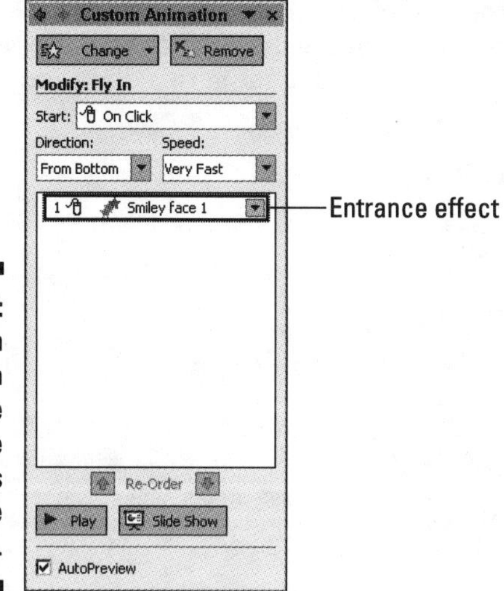

Figure 19-5: The Custom Animation Task Pane lists the animations you have created.

6. **Adjust the property settings for the animation if you want.**

   In Figure 19-5, the effect has two property settings: Direction and Speed. The Direction setting indicates which direction the smiley face should fly in from, and the Speed setting indicates how fast it should move.

7. **To preview the animation, click the Play button at the bottom of the Custom Animation Task Pane.**

   Or, if you prefer, just run the slide show to see how the animation looks. If nothing happens, try clicking the mouse to get the animation started.

If you add more than one effect to a slide, the effects are initiated one at a time by mouse clicks, in the order you create them. You can drag effects up or down in the custom animation list to change the order of the effects. For information about changing the order or setting up automatic effects, see the section "Timing your animations" later in this chapter.

Notice in Figure 19-5 that the Add Effect button has changed to Change Effect because the Smiley face Entrance effect is selected in the custom animation list. If you want to change the effect — for example, use the Magnify entrance effect instead of the Fly In effect — click the Change Effect button and choose a new effect.

You can further tweak an effect by clicking the down arrow that appears next to the effect in the custom animation list, then choosing Effect Options. This brings up a dialog box similar to the one shown in Figure 19-6. This dialog box has settings that let you add a sound to the animation, change the color of the object after the animation completes, and specify how text is to be animated (all at once, one word at a time, or one letter at a time). Depending on the type of effect, additional controls may appear in this dialog box.

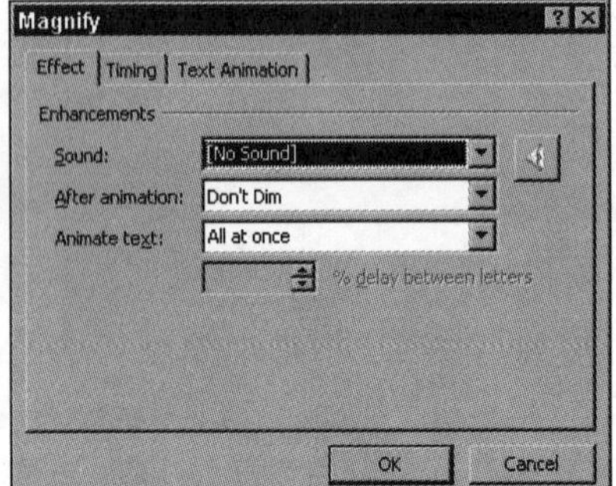

Figure 19-6: The Effect settings dialog box

Animating Text

The most common reason for animating text is to draw attention to your text one paragraph at a time as you show your presentation. One way to do this is to create an entrance effect for the text placeholder; then adjust the effect settings so that the entrance effect is applied one paragraph at a time. When you do that, your slide initially appears empty except for the title. Click the mouse once and the first paragraph appears. Talk about that paragraph for awhile, then click the mouse again to bring up the second paragraph. You can keep talking and clicking until all the paragraphs have appeared. Then, when you click again, PowerPoint calls up the next slide.

Another approach is to use an emphasis effect instead of an entrance effect. This allows all the paragraphs to be displayed on the slide initially. When you click the mouse, the entrance effect is applied to the first paragraph — it changes colors, increases in size, spins, whatever. Each time you click, the effect is applied to the next paragraph in sequence.

Either way, you must first add the effect for the text placeholder, then call up the effect settings dialog box by clicking the down arrow next to the effect in the custom animation list and choosing Effect Settings. This summons the settings dialog box for the text object. Click the Text Animation tab to see the animation settings shown in Figure 19-7.

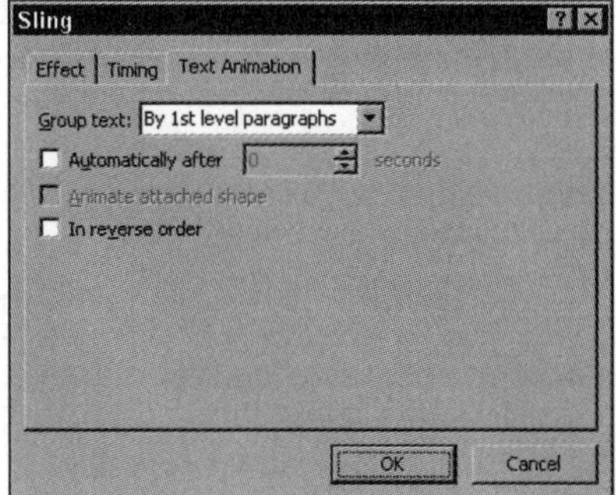

Figure 19-7: Animating text.

The Group Text By setting is the one that controls how paragraphs appear when you click the mouse during the show, based on the paragraph's outline level. If you have only one outline level on the slide, Group By 1st Level Paragraphs will do. If you have two or more levels, leaving Group Text By set to Group By 1st Level Paragraphs causes each paragraph to be animated along with any paragraphs that are subordinate to it. If you'd rather animate the second-level paragraphs separately, choose Group By 2nd Level Paragraphs instead.

The other controls on this tab let you animate each paragraph automatically after a certain time interval or display the paragraphs in reverse order. (David Letterman, if you're reading this, you can use this feature when you present your Top Ten lists.)

Timing your animations

Most animations are initiated by mouse clicks. But you can set up several animations to activate automatically; in sequence or all at the same time. To do so, you must use PowerPoint's animation timing features.

The first trick to controlling animation timing is to get the effects listed in the custom animation list in the correct order. Effects are added to the list in the order you create them. If you plan carefully, you may be able to create the effects in the same order that you want to animate them. But more likely, you'll need to change the order of the effects. Fortunately, you can do that easily enough by dragging the effects up or down in the custom animation list.

After you get the effects in the right order, use the Start control that's near the top of the Custom Animation Task Pane to set the start option for each effect. This control has three options:

- **On Click:** Starts the effect when you click the mouse or press Enter.
- **With Previous:** Starts the effect when the effect immediately above it starts. Use this option to animate two or more objects simultaneously.
- **After Previous:** Starts the effect as soon as the preceding effect finishes.

Starting with the first effect in the list, click each effect to select it, then choose the Start option for the effect. If all the effects except the first are set to With Previous or After Previous, the entire slide's animations run automatically once you start the first effect by clicking the mouse.

For example, Figure 19-8 shows a slide with three polygons drawn to resemble pieces of a puzzle. You can animate this puzzle so that the three pieces come together at the same time like this:

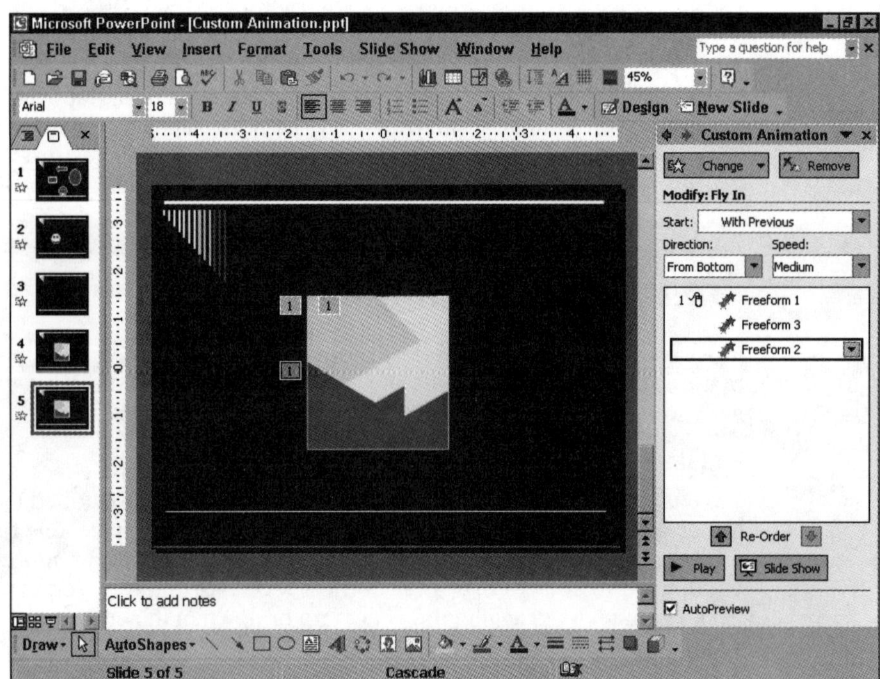

Figure 19-8: An animated puzzle.

Follow these steps to set up an animated puzzle like the one in Figure 19-8:

1. **Add a Fly In entrance effect for the top left piece with the following settings:**

   Start: On Click

   Direction: From Top-Left

   Speed: Medium

2. **Add a Fly In entrance effect for the top right piece with the following settings:**

   Start: With Previous

   Direction: From Top-Right

   Speed: Medium

3. **Add a Fly In entrance effect for the bottom piece with the following settings:**

   Start: With Previous

   Direction: From Bottom

   Speed: Medium

For even more control over an effect's timings, click the down arrow to the right of the effect and choose Timing. A dialog box similar to the one in Figure 19-9 appears. Here's the lowdown on the timing controls:

- **Start:** The same as the Start control in the Custom Animation Task Pane.
- **Delay:** Lets you delay the start of the animation by a specified number of seconds.
- **Speed:** The same as the Speed control in the Custom Animation Task Pane.
- **Repeat:** Lets you repeat the effect so the object is animated several times in succession.
- **Rewind when done playing:** Certain effects leave the object in a different condition than the object was when you started. For example, the object may change color or size or move to a new position on the slide. If you check the Rewind when done playing option, the object is restored to its original condition when the animation finishes.

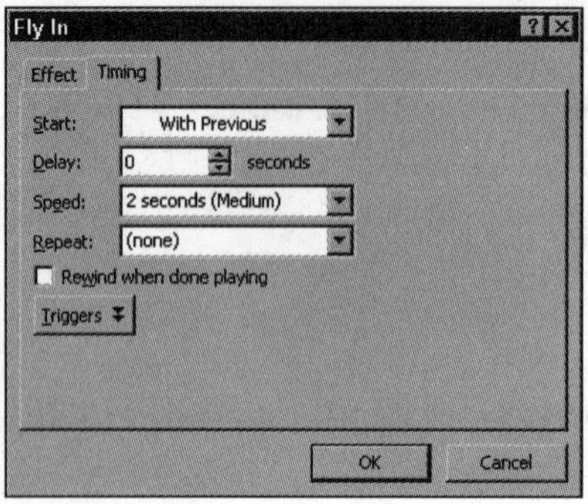

Figure 19-9: Setting the timing controls.

Part V

PowerPoint and the Net

"Come on Walt—time to freshen the company Web page."

In this part . . .

Some of the hottest new features of PowerPoint are Web-compatibility features. Bill Gates is riding the wave of the future again, and the results include zupped-up online collaboration, cool stuff for your intranet, and HTML formatting ability that makes PowerPoint fit the Internet like an expensive suit. If you, too, have been caught up in the hype of the Internet, and you sleep with your cable modem under your pillow, you'll appreciate the chapters in this part.

Chapter 20

Going Online with PowerPoint

In This Chapter

- Opening presentations on the Web using PowerPoint
- Accessing FTP sites from PowerPoint
- Using the Web toolbar
- Broadcasting a presentation

Office 2002 has one big, gigantic goal — to make everything in the entire Office suite work compatibly with the Internet. In keeping with the times, Office 2002 has been designed with the idea that users will use the Internet, so the software that users select must be Internet compatible.

I know what you're thinking: You think you have to use special Internet software — such as Microsoft Internet Explorer or Netscape Navigator — to access the Internet. Isn't a browser program required to access the World Wide Web?

Until Microsoft released Office 97, it was. But since then, all the Office programs — including of course PowerPoint — let you access files on the Internet directly, without going through a Web browser. PowerPoint lets you open PowerPoint presentation files whether they reside on your computer or on the Internet.

The Internet features described in this chapter also apply to a type of network that has lately become cutting edge in companies around the world, called an *intranet*. An intranet is like a local version of the Internet. It looks, feels, and behaves just like the Internet but is local to a specific company and cannot be accessed by outside users. If your company has an intranet, you can use PowerPoint to open presentations that have been stored on it. Corporations think using an intranet is a "value-added exercise." (Who makes up these hot buzzwords, anyway?)

This entire chapter assumes that you have access to the Internet. If you do not, you should first pick up a copy of my book, *Internet Explorer 5.5 For Windows For Dummies,* published by Hungry Minds, Inc., which shows you how to get connected to the Internet. And as a bonus, shows you how to use Internet Explorer 5.5 to access the Internet.

Internet jargon you can't avoid

Unfortunately, there's no way to discuss using PowerPoint to access Internet presentations without using some farily heavy Internet terminology. Here are some basics — an overview of some of the more important Internet terms used in this chapter. (Although I'm sure many of you know these, there is always someone hiding his or her head in the sand.)

- **Internet:** The Internet is a huge global network that consists of literally millions of computers.
- **World Wide Web:** The fastest-growing segment of the Internet. The Web (as it is usually called) consists of millions of pages of information that can be displayed at will by a Web browser program.
- **Web browser:** A program designed to access the World Wide Web. The two most popular Web browsers are Netscape Navigator and Microsoft Internet Explorer.
- **HTML:** HyperText Markup Language, the codes used to format a page for the World Wide Web. As a casual Web user, you don't have to concern yourself with HTML. If you want to create Web pages of your own, you need to get user-friendly Web-page creating software to sidestep knowing some HTML, or check out *HTML For Dummies,* 3rd Edition, by Ed Tittel and Steve James (published by Hungry Minds, Inc.).

You've probably noticed that there are many software applications available for creating your own Web site these days, and many user-friendly Web server communities. All you need to do to publish your own Web site is be able to breathe, able to type, and have Internet access.

- **Web page:** A single page of information on the World Wide Web.
- **Web server:** A computer that stores Web pages so the pages can be retrieved by Internet users such as yourself.
- **Home page:** A Web page that serves as a starting point for a collection of related Web pages (often called a Web site).
- **FTP:** File Transfer Protocol, a way of copying individual files from one computer to another.
- **FTP server:** A server computer that stores files that can be accessed via FTP.
- **URL:** Uniform Resource Locator, an Internet address. A URL identifies a Web server or FTP server, plus the filename for the document or file to be retrieved. These days, folks refer to Web page addresses as URLs.

Opening a Presentation at a Web Site Using PowerPoint

Suppose that you create a PowerPoint presentation and decide to make it available to the general public via the Internet. You can do that by saving the presentation as an HTML file so that anyone with a Web browser can access the presentation. Or, you can post the .ppt file on the Web server so that anyone with PowerPoint can open the presentation directly from the Web server and view the file from within PowerPoint. You have to determine who your audience is and what they're going to do with the presentation.

If you want to make your PowerPoint presentation available to other PowerPoint users on, let's say, your intranet, then saving your presentation to the intranet in .ppt format makes sense. If you want to make your presentation available to users without PowerPoint, then saving your presentation in HTML makes sense, as users can access the presentation with only a browser. You can find more information about saving HTML presentations to the Web and using browsers to access HTML files created in PowerPoint in Chapter 22.

You can open .ppt presentations that reside on Internet Web servers by using the standard File➪Open command. When you open an Internet-based presentation, PowerPoint opens the presentation in read-only mode, which means that you can view the presentation but can't save any changes you make.

To open a presentation located on a Web server, you must know the complete address (called a *URL*) of the presentation that you want to open. This address usually consists of three parts: a server address, one or more directory names, and a filename for the presentation. The address must always begin with `http://` so that PowerPoint can distinguish the address from a normal filename. And the other parts of the URL are separated by slashes.

For example, consider this address:

```
http://www.con.com/river/trouble.ppt
```

Here, the server name is `www.con.com`, the directory is `river`, and the filename is `trouble.ppt`.

When you know the URL, all you have to do to open a presentation is type its URL in the File Name field on the standard Open dialog box. Here's the complete procedure for opening a presentation at an Internet Web site:

1. **Find out the complete URL of the presentation that you want to open.**
2. **Choose the File➪Open command.**

   Alternatively, click the Open button or use the keyboard shortcut Ctrl+O. One way or the other, the Open dialog box appears.
3. **In the File Name field, type the URL of the presentation that you want to open.**

   For example, type `http://www.con.com/river/trouble.ppt`.
4. **Click Open.**

   If you're not already connected to the Internet, a Connect To dialog box appears so that you can make a connection.

   Copying the file over the Internet to your computer takes a few moments — perhaps a few minutes if the presentation is large. When the transfer is finished, the presentation is displayed as normal.

If you have the Web toolbar displayed, you can enter the address in the Address box, press Enter, and voilà! The presentation is displayed. You can find more about the Web toolbar at the end of this chapter.

You have just successfully opened a .ppt presentation residing on the Internet using PowerPoint. In Chapter 22, you discover how to save a PowerPoint presentation to the Web using the Save As dialog box, in HTML format, as well as open the presentations in your browser just for kicks, too. Don't put the book down now! Everyone loves a good mystery.

PowerPoint doesn't care if the file identified by the URL is on a computer halfway around the globe, on a computer two floors up from you, or on your own computer. So long as the URL is valid, PowerPoint retrieves the presentation and displays it.

Using an FTP Site

FTP, which stands for *File Transfer Protocol,* is one of the oldest parts of the Internet. FTP is designed to create Internet libraries where files can be stored and retrieved by other Internet users.

FTP uses a directory structure that works much like Windows 95 or 98 folders. The main directory of an FTP site is called the *root.* Within the root are other directories, which may contain files, additional directories, or both. For example, a typical FTP server for a business may have directories such as Products (for storing files that contain product information), Company (for company information), Software (for software files that can be downloaded), and Docs (for documentation about the company's products).

Until Office 97, you had to use separate FTP software to retrieve files from an FTP site. Since Office 97 (and in PowerPoint 2002, of course), you can access FTP sites from the standard Open and Save As dialog boxes. Since PowerPoint 97, you can set up FTP sites so that you can access them as if they were disk drives attached to your computer.

The following section — "Adding an FTP Site to Your Computer" — explains how you can set up an FTP site so that you can access it from within PowerPoint. The section after that — "Opening a presentation from an FTP site" — shows how to actually access an FTP site from PowerPoint.

Adding an FTP Site to Your Computer

Before you can access files in an FTP site, you must add the address (URL) of the FTP site to your computer's list of FTP sites. To do that, follow these steps:

1. **In PowerPoint, summon the File⇨Open command.**

   This command summons the Open dialog box, which is illustrated in Figure 20-1.

2. **Click the down arrow for the Look in list box and then scroll down to select Add/Modify FTP Locations.**

   The dialog box shown in Figure 20-1 appears.

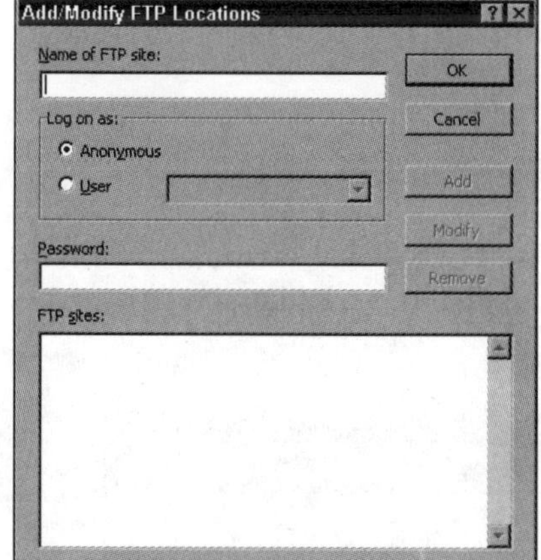

Figure 20-1: Adding an FTP site.

3. **Type the URL of the FTP site in the Name of FTP site field.**

   Be sure to include `ftp://` at the start of the URL.

4. **If this FTP site requires you to enter a user name and password to gain access, click the User button and then type your user name and password.**

   You have to get the name and password to use from the administrator of the FTP site you are accessing. (At many FTP sites, the user name of "Anonymous" works, with the password being your e-mail address.)

5. **Click Add.**

   The new FTP site is added.

6. **Click OK.**

   The Add/Modify FTP Locations dialog box vanishes, returning you to the Open dialog box.

7. **Click Cancel to return to PowerPoint.**

   The FTP site is now added to the list of FTP sites that are available from within PowerPoint. To open a presentation from this site or another site you have previously added, follow the steps detailed in the next section.

Opening a presentation from an FTP site

To open a presentation from an FTP site, follow these steps:

1. **Choose the File⇨Open command.**

   This summons the Open dialog box.

2. **Click the down arrow of the Look in list box and then scroll down to find and select the FTP site containing the presentation that you want to open.**

   Your computer hesitates for a moment as it connects with the FTP site. Then the Open dialog box is displayed, listing the directories that appear at the FTP site's root. See Figure 20-2.

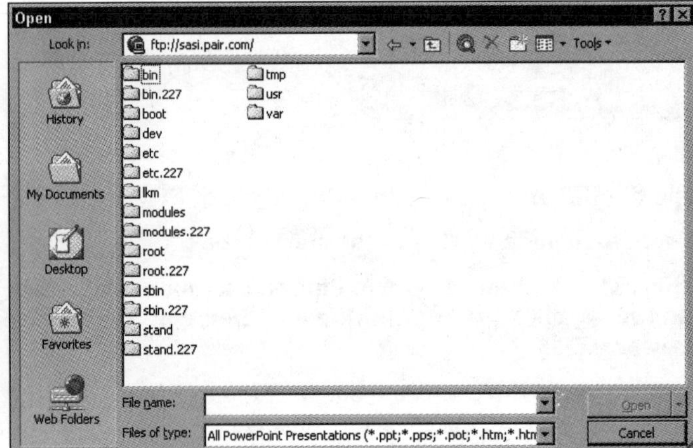

Figure 20-2: Opening a file from an FTP site.

3. **Select the file that you want to open.**

   To open a directory, double-click the directory's icon. Click the icon of the file you want to select.

4. **Click Open.**

   Depending on the size of your presentation, you may have to wait for a few minutes for PowerPoint to download the presentation.

You're done!

Saving a presentation to an FTP site

If you have access to an FTP site that lets you store your file (that is, if you have "write privileges" for the FTP site), you can also save a presentation directly to the FTP site from PowerPoint using the File➪Save As command. Here is the procedure:

1. **Choose the File➪Save As command.**

   The familiar Save As dialog box appears.

2. **Click the down arrow for the Look in list box and then scroll down to find and select the FTP site on which you want to save the presentation.**

   Your computer connects to the FTP site (this may take a moment) and then displays the FTP site's root directory in the Save As dialog box.

3. **Navigate to the directory where you want to save the file.**
4. **Type a name for the file.**
5. **Click Save.**

   The file is copied to the FTP server. Depending on the size of the file, this may take a while. If the file has dozens of slides, each with large graphics, you may have enough time to catch a quick lunch while the file is copied to the FTP server.

Using the Web Toolbar

PowerPoint 2002 sports a toolbar called the Web toolbar. The Web toolbar is designed to make it easier for you to view documents that contain hyperlinks or that were retrieved from the World Wide Web. Figure 20-4 shows a presentation with the Web toolbar active, and Table 20-1 lists the function of each button and control on the Web toolbar. (In Figure 20-3, the Web toolbar is located just above the ruler.)

To summon the Web toolbar, choose the View➪Toolbars➪Web or click the Web toolbar button in the standard toolbar.

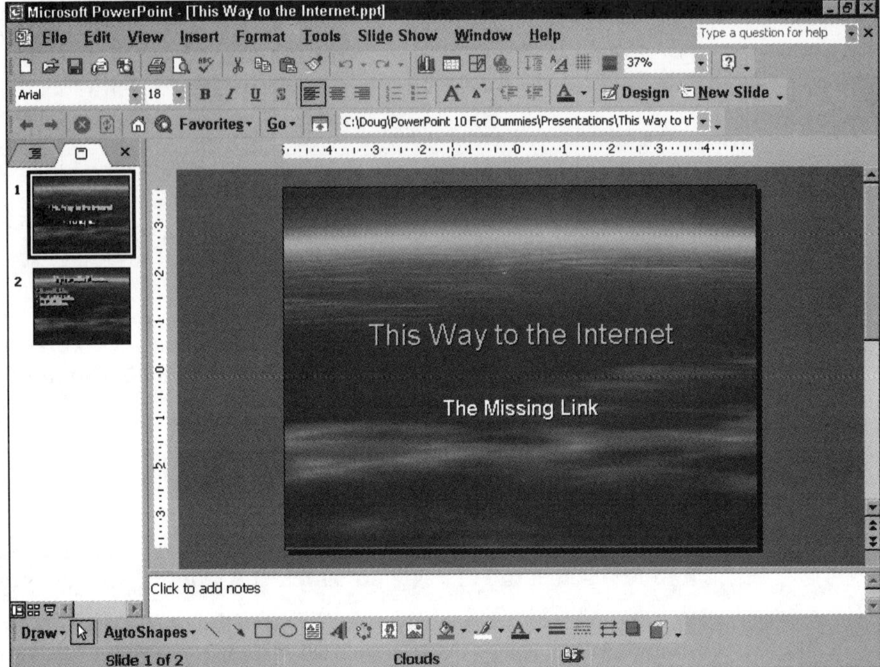

Figure 20-3: The Web toolbar in action.

Table 20-1 Buttons on the Web Toolbar

Button	*Name*	*What It Does*
	Back	Goes to the previously displayed slide.
	Forward	Returns to the slide you went back from.
	Stop	Stops downloading the current page.
	Refresh Current Page	Reloads the current page.
	Start Page	Displays your designated start page.
	Search Page	Displays your designated search page.
Favorites	Favorites	Displays your favorites list, similar to clicking the Look In Favorites button in an Open or Save As dialog box.

Button	*Name*	*What It Does*
Go	Go	Displays a menu that includes the Back, Forward, Start, and Search commands that correspond to the Back, Forward, Start, and Search buttons. Also includes an Open command and commands to designate the current page as your start page or search page.
	Show only Web toolbar	Temporarily hides everything on the screen except the slide area and the Web toolbar. Click this button again to get the screen back to normal.
(None)	Address	A large combination text box and drop-down list box that shows the address of the current page. I don't picture it here in this table because it's too dang big, but you can't miss it: It takes up almost the whole right half of the Web toolbar.

If you find that you don't have all the buttons you want on your Web toolbar, remember the down arrow that leads you to the Add or Remove Buttons button. Chant, "Button, button, who's got the button?" while performing this task, and it works a lot better.

The Web toolbar is most useful when used in a slide show that is browsed by an individual rather than one that is printed out as slides or transparencies and shown with a projector. For example, suppose that you create a presentation that describes your company's employee benefits programs, and the presentation contains dozens of hyperlinks that bounce back and forth from slide to slide and perhaps even lead to other presentations. When individuals view this presentation, they'll want to activate the Web toolbar so they can use its controls to follow the presentation's hyperlinks and to go back to slides they've already viewed.

Using Presentation Broadcast

Presentation Broadcast is a nifty PowerPoint that lets you show a presentation over the Internet. Other Internet users can tune in to watch your presentation. And the best part is, they don't even have to have PowerPoint to watch; any old Web browser will do. (Well, *really* old Web browsers won't work. Presentation Broadcasts are best viewed with Internet Explorer 5.1 or later.)

When you broadcast a presentation, the viewers can see the presentation's slides along with a table of contents that lets them click to move forward or backward through the presentation. In addition, viewers can hear your voice or see your picture if your computer has a microphone and a camera.

Here's what you need to broadcast a presentation:

- A presentation interesting enough to broadcast to someone who cares, who can't just walk across the hall to watch the presentation on your computer. This may seem like an obvious point, but sometimes we get so wrapped up in technology that we forget the simple solutions. Presentation broadcast is too much fuss to use unless you really need it.
- A high-speed Internet connection such as ISDN, DSL, Cable, or some such. Avoid using presentation broadcast with a dial-up connection.
- A microphone and video camera if you want to broadcast your voice or picture.
- A server computer that can host your broadcast unless only one or two people will view your presentation. If more than ten people will view your presentation, the server should run Windows Media Server software. (If you're sharing a presentation from your own computer, you must first save the presentation to a shared folder.)

To set up a Presentation Broadcast, choose Slide Show➪Online Broadcast➪Settings command to summon the Broadcast Settings dialog box, pictured in Figure 20-4. Use this dialog box to set options such as whether your presentation will include audio and video and what kind of server to use.

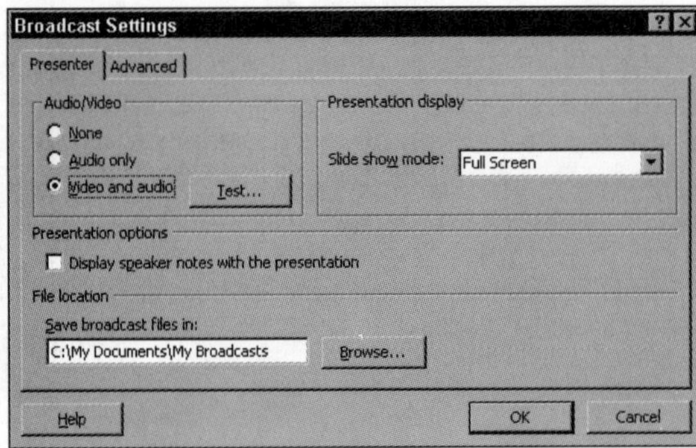

Figure 20-4: The Broadcast Settings dialog box.

To start an online presentation, choose the Slide Show➪Online Broadcast➪Start Live Broadcast Now command. This summons a dialog box on which you can indicate the title and subject of your presentation, who will be making the presentation, and who should be invited to the broadcast. You can then proceed with the broadcast.

Chapter 21

Working with Hyperlinks and Action Buttons

In This Chapter

- Getting to know hyperlinks
- Using action buttons

Imagine you, a community-minded businessperson, giving a presentation on how a marching band can cure your town's budding juvenile problem when the librarian — you know, the one named Marian — interrupts. She wants you to go back to that section about how pool halls are breeding grounds for all sorts of ills, something you finished several slides ago. How do you skip back to the section quickly?

Now imagine that you're giving a presentation before the executive committee of your company, and the vice president of finance raises a question about some information on a slide. You anticipated the question, and you know that another presentation has a slide that will put the matter to rest, but how do you get to that slide?

With hyperlinks and action buttons, that's how. And this chapter explains the way to use them.

Using Hyperlinks

In PowerPoint, a *hyperlink* is simply a bit of text or a graphic image that you can click when viewing a slide to summon another slide, another presentation, or perhaps some other type of document such as a Word document or an Excel worksheet. The hyperlink may also lead to a page on the Internet's World Wide Web.

For example, suppose that you have a slide that contains a chart of sales trends. You can place a hyperlink on the slide that, if clicked during a slide show, summons another slide presenting the same data in the form of a table.

That slide can in turn contain a hyperlink that, when clicked, summons an Excel spreadsheet that contains the detailed data on which the chart is based.

Another common use for hyperlinks is to create a table of contents for your presentation. A slide — usually the first or second slide in the presentation — is created that contains links to other slides in the presentation. The table of contents slide may include a link to every slide in the presentation, but more likely it contains links to selected slides. For example, if a presentation contains several sections of slides, the table of contents slide may contain links to the first slide in each section.

Hyperlinks are not limited to slides in the current presentation. Hyperlinks can lead to other presentations. When you use this kind of hyperlink, a person viewing the slide show clicks the hyperlink, and PowerPoint automatically loads the indicated presentation. The hyperlink can lead to the first slide in the presentation, or it can lead to a specific slide within the presentation.

A common use for this type of hyperlink is to create a menu of presentations that can be viewed. For example, suppose that you have created the following four presentations:

- The Detrimental Effects of Pool
- Case Studies in Communities Destroyed by Pool Halls
- Marching Bands through the Ages
- Understanding the Think System

You can easily create a slide listing all four presentations and containing hyperlinks to them. The person viewing the slide show simply clicks on a hyperlink, and off he or she goes to the appropriate presentation.

Here are a few additional thoughts to ponder concerning hyperlinks:

- Hyperlinks aren't limited to PowerPoint presentations. In PowerPoint, you can create a hyperlink that leads to other types of Microsoft Office documents, such as Word documents or Excel spreadsheets. When the person viewing the slide show clicks one of these hyperlinks, PowerPoint automatically runs Word or Excel to open the document or worksheet.
- A hyperlink can also lead to a page on the Internet's World Wide Web. When the user clicks the hyperlink, PowerPoint runs Internet Explorer to connect to the Internet and displays the Web page.

  For more information about browsing the World Wide Web, see my book *Internet Explorer 5.5 For Windows For Dummies,* published by Hungry Minds, Inc.

- Hyperlinks work only when the presentation is shown in Slide Show View. You can click on a hyperlink all you want while in Slide View, Outline View, or Slide Sorter View, and the only thing that happens is that your finger gets tired. Links are active only when viewing the slide show.

Creating a hyperlink to another slide

Adding a hyperlink to a presentation is easy. Just follow these steps:

1. **Select the text or graphic object that you want to make into a hyperlink.**

   The most common type of hyperlink is based on a word or two of text in a slide's body text area. For example, in Figure 21-1, I've selected some text ("Trouble in River City") that I want to make into a hyperlink.

2. **Choose the Insert⇨Hyperlink command.**

   Alternatively, click the Insert Hyperlink button (shown in the margin) found on the standard toolbar or use the keyboard shortcut Ctrl+K. One way or the other, the Insert Hyperlink dialog box shown in Figure 21-1 is summoned.

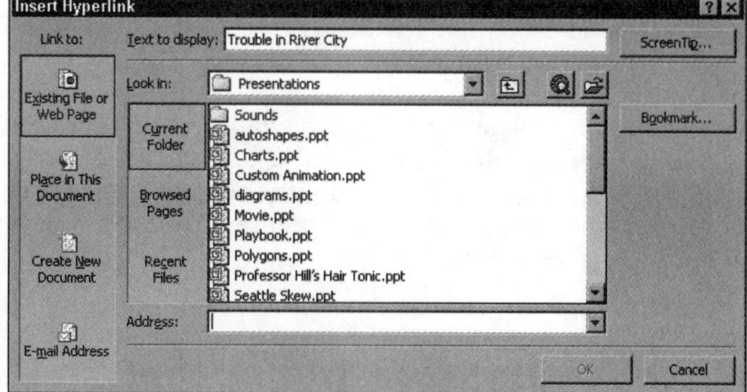

Figure 21-1: The Insert Hyperlink dialog box.

3. **Click the Place in This Document icon in the list of four icons on the left side of the Insert Hyperlink Dialog box.**

   The four icons are:

   - **Existing File or Web Page:** This means you can link to another file in another application, or to a Web page on the Internet.
   - **Place in This Document:** This means you can link one part of your PowerPoint presentation to another part.
   - **Create New Document:** This is just what it says it is. You can, however, choose now or another time to edit the new document by clicking the appropriate button.

- **E-mail Address:** Use this to link to an e-mail address. This feature is useful in an intranet or Internet setting because this link allows the reader to write e-mail to the e-mail address you link to.

If you click Existing File or Web Page, you can then select your link from the following:

- **Current Folder:** Allows you to choose any page in the current folder.
- **Browsed Pages:** Allows you to choose any page you have browsed using your Web browser recently.
- **Recent Files:** Enables you to view recently used files, which is a subdirectory in windows.

You can then make up your mind whether you want to browse for a file, a Web file, or a bookmark, or if you want to turn off the computer and go for coffee. Don't ask me which one I suggest. Then after you've found it and clicked it, click OK. And you have lift off — er, I mean hyperlink.

Suppose you want to just link something to something else in the same presentation. Click Place in this Document, and the text box to the right displays the list of slides in your document. As you click each slide, you can see a slide preview.

4. **Click the slide that you want the hyperlink to lead to, and then click OK.**

   You return to Normal View. The Insert Hyperlink dialog box vanishes, and the hyperlink is created.

If you create the hyperlink on text, the text changes color and is underlined. Graphic objects such as AutoShapes, WordArt, or clip art pictures are not highlighted in any way to indicate that they are hyperlinks. However, the mouse pointer always changes to a hand pointer whenever it passes over a hyperlink, providing a visual clue that the user has found a hyperlink.

Creating a hyperlink to another presentation

Creating a hyperlink that opens another presentation is much like the procedure described in the section "Creating a hyperlink to another slide," but with a couple important differences. Here are the steps:

1. **Select the text or graphic object that you want to make into a hyperlink.**

2. **Choose the Insert⇨Hyperlink command or click the Insert Hyperlink button.**

   The Insert Hyperlink dialog box appears.

3. **Click Existing File or Web Page from the list of icons on the left side of the dialog box.**
4. **Click Current Folder.**
5. **Choose the file that you want to link to.**

   You may have to rummage about your hard disk to find the presentation.
6. **Click OK.**

The presentation that you link to does not have to be in the same folder or even on the same drive as the current presentation. In fact, you can link to a presentation that resides on a network file server if you want.

You can also link to a specific slide within another presentation by clicking the Bookmark button. This brings up a dialog box listing the slides in the selected presentation. Choose the slide you want to link to; then click OK to return to the Insert Hyperlink dialog box.

If you want to create a hyperlink to an existing Web page, just type the address of the Web page in your outline or on your slide and a hyperlink automatically appears. You can select any page of a Web site as long as you know the URL for that specific page.

When you follow a link to another presentation, PowerPoint automatically opens the other presentation. That means you now have both presentations open. When you're finished viewing the second presentation, close it to return to the original presentation.

Removing a hyperlink

To remove a hyperlink, right-click the hyperlink you want to zap, then choose Remove Hyperlink from the menu that appears.

Using Action Buttons

An *action button* is a special type of AutoShape that places a button on the slide. When the user clicks the button during a slide show, PowerPoint takes whatever action you have designated for the button. The following sections describe how action buttons work and show you how to add them to your presentations.

Button actions

When you create a button, you assign a shape for the button (you have 12 shapes to choose from; the shapes are described a bit later in this section) and an action to be taken when the user clicks the button or merely points the mouse pointer at it. The action for a button can be any of the following:

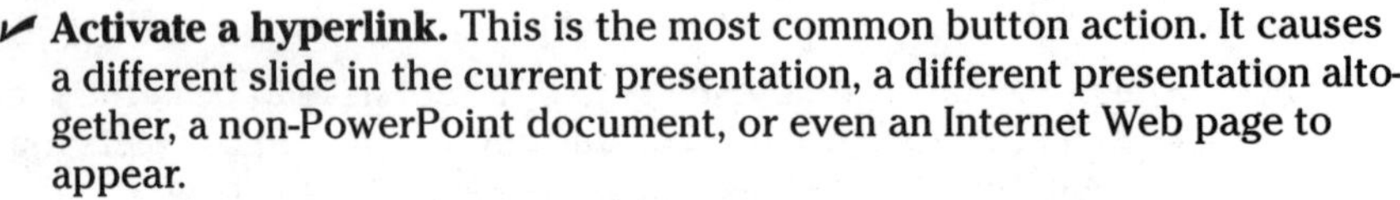

- **Activate a hyperlink.** This is the most common button action. It causes a different slide in the current presentation, a different presentation altogether, a non-PowerPoint document, or even an Internet Web page to appear.
- **Run a program.** For example, you can set up a button that runs Microsoft Word or Excel.
- **Run a macro.** PowerPoint lets you create *macros,* which are programs written in a powerful programming language called Visual Basic for Applications.
- **Play a sound.** Adding sound is explained in Chapter 18.

Action buttons are usually set up as hyperlinks, so that when the user clicks the button, a different slide in the current presentation or a different presentation altogether is displayed. A well-planned arrangement of action buttons scattered throughout a presentation can make it easy for someone to view the presentation in any order he or she wants.

Button shapes

PowerPoint provides a selection of built-in shapes for action buttons. Table 21-1 lists the action button shapes that you can place in your presentation and indicates what type of hyperlink is associated with each type.

Table 21-1 Action Buttons

Button Image	*Name*	*What Button Does*
	Custom	No default action for this button type.
	Home	Displays the first slide in the presentation.
	Help	No default action for this button type.
	Information	No default action for this button type.

Button Image	Name	What Button Does
◁	Back or Previous	Displays the previous slide in the presentation.
▷	Forward or Next	Displays the next slide in the presentation.
|◁	Beginning	Displays the first slide in the presentation.
▷|	End	Displays the last slide in the presentation.
	Return	Displays the most recently viewed slide.
	Document	No default action for this button type.
	Sound	No default action for this button type.
	Movie	No default action for this button type.

Creating a button

To add a button to a slide, follow these steps:

1. **Move to the slide on which you want to place a button.**
2. **Click the AutoShapes button in the drawing toolbar and then click Action Buttons.**

   The Action Buttons toolbox appears.
3. **Click the button for the action button shape that you want to create.**
4. **Draw the button on the slide.**

   Start by pointing to the spot where you want the upper-left corner of the button to appear. Then press and hold the left mouse button and drag the mouse to where you want the lower-right corner of the button to appear.

   When you release the mouse button, the Action Settings dialog box appears
5. **If you want, change the action settings for the action button.**

   In most cases, the default setting for the action button that you chose is appropriate for what you want the button to do. For example, the action setting for a Forward or Next Button is Hyperlink to Next Slide. If you want the slide to hyperlink to some other location, change the Hyperlink to setting.

6. **Click OK.**

   The Action Settings dialog box vanishes, and the button is created.

Here are some additional thoughts concerning action buttons:

- Like many other AutoShapes, the action button shapes have an adjustment handle — a little diamond-shaped handle that floats nearby. You can drag the adjustment handle to change the apparent depth of the button image.
- To move a button, just click it to select it. Then drag the button with the mouse to a new location.
- You can change the action setting for a button by right-clicking the button and choosing the Action Settings command.
- Action buttons by default assume the fill color from the slide's color scheme. You can apply any fill color you want to the button, just like you can to any other drawing object. Refer to Chapter 14 for details.

Creating a navigation toolbar

Grouping action buttons into a navigation toolbar makes a slide show easy to navigate. You can add a set of navigation buttons to the bottom of your Slide Master. For this example, I use Beginning, Backward or Previous, Forward or Next, and Ending buttons, but you can include any buttons you want. To create a navigation toolbar that appears on every slide, follow these steps:

1. **Switch to Slide Master View.**

   Choose the View⇨Master⇨Slide Master command. Or, if you like shortcuts, hold down the Shift key and press the Normal View button at the lower-left corner of the PowerPoint window.

2. **Create the action buttons that you want to include.**

   Follow the procedure described in the section "Creating a button" to create each button. Make sure all the buttons are the same size and line them up to create a tight cluster of buttons.

3. **Return to Slide View.**

   Click the Slide View button or choose the View⇨Slide command.

The buttons that you created appear on every slide in your presentation.

Chapter 22

Creating Web Pages with PowerPoint

In This Chapter

- Saving presentations as Web pages
- Publishing options
- Publishing a presentation or HTML file to the Web
- Opening a PowerPoint presentation on the Web using your browser

PowerPoint lets you save your presentations in HTML format so they can be viewed using a Web browser such as Internet Explorer. By using this feature, you can distribute your presentations to users who do not have PowerPoint installed on their computers.

This chapter explores using PowerPoint as a tool for creating HTML pages. PowerPoint isn't really the best tool to use for creating Web pages — you're better off using a Web page editor such as Microsoft FrontPage. However, HTML format gives you the option of creating PowerPoint presentations that can be viewed over the Internet or by users who don't have PowerPoint.

Creating Web pages is just the beginning of having an "up-and-running" Web site. This chapter shows you what you need to know to convert PowerPoint presentations to HTML files so that they can be placed on the Web. To set up and manage your own Web site, however, you need to know much more than what's in this chapter. For more information, I recommend that you consult *HTML For Dummies,* 3rd Edition, by Ed Tittel and Steve James (published by Hungry Minds, Inc.).

About the Save as a Web Page Feature

The Save as a Web Page feature converts PowerPoint presentations to HTML files that can be published on the World Wide Web and displayed by Web browsers such as Microsoft Internet Explorer and Netscape Navigator. By selecting Save as a Web Page in the File menu, you instantly summon the Save As dialog box that gives you access to Web publishing features. When you save a .ppt file in HTML format, PowerPoint creates a separate Web page for each slide in your presentation. All of these Web pages, with the exception of the starting page, are stored in a single folder using the name of the presentation that you are converting.

For example, if you convert a presentation named Trouble in River City.ppt, the Save as a Web Page feature creates the presentation's HTML files in a folder named Trouble in River City_files. It also creates a file called Trouble in River City.htm.

The first thing you see when you select Save as a Web Page is the Save As dialog box shown in Figure 22-1.

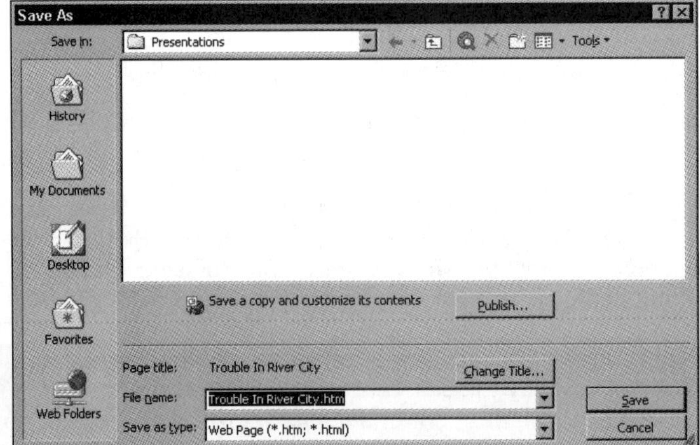

Figure 22-1: The Save As Web Page dialog box.

To save a PowerPoint presentation as a Web page, follow these steps:

1. **Select File⇨Save as Web Page.**

   Notice that the name of your presentation appears in the File Name text box and that the Save as Type text box says: Web Page (*.htm; *.html).

2. **If you want, change the page title by using the Change Title button.**

   The Page Title field (above the File Name text box) indicates the text that will be displayed in the Title bar when your presentation is displayed in a Web browser. The page title defaults to the title of your presentation taken from the title slide. If you want, you can change the page title by clicking the Change Title button. This brings up a separate dialog box where you can type a new title. Click OK to return to the Save As dialog box.

3. **Click the Publish button.**

The Publish button is located near the center of the Save As dialog box. When you click it, the Publish as Web Page dialog box appears, as shown in Figure 22-2.

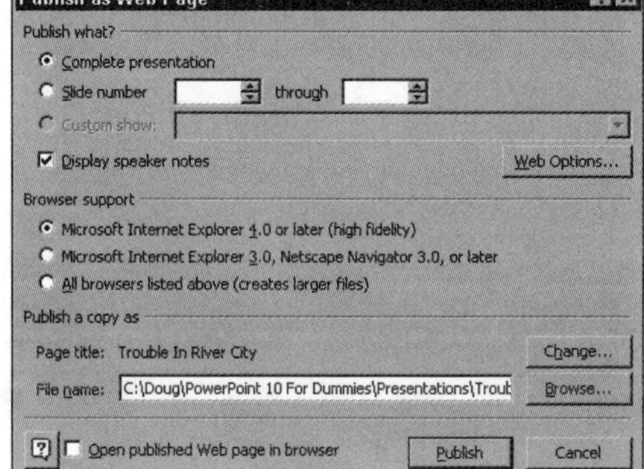

Figure 22-2: The Publish as Web Page dialog box.

4. **Make your selections in the "Publish What?" section of the dialog box.**

   Here you decide if you are going to publish the whole presentation or just a number of slides from the presentation. You also get to choose whether or not to include your speaker notes. Make the appropriate selections, and you are ready to move on.

5. **Click the Web Options button.**

   Time for a new dialog box. This dialog box, aptly named Web Options and shown in Figure 22-3, leads you through a variety of choices necessary to set up your published Web page files as you like them.

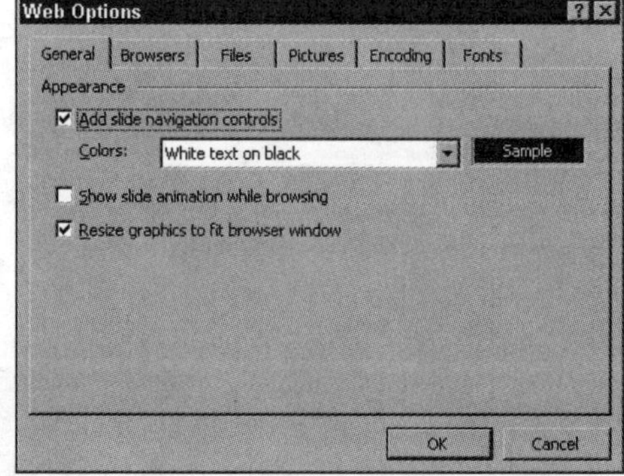

Figure 22-3: The Web Options dialog box.

Here you see six different tabs: General, Browsers, Files, Pictures, Encoding, and Fonts. You don't have to be a Web wizard to figure this out; the default settings work for most saved presentations. The General tab allows you to make appearance selections, the Files tab makes determinations about how your files will be organized, the Pictures tab allows you to mess around with the picture files in a presentation, and the Encoding tab is set for Western European (Windows). Notice, if you click the drop-down text box, you have other choices.

6. **Click OK.**

   You are whisked back to the Publish as Web Page dialog box.

   Now, take a gander at the browser support area. This is important. Not everyone has the most recent version of Internet Explorer. To make sure that every Tom, Dick, and Barbara can open your presentation in their browser, select All browsers listed above.

7. **Check the Open Published Web Page in Browser check box.**

   This tells PowerPoint to start your Web browser so you can see the Web page after you complete the next step.

8. **Click Publish.**

   Your publication is saved as an HTML file. If you checked the Open Published Web Page in Browser option in Step 6, your Web browser magically starts up and displays your presentation in HTML format, as shown in Figure 22-4.

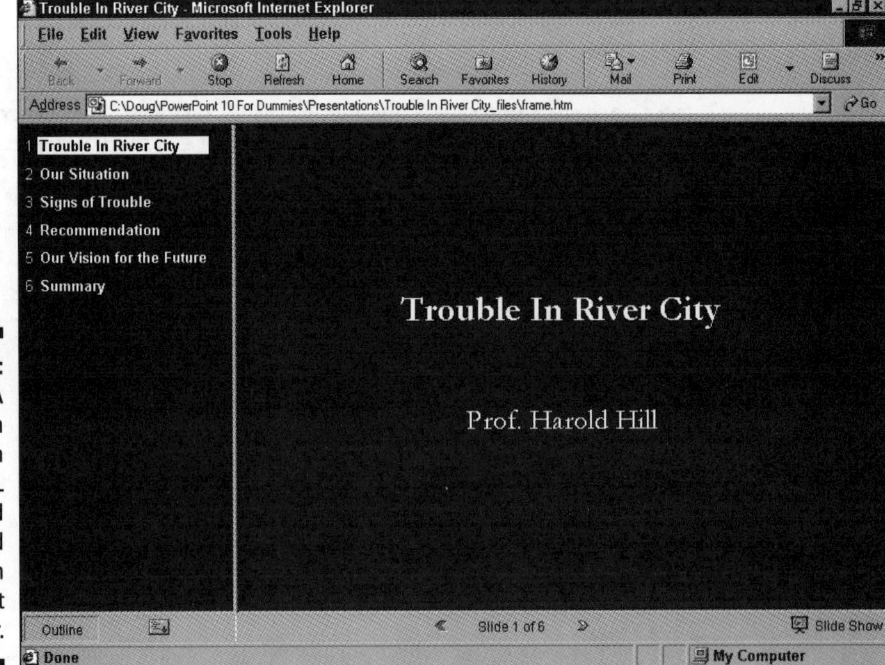

Figure 22-4: A presentation saved in HTML format and displayed with Internet Explorer.

Publishing a Presentation or HTML File to the Web

Saving a presentation as a Web page creates the HTML files you need to publish your presentation on the Internet, but it doesn't actually post the presentation on a Web site. To do that, you'll first have to obtain space on a Web server and gather the details you need to publish files to the server. After you do that, you can follow these steps:

1. **Open your presentation that you have saved in HTML.**

   Just click File⇨Open and select the right .htm presentation.

2. **Select Save as Web Page from the File menu.**

3. **Now type the Web server's URL that you would like to save the .htm file to in the File Name text box.**

   Remember URL addresses always begin with `http://`.

4. **Click Save.**

   PowerPoint connects to the Web server and displays the folders that are currently housed on the site.

5. **Place your cursor over the File Name text box and watch the name of your .htm file reappear.**

   Just like that.

6. **Click Save.**

Guess what, you're done. Now, for fun, find it using your Web browser. Type the URL address to the server you sent it to and add the name of your file, dividing the server URL and your filename (including the extension, such as Trouble.htm) by a slash. Click Go, and your file appears. Make sure you are connected to the Internet or your intranet, or it won't work.

What the heck are all those files that you see in your file folder with the strange extensions? Thought you'd ask me. Some of the most interesting are:

- **.htm:** These are the HTML files for your presentation. Each slide has a separate HTML file (`slide0001.htm`, `slide0002.htm`, and so on).
- **.gif:** Buttons, icons, bullets, and other goodies that display on the HTML pages are rendered as GIF files, a popular graphics format for Web pages.
- **.jpg:** You may also find images stored as JPEG files, a format that lets large images be compressed for efficient transmission over the Internet.

- **.xml:** Another type of file created by the Save as Web Page feature. PowerPoint uses XML files for your presentation's masters.
- **.css:** A style sheet file that includes information that helps format your presentation.

After you convert your presentation, you must upload it to your Web server's disk in order to make it available on the World Wide Web. You must copy all the files in the presentation's folder to the Web server.

Unfortunately, the procedures you have to follow to copy your files to the Web server depend on how your Web server has been set up. This is one of those times when being friends with the person responsible for administering the Web site can pay off.

Viewing a Converted Presentation

After you finish converting a presentation to HTML using the Save as Web Page command, you will naturally want to view it to make sure the conversion worked as you expected. To view your converted HTML presentation, just select File⇨Web Page Preview. This summons your Web browser and displays the presentation.

Chapter 23

Online Collaborations

In This Chapter

- Sending your presentation out for review
- Holding Web discussions
- Keeping in touch with e-mail subscriptions
- Meeting now with NetMeeting

"Works well with others" is more than standard fare for rookie resumes. It's also one of the PowerPoint 2002 mantras. For years, the other Office programs, most notably Word and Excel, have had great collaboration features. But PowerPoint always got the leftovers. PowerPoint 2002 finally has decent collaboration features that simplify the task of working together to create a presentation. These features work especially well if you and your collaborators are all connected to the Internet. This chapter shows you how to use those features.

Using PowerPoint's Reviewing Features

One of PowerPoint most useful collaboration features is the Reviewing feature. The Reviewing feature allows you to e-mail a presentation to one or more of your buddies so they can make changes and add comments. Your reviewers can then return their marked- up copies of your presentation to you so you can review their changes and comments one by one, accepting the good ones and rejecting the stupid ones. You can then combine all the changes into a final version of the presentation.

PowerPoint's reviewing features work best if everyone in the process uses Outlook as their e-mail program. Outlook automatically keeps track of presentations you have sent out for review and offers to automatically combine them when the reviews come back. If you use another e-mail program, you must manually keep track of who has returned reviewed copies so you can combine them to create a final version.

Sending a presentation to reviewers

When you're ready to put a presentation out for review, follow these steps:

1. **Open the presentation you want to send out for review.**

   If the presentation is already open, use the File➪Save command to save any changes you've made since you opened it.

2. **Choose the File➪Send To➪Mail Recipient (for Review) command.**

   PowerPoint summons Outlook (or whatever e-mail program you use) and creates a new message with the Subject line filled in ("Please review . . ."), the presentation attached to the message, and the message text set to "Please review the attached document."

3. **In the To field, add an e-mail address for each person you want to send a review copy to.**

   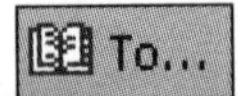

   You can type the e-mail addresses directly into the To field, or you can click the To button (shown in the margin) to call up the Address Book. You can then use the Address Book to select your reviewers.

   If you want to send the presentation to more than one person, separate the e-mail addresses with semicolons.

4. **If you want, change the Subject field or message body.**

   You'll probably want to say something a little more cordial than the bland "Please review. . . ." messages created automatically by PowerPoint.

5. 

   If you want to add a deadline to motivate the reviewers, click the Follow-Up icon (shown in the margin).

   This summons the Flag for Follow Up dialog box, shown in Figure 23-1. Set the date and time the review must be returned by using the two Due By drop-down boxes, then click OK.

Flag for Follow Up
Flagging marks an item to remind you that it needs to be followed up. After it has been followed up, you can mark it complete.
Flag to: Review | Clear Flag
Due by: None | None
OK | Cancel

Figure 23-1: Setting the Flag for Follow Up options.

6. **Set any other Outlook options you want for the message.**

   There's a whole bevy of options you can set for Outlook messages, such as high or low importance, signatures, stationery, plain or HTML formatting, and more. But this isn't an Outlook book; I won't go into them here.

7. **Click the Send button (shown in the margin).**

   Your message is whisked away, to be delivered as soon as possible.

If you do not use Outlook for your e-mail, you can still send a presentation to other users for review. Instead of using the File⇨Send To command, use the File⇨Save As command instead. In the Save As dialog box, choose "Presentation for Review" as the file type and change the file name to something like "Trouble in River City — Review Copy for Marcellus." Then use one of the following methods to distribute the presentation:

- To send the review copy presentation as e-mail, use your e-mail program to send a message to the reviewer with the presentation as an attachment.
- If you and your reviewers are on the same network, save the review copies on a shared folder on a network server. Then tell your reviewers where they can access their review copies and have them tell you when they have finished their review.
- You can save the presentation to a diskette, then give the diskette to your reviewer. When the reviewer finishes, he or she can return the reviewed presentation on the same disk.

Another way to send a presentation out for review is to use the File⇨Send To⇨Routing Recipient command. This command enables you to send a single copy of a presentation to a list of recipients. Each recipient in the list can review the presentation, make changes and add comments, then forward the presentation to the next recipient on the list. When the last recipient finishes his or her review, the presentation is sent back to you. You can then see the changes and comments made by all your reviewers at once.

Reviewing a presentation

If someone sends you a presentation for review, you can edit the presentation any way you want. PowerPoint keeps track of any changes you make to the presentation so your changes can be combined with changes made by other reviewers and then considered one by one.

In addition to making changes, you can also post comments to ask questions, make suggestions, or brag about your kids. To add a comment to a presentation, follow these steps:

1. **Call up the slide you want to add a comment to.**

2. **Choose Insert⇨Comment or click the Insert Comment button (shown in the margin).**

   A comment bubble appears on the slide, as shown in Figure 23-2. Your initials and a comment number appear in the small box next to the bubble. (For example, in Figure 23-2, the reviewer's initials are MW and the comment number is 3.)

MW3 Marcellus Washburn 3/14/01

Figure 23-2: Creating a comment.

3. **Type whatever you want in the comment bubble.**

   Offer some constructive criticism. Suggest an alternative approach. Or just comment on the weather.

4. **Click anywhere outside the comment bubble to make it disappear.**

   Only the comment tag (the little box with the reviewer's initials and comment number) remains.

5. **If you want, move the comment tag.**

   You can move the comment closer to the slide item you're commenting on by dragging the comment tag around the slide.

To change a comment, double-click the comment tag, then edit the text in the comment until you are satisfied.

To delete a comment, click the comment to select it, then press the Delete key.

Reading the reviews

When a reviewer returns a reviewed presentation to you via Outlook, you can open the reviewed presentation by double-clicking the presentation in the e-mail message. PowerPoint displays a dialog box informing you that you are opening a reviewed presentation and offering to combine the changes and comments from the review with the original presentation. Click Yes.

If you aren't using Outlook, PowerPoint doesn't automatically offer to combine reviewed presentations with the original. So you must follow these steps to incorporate your reviewer's changes into your original presentation:

1. **Open the original presentation.**

2. **Choose Tools⇨Compare and Merge Presentations.**

   This brings up the Choose Files to Merge with Current Presentation dialog box, which looks pretty much like a standard Open dialog box.

3. **Select the presentation you want to combine with the original.**

   You may have to hunt around your hard disk for awhile to find the copy of the presentation your reviewer sent back to you. When you find the presentation, click it.

4. **Click Merge.**

   If a dialog box appears telling you that you didn't use the File⇨Send To command to send the presentation out for review, say "Well, Duh" and click Continue. PowerPoint then merges the presentations.

When you review changes made by other users, PowerPoint places a special change icon next to any object that was changed by a reviewer, as shown in Figure 23-3. As you can also see, a Revisions Pane appears to the right of the slide.

To see a change made by your reviewers, click the Change icon (shown in the margin). The icon expands into a bubble listing the changes made to that item. For example, Figure 23-4 shows a change bubble that indicates two changes made to a slide title.

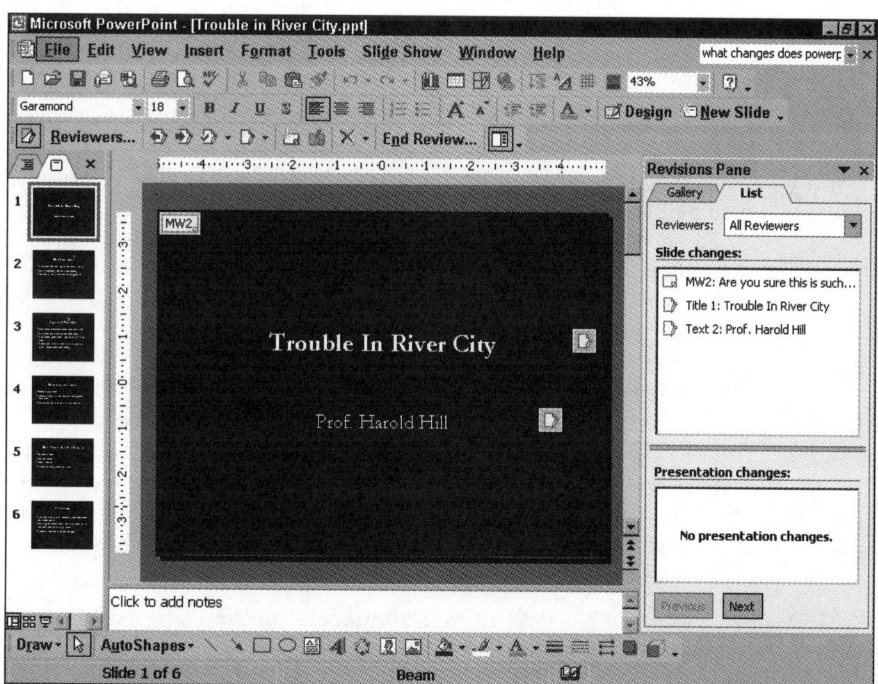

Figure 23-3: PowerPoint highlights changes.

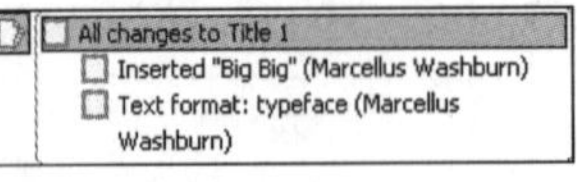

Figure 23-4: Click the change icon to list changes for an item.

To apply a change made by one of your reviewers, click the checkbox next to the change. For example, to apply the typeface change suggested by Marcellus, click the checkbox next to "Text format: typeface (Marcellus Washburn)." If you don't like the effect of the change, click the checkbox again to uncheck it.

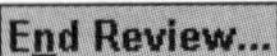

When you have reviewed all the changes in your presentation — checked the ones you like and unchecked the ones you don't like — click the End Review button in the Reviewing toolbar (shown in the margin). This applies the changes you checked and discards the changes you unchecked. After you save the file, those changes become permanent.

Web Discussions

Web Discussions allow you and your buddies to review a presentation and use a nifty discussion panel at the bottom of your screen to make remarks. (Remember, this feature does require that Office Server Extensions are installed on your company's Web server. But a simple phone call to your network administrator or a quick stop by his or her office with a box of Ding Dongs should help you secure the server address to connect to.)

To start a Web Discussion in PowerPoint, follow these steps:

1. **Make some friends at work.**

   You can have a discussion with yourself, but people will talk. You and your colleagues will find that it is easy to view documents from your individual computers, even if you are in the same office. This makes even more sense for branch offices miles away.

2. **Choose Tools⇨Online Collaboration⇨Web Discussions.**

   Your computer will buzz and whir for just a bit, then the Web Discussions toolbar appears on your screen. Not much else seems to happen, yet. . . .

3. **Click Discussions in the Web Discussions toolbar, then choose Discussion Options.**

   Suddenly a dialog box appears, like the one shown in Figure 23-5, giving you the opportunity to add a discussion server. Now's the time to bribe the network administrator with some snacks.

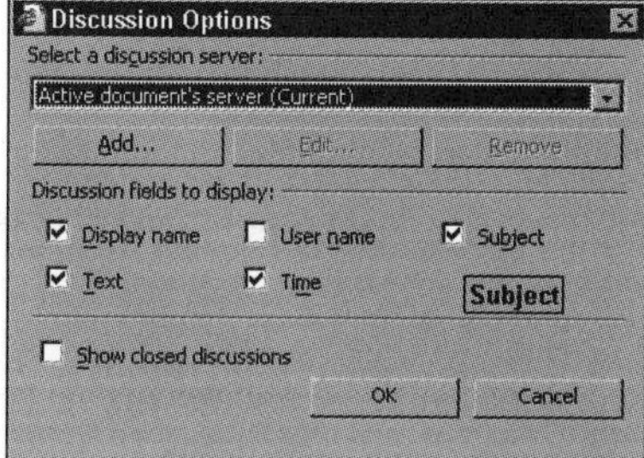

Figure 23-5: Discussion Options.

   In this spot you can edit, add, or remove your server selections, as well as set up how you would like your discussion to appear. You can set up your discussion fields here including Display name, User name, Subject, Text, and Time. This is all very logical.

4. **Click Add.**

   The dialog box shown in Figure 23-6 appears. Here is where you actually type in the address and name of your discussion server. You'll have to get that information from your network administrator. Hope he enjoyed the snacks.

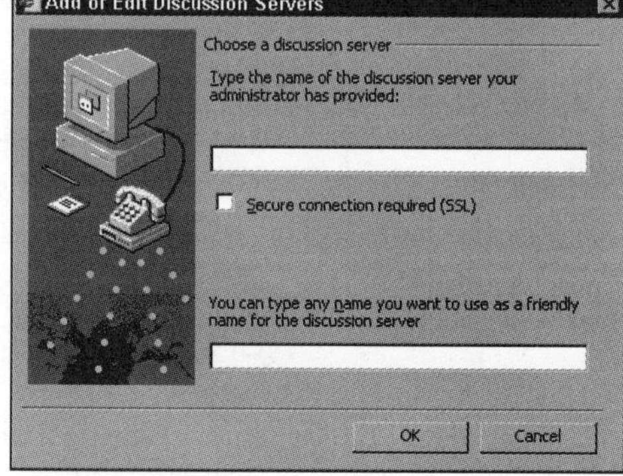

Figure 23-6: The Add or Edit Discussion Servers dialog box.

5. **Type the address and name of your discussion server in the appropriate fields, then click OK.**

   You are whisked back to the Discussion Options dialog box, only this time the discussion server you added is selected in the Select a discussion server drop-down.

6. **Click OK.**

Watch as your screen morphs into a discussion, with a special discussion pane appearing below the slide.

You can participate in Web Discussions by using the buttons on the Web Discussions toolbar, as described in Table 23-1.

Table 23-1 The Web Discussion Toolbar Buttons

Button	*Description*	*What It Does*
Discussions ▾	Discussions	Leads you to a pull-down menu of options to insert, refresh, filter, or print the discussions. Also gives you a return trip to the Discussion Options dialog box.
	Insert Discussion	Shortcut to the same function on the Discussions pull-down menu.
Subscribe...	Subscribe	This feature allows you to be notified by e-mail when any changes are made to a document or the contents of a file folder.
	Stop Communication	Disconnects you from the discussion server.
	Show/Hide Discussion Pane	Clicking this button hides or displays (whichever you aren't already doing) the discussion pane. It does not disconnect you from the discussion server.
Close	Close	Closes the whole Web Discussion, including the discussion pane, and disconnects you from the server.

Meet Now with NetMeeting

You know how PowerPoint includes various tools that are actually applications in and of themselves. The Meet Now feature hooks you up with yet another — NetMeeting. You may already be familiar with NetMeeting, and if you aren't, you need to sit down and spend a day or two with it. However, here are a few basics to get you pointed in the right direction.

I'm not going to be able to squeeze in a whole *NetMeeting For Dummies* book at the end of Chapter 23. NetMeeting has been around long enough to have a mature set of features that support any size meeting and any level of complexity. It works so well, in fact, that it is fast becoming a staple in large corporate intranets and making it hard for business travelers to keep their budgets. You can figure it out just by having a friend at the other end and playing with it for a while. The Help text for this feature in PowerPoint, in NetMeeting itself, and at `www.microsoft.com/netmeeting/` are all pretty good.

What's so hot about NetMeeting, you ask? Well, for starters, it's a collaborative application that allows you and your colleagues to work on the same presentation, using a whiteboard, chat, audio, and video broadcast, and of course the Windows application of your choice. One big difference between NetMeeting and Presentation Broadcast is that NetMeeting users can take turns driving the application. And PowerPoint in NetMeeting isn't limited to a mere slide show presentation. NetMeeting viewers get to see the presenter edit changes in PowerPoint (or Word or Excel).

Check your company's policy on lunchtime video gaming before connecting with your pals in another time zone and setting up that chess match. Some companies frown on their employees creating virtual casinos by combining NetMeeting with a $10 piece of roulette or blackjack software.

To fire up NetMeeting, choose Tools⇨Online Collaboration⇨Meet Now. The first time you use NetMeeting, you'll be asked to identify yourself. After you've done that, you can call up someone to meet with by using the Find Someone dialog box.

Click the person you want to meet with. If the other person accepts your invitation to meet, you'll return to PowerPoint, from which you and the other meeting participants share access to the presentation that was open when you started the meeting. You or anyone else in the meeting can make changes to the presentation. After a slight delay, changes will be visible in everyone's copy of the shared presentation.

You can also use the buttons in the Online Meeting toolbar to start a chat, display a whiteboard you can all doodle on, invite more people to the meeting or kick people out of the meeting, or leave the meeting (see Table 23-2).

Table 23-2 The Online Meeting Toolbar Buttons

Description	*Button*	*What it Does*
	Participant List	A pull-down menu of those folks who are actively on your call at that moment.
	Call Participant	Lets you invite more people to participate.
	Remove Participants	Kicks people out.
	Allow Others to Edit	Lets other people edit your presentation.
	Display Chat Window	Opens a chat window where you can type messages that are seen by other meeting participants.
	Display Whiteboard	Calls up the whiteboard, a shared drawing window that you and other meeting participants can doodle on if you're bored.
	End Meeting	I'll give you three guesses, and the first two don't count.

NetMeeting is like craps. It's pretty intimidating the first time you try it — or even watch. Of course, so is calamari. Even if you have the feel for it, your novice collaborators (*newbies* in Net lingo) may be overwhelmed and need some handholding. Until everyone you work with is comfortable with the application, I strongly suggest you plan some extra time at the beginning of your meeting for getting everyone acclimated with how to find the server, how to share applications, how to chat, take turns on the Whiteboard, know who is driving, and so on. You may even plan a whole training/familiarization session in advance to take all the thrills and chills out of the experience and allow you to get down to work without distractions when you really need to. More than one meeting has been blown by intrigued newbies playing with the collaboration features. It's worse when that newbie is the one who is hosting the meeting.

Now get out there and host a meeting!

Part VI
The Part of Tens

The 5th Wave
By Rich Tennant
WHAT'S THE DIGITAL BATHROOM SCALE DOING IN MY LAPTOP CASE?
...PROMPT...?

In this part . . .

PowerPoint is pretty good at slinging bullets, so I figured it would be fitting to end this book with a bevy of chapters that aren't much more than glorified bulleted lists. Each chapter in this part covers ten things (more or less) worth knowing about PowerPoint. Without further ado, here they are, direct from the home office in Fresno, California.

Chapter 24

Ten PowerPoint Commandments

And the Hapless Windows user said, "But who am I to make this presentation? For I am not eloquent, but I am slow of speech and of tongue, and my colors clasheth, and my charts runneth over." And Microsoft answered, "Fear not, for unto you this day is given a program, which shall be called PowerPoint, and it shall make for you slides, which shall bring forth titles and bullets and yea, even diagrams."

— Presentations 1:1

And so it came to pass that these ten PowerPoint commandments were passed down from generation to generation. Obey these commandments and it shall go well with you, with your flip chart, and with your overhead projector.

I. Thou Shalt Frequently Savest Thy Work

Every two or three minutes, press Ctrl+S. It takes only a second to save your file, and you never know when you'll be the victim of a rotating power outage (even if you don't live in California).

II. Thou Shalt Storeth Each Presentation In Its Proper Folder

Whenever you save a file, double-check the folder you're saving it to. It's all too easy to save a presentation in the wrong folder and then spend hours searching for the file later. You'll wind up blaming the computer for losing your files.

III. Thou Shalt Not Abuseth Thy Program's Formatting Features

Yes, PowerPoint lets you set every word in a different font, use 92 different colors on a single slide, and fill every last pixel of empty space with clip art. If you want your slides to look like ransom notes, go ahead. Otherwise, keep things simple.

IV. Thou Shalt Not Stealeth Copyrighted Materials

Yup, Napster was cool while it lasted. But music is copyrighted. So are many of the pictures and clip art you stumble across on the Internet. Don't use it if you don't have permission.

V. Thou Shalt Not Departeth from the Way of Thy Color Scheme; Neither Shalt Thou Neglect the Pattern of Thine AutoLayout or the Appearance of Thy Template

Microsoft hired a crew of out-of-work artists to pick the colors for the color schemes, arrange things with the slide layouts, and create beautiful backgrounds for the Design Templates. Humor them. They like it when you use their stuff.

VI. Thou Shalt Not Abuse Thine Audience With Cute Animations

PowerPoint animations are cute, and sometimes quite useful. But if you do a goofy animation on every slide, pretty soon your audience will just think you're strange.

VII. Remember Thy Computer Gurus, to Keep Them Happy

If you have a friend or coworker who knows more about computers than you do, keep that person happy. Throw him or her an occasional Twinkie or a bag of Cheetos. Treat computer nerds as if they are human beings. After all, you want them to be your friends.

VIII. Thou Shalt Backeth Up Thy Files Day by Day

Yes, every day. One of these days, you'll come to work only to discover a pile of rubble where your desk used to be. A federal agent will pick up what's left of your computer's keyboard and laugh. But if you back up every day, you won't lose more than a day's work.

IX. Thou Shalt Fear No Evil, for Ctrl+Z Is Always With Thee

March ahead with boldness. Not sure what a button does? Click it! Click it twice if it makes you feel powerful! The worse that it can do is mess up your presentation. If that happens, you can press Ctrl+Z to set things back the way they should be.

X. Thou Shalt Not Panic

You're the only one who knows you're nervous. You'll do just fine. Imagine the audience naked if that will help. (Unless, of course, you're making a presentation to a nudist club and they actually are naked, in which case try to imagine them with their clothes on.)

Chapter 25

Ten Tips for Creating Readable Slides

This chapter gives you a few random tips and pointers that will help you produce readable slides.

Try Reading the Slide from the Back of the Room

The number-one rule of creating readable slides is that everyone in the room must be able to read them. If you're not sure, there's one sure way to find out: Try it. Fire up the projector, call up the slide, walk to the back of the room, and see if you can read it. If you can't, you'll have to make an adjustment.

Remember that everyone's eyesight may not be as good as yours. If you have perfect vision, squint a little when you get to the back of the room to see how someone whose vision isn't perfect might see the slide.

No More than Five Bullets, Please

Ever notice how David Letterman uses two slides to display his Top Ten lists? Dave's producers know that ten items is way too many for one screen. Five is just right. You might be able to slip in six now and again, but if you're up to seven or eight, try breaking the slide into two slides.

Avoid Small Text

If you can't read a slide from the back of the room, it's probably because the text is too small. The rule of thumb is that 24-point type is the smallest you should use for text you want people to read. A 12-point type may be perfectly readable in a Word document, but it's way too small for PowerPoint.

Avoid Excessive Verbiage Lending to Excessively Lengthy Text That Is Not Only Redundant But Also Repetitive and Reiterative

See what I mean? Maybe the heading should have been "Be Brief."

Use Consistent Wording

One sign of an amateur presentation is when the wording in bullet lists is not grammatically consistent. Consider this list:

- Profits will be improved
- Expanding markets
- It will reduce the amount of overseas competition
- Production increase

Each sentence uses a different grammatical construction. The same points made with consistent wording have a more natural flow and make a more compelling case:

- Improved profits
- Expanded markets
- Reduced overseas competition
- Increased production

Avoid Clashing Colors

The professionally chosen color schemes that come with PowerPoint are designed to create slides that are easy to read. If you venture away from them, be careful about choosing colors that are hard to read.

Watch the Line Endings

Sometimes PowerPoint will break a line at an awkward spot which can make slides hard to read. For example, a bullet point might be one word too long to fit on a single line. When that happens, you might want to break the line elsewhere so the second line has more than one word. (Use Shift+Enter to create a line break that doesn't start a new paragraph.)

Alternatively, you might want to drag the right margin of the text placeholder to increase the margin width so that the line doesn't have to be broken at all.

Keep the Background Simple

Don't splash a bunch of distracting clip art on the background unless it is essential. The purpose of the background is to provide a well-defined visual space for the slide's content. All too often, presenters put up slides that have text displayed on top of pictures of the mountains or city skylines, which makes the text almost impossible to read.

Use Only Two Levels of Bullets

Sure, it's tempting to develop your subpoints into sub-subpoints and sub-sub-subpoints, but no one will be able to follow your logic. Don't make your slides more confusing than they need to be. If you need to make sub-sub-subpoints, you probably need a few more slides.

Keep Charts and Diagrams Simple

PowerPoint can create elaborate graphs that even the best statisticians will marvel at. But the most effective graphs are simple pie charts with three or four slices and simple column charts with three or four columns. Likewise, Pyramid, Venn, and other types of diagrams lose their impact when you add more than four or five elements. (See Chapter 15 for more on diagrams.)

If you remember only one rule when creating your presentations, remember this one: *Keep it simple, clean, and concise.*

Chapter 26

Ten Ways to Keep Your Audience Awake

Nothing frightens a public speaker more than the prospect of the audience falling asleep during the speech. Here are some things you can do to prevent that from happening. (Yawn.)

Don't Forget Your Purpose

Too many presentations ramble on and on with no clear sense of purpose. The temptation is to throw in every clever quotation and every interesting tidbit you can muster that is even remotely related to the topic of your presentation. The reason that this temptation is so big is that you mostly likely haven't identified what you hope to accomplish with your presentation. In other words, you haven't pinned down your *purpose*.

Don't confuse a presentation's title with its purpose. Suppose that you're asked to give a presentation to a prospective client on the advantages of your company's new, improved deluxe model ChronSimplastic Infindibulator. Your purpose in this presentation is not to convey information about the new Infindibulator, but to persuade your client to buy one of the $65 million beasties. The title of your presentation may be *Infindibulators for the Twenty-First Century* but the purpose is "convince these saps to buy one, or maybe two."

Don't Become a Slave to Your Slides

PowerPoint makes such beautiful slides that the temptation is to let them be the show. That's a big mistake. *You* are the show, not the slides. The slides are merely visual aids, designed to make your presentation more effective, not to steal the show.

It's tempting to dim the lights, hide behind the lectern, and let your slides do all the talking. Don't succumb. Keep the slides in their rightful place.

Don't Overwhelm Your Audience with Unnecessary Detail

On November 19, 1863, a crowd of 15,000 gathered in Gettysburg to hear Edward Everett, one of the greatest orators of the time. Mr. Everett spoke for two hours about the events that had transpired during the famous battle. When he finished, Abraham Lincoln rose to deliver a brief two-minute postscript that has become the most famous speech in American history.

If PowerPoint had been around in 1863, Everett probably would have spoken for four hours. PowerPoint practically begs you to talk too much. Once you start typing bullets, you can't stop. Pretty soon, you have 40 slides for a 20-minute presentation. That's about 35 more than you probably need. Try to shoot for one slide for every two to five minutes of your presentation.

Don't Neglect Your Opening

As they say, you only get one opportunity to make a first impression. Don't waste it by telling a joke that has nothing to do with the topic, apologizing for your lack of preparation or nervousness, or listing your credentials. Don't pussyfoot around; get right to the point.

The best openings are those that capture the audience's attention with a provocative statement, a rhetorical question, or a compelling story. A joke is okay, but only if it sets the stage for the subject of your presentation.

Be Relevant

The objective of any presentation is to lead your audience to say, "Me, too!" Unfortunately, many presentations leave the audience thinking, "So what?"

The key to being relevant is giving your audience what they need, not what you think is interesting or important. The most persuasive presentations are those that present solutions to real problems rather than opinions about hypothetical problems.

Don't Forget the Altar Call

What would a Billy Graham crusade be without the altar call? A wasted opportunity.

You've spent hours putting your presentation together. Don't forget to ask for the order. Invite your audience to respond and show them how. Make them an offer they can't refuse. Tell them your 800 number. Roll the pen across the table. Sing *Just As I Am*. Do whatever it takes.

Practice, Practice, Practice

Back to good ol' Abe: Somehow a rumor got started that Abraham Lincoln hastily wrote the Gettysburg Address on the train, just before pulling into Gettysburg. In truth, Lincoln agonized for weeks over every word.

Practice, practice, practice. Work through the rough spots. Polish the opening and the altar call and all the awkward transitions in between. Practice in front of a mirror. Video tape yourself. Time yourself.

Don't Panic

Don't worry! Be happy! Even the most gifted public speakers are scared silly every time they step up to the podium. Whether you're speaking to one person or ten thousand, relax. In 20 minutes, it will all be over.

No matter how nervous you are, no one knows it except you. That is, unless you tell them. The number one rule of panic avoidance is to never apologize for your fears. Behind the podium, your knees may be knocking hard enough to bruise yourself. But no one else will notice. After you swab down your armpits and wipe the drool off your chin, people will say, "Weren't you nervous? You seemed so relaxed!"

Expect the Unexpected

Plan on things to go wrong, because they will. The projector won't focus, the microphone won't listen, you'll drop your notes on the way to the podium. Who knows what else will happen?

Take things in stride, but be prepared for problems you can anticipate. Carry an extra set of notes in your pocket. Bring your own microphone if you have one. Have a backup projector ready if possible.

Don't Be Boring

An audience can overlook almost anything, but one thing they'll never forgive you for is boring them. Above all, do not bore your audience.

This guideline doesn't mean you have to tell jokes, jump up and down, or talk fast. Jokes, excessive jumping, and rapid speech can be as boring as formatting disks. If you obey the other commandments — if you have a clear cut purpose and stick to it, avoid unnecessary detail, and address real needs — you'll never be boring. Just be yourself and have fun. If you have fun, so will your audience.

Chapter 27

Ten Things That Often Go Wrong

There are probably closer to 10,000 things that can go wrong when you're working with PowerPoint, but these ten are among the things that go wrong most often.

I Can't Find My File!

You spent hours polishing that presentation and now you can't find the file. You know that you saved it, but it's not there! The problem is probably one of two things: Either you saved the file in a folder other than the one you thought you did, or you used a different name to save it than you intended. The solution? Use the File⇨Open command's search features. Also, for a quick look, click the History icon in the upper-left-hand corner of the Open dialog box. You'll see the history of your recently used files, displaying the contents of an appropriately titled folder: Recent.

I've Run Out of Disk Space!

Nothing is more frustrating than creating a fancy PowerPoint presentation and then discovering that you're completely out of disk space. What to do? Start up a My Computer window and rummage through your hard disk, looking for files you don't need. Delete enough files to free up a few megabytes and then press Alt+Tab to move back to PowerPoint and save your file. I did this just a few days ago: I had to delete a bunch of music files that I had accumulated to make my own CDs. (It was either them or the Word document files for the first few chapters of this book. Not an easy decision.)

If your disk is full and you can't find more than a few files to delete, try double-clicking on the Recycle Bin icon and choosing the File⇨Empty Recycle Bin command. This often frees up additional disk space. If that doesn't work, click the Start menu, then choose Program Files⇨Accessories⇨System Tools⇨Disk Cleanup. The Disk Cleanup program scans your hard disk for unnecessary files and offers to remove them for you. It can often free up many megabytes of disk space.

If you run out of disk space often, consider adding a larger disk drive to your computer. For $200 or so, you can add umpteen gigabytes of disk storage to your computer.

I've Run Out of Memory!

Many people are still using computers with only 32MB of internal memory. Although you can run PowerPoint 10 with as little as 32MB of memory, 64MB is a more reasonable minimum, and even 128MB isn't an outrageous amount of memory these days. Make sure that you have enough memory to keep the time that tasks take to the minimum. The additional memory helps your computer to not give up and crash from the overload of open applications. Memory is cheap! Why not make sure you have enough?

PowerPoint Has Vanished!

You're working at your computer, minding your own business, when suddenly — whoosh! — PowerPoint disappears. What happened? Most likely, you clicked some area outside the PowerPoint window or you pressed Alt+Tab or Alt+Esc, which whisks you away to another program. To get PowerPoint back, press Alt+Tab. You may have to press Alt+Tab several times before PowerPoint comes back to life.

PowerPoint can also vanish into thin air if you use a screen-saver program. Try giving the mouse a nudge to see whether PowerPoint reappears.

I Accidentally Deleted a File!

Just learned how to delete files and couldn't stop yourself, eh? Relax. It happens to the best of us. Odds are that you can get the deleted file back if you act fast enough. Double-click the Recycle Bin icon that sits on your desktop. There, you'll probably find the deleted file. Copy it back to the folder where it belongs.

It Won't Let Me Edit That!

No matter how hard you click the mouse, PowerPoint won't let you edit that doohickey on-screen. What gives? The doohickey is probably a part of the Slide Master. To edit it, use the View⇨Master⇨Slide Master command. This step displays the Slide Master and enables you to edit it.

Something Seems to Be Missing!

You just read the chapter about Diagrams, but nothing happens when you try to insert a diagram. Or worse, PowerPoint locks up when you choose the Insert⇨Diagram command. Arghhhh!

It's possible that your PowerPoint installation has somehow become corrupted. Perhaps an important system file was accidentally deleted, or a problem has somehow managed to creep into the Windows Registry (the file that keeps track of settings for Windows itself as well as for programs you have installed on your computer).

Fear not! PowerPoint includes a feature called Detect and Repair that can correct such problems. Just fire up PowerPoint, choose the Help⇨Detect and Repair command, and follow the instructions that appear on the screen.

What Happened to My Clip Art?

You just purchased and installed an expensive clip art collection that has 500 stunning photographic-quality images from the theatrical re-release of Stanley Kubrick's classic *2001: A Space Odyssey*, but you can't find them in the Media Gallery. Where did they go? Nowhere. You just have to tell Media Gallery about them. Fire up the Gallery by clicking the Insert Picture button or by selecting Insert⇨Picture⇨Clip Art. Then click the Import Clips button. Then insert the filename of the images you want to add in the File Name text box, click the appropriate clip import option, and click Import.

One of the Toolbars (Or Toolbar Features) Is Missing!

One of the most useful features of PowerPoint is that it lets you completely customize its menus and toolbars. Unfortunately, this feature has a downside: it's all too easy to mess up a menu or toolbar, sometimes quite by accident and without even realizing it. Then all of a sudden, one day you reach for the Bold button and it's not there. Or maybe the whole Formatting toolbar seems to be missing.

What gives? Perhaps it's the new IntelliSense feature deciding which buttons on your toolbar you use 95 percent of the time. Luckily, menu choices are at the end of each menu, and down-arrow buttons on the toolbars enable you to see all the toolbar and menu commands so that you can select what is missing.

If your toolbar is missing altogether, you can't see all the choices available to you. Aside from the Standard and Formatting toolbars, you sometimes have to summon a toolbar if it somehow gets lost. It happens all the time, so don't feel bad. Just look in the mirror and say to yourself, "It's not my fault that the toolbar disappeared. It happens even to experts like that nice Mr. Lowe, who wrote a whole book about PowerPoint. I shouldn't blame myself. After all, I'm good enough, I'm smart enough, and, doggone it, people like me."

Then use the View⇨Toolbars command to reactivate the missing toolbar.

You may also want to check out the Standard toolbar and select Tools⇨Customize⇨Options. By doing so, you have an opportunity to check a text box that combines the Standard and Formatting toolbar on one line! Some people have been known to go clinically insane when this text box was checked without their knowledge. Don't be caught unaware!

The Projector Doesn't Work!

There are many reasons why an LCD projector might not be working. Assuming that the computer and projector are both plugged in and turned on and you have used the correct video cable to connect your computer to the projector, here are two common problems you should check:

- Most projectors have two or more video input ports. The projector must be configured to use the input port your computer is connected to. Look for a button on the projector to set the input source. The projector might use a menu to set the input source: In that case, use the button that calls up the menu, scroll through the choices to find the video input source, and then select the input port your computer is connected to.
- If you're using a laptop, make sure that the external video port is activated. Most laptops have a function key on the keyboard to do this. Look for a key with an icon that represents a video monitor. You may have to hold down a function key (probably labeled "FN") while you press the monitor key.

Chapter 28

Ten PowerPoint Shortcuts

You can do just about anything you can do with PowerPoint by hacking your way through the menus or clicking the correct toolbar button. But you can sometimes work more efficiently if you know a few keyboard and mouse shortcuts.

Keyboard Shortcuts for Multiple Windows

Most Windows programs that enable you to open multiple documents, including Word for Windows and Excel, work the same way PowerPoint works. Memorizing the menu commands and keyboard shortcuts for working with more than one presentation window in PowerPoint pays off, because you use the same menu commands and keyboard shortcuts in other programs.

Shortcut	*Action*
Ctrl+F6	Moves you to the next presentation window.
Shift+Ctrl+F6	Moves you to the previous presentation window.
Ctrl+F10	Maximizes a presentation window.
Ctrl+F5	Returns a window to its normal size.
Ctrl+F4	Closes a document window.

Right-Click Anywhere to Get a Quick Menu

You can right-click just about anything with the mouse button to get a quick menu of common things you can do to the object. Try it — it's kind of fun.

Ctrl+X, Ctrl+C, or Ctrl+V to Cut, Copy, or Paste

Just about all Windows applications respond to these keyboard shortcuts.

Shortcut	*Action*
Ctrl+X	Cuts the selection to the Clipboard.
Ctrl+C	Copies the selection to the Clipboard.
Ctrl+V	Inserts the contents of the Clipboard.

Note: Before you use Ctrl+X or Ctrl+C, select the object you want to cut or copy.

Ctrl+Z to Undo a Mistake

Oops! Didn't mean to double-click there? Don't panic. Press Ctrl+Z, and whatever you did last is undone.

Ctrl+B or Ctrl+I for Bold or Italics

Like most Windows applications, PowerPoint accepts the following keyboard shortcuts for text formatting:

Shortcut	*Action*
Ctrl+B	Bold
Ctrl+I	Italic
Ctrl+U	Underline
Ctrl+spacebar	Return to normal format

Note: Before using these shortcuts, highlight the text that you want to format.

Ctrl+S to Save a File

Press Ctrl+S to save the current presentation to a file. The first time you save a new file, PowerPoint displays the Save As dialog box, in which you can assign a name to the file. Thereafter, Ctrl+S saves the file by using the same name.

Ctrl+G to Show the Guides

Need help aligning drawn objects? Press Ctrl+G to call up the Grids and Guides dialog box. You can then set up grid lines and guide lines which help you snap objects in place.

Shift While Drawing to Constrain Objects

If you hold down the Shift key while drawing an object, the object is drawn perfectly straight or perfectly round. Circles will be circles, squares will be squares, and lines will stick to 45-degree angles.

Alt+Esc, Alt+Tab, or Ctrl+Esc to Switch to Another Program

This isn't really a PowerPoint shortcut; it's a Windows shortcut. To switch to another application that you have minimized or that is hiding behind your active window, use one of these keyboard combinations:

- **Alt+Esc:** Switches to the next program in line.
- **Alt+Tab:** Displays the name of the next program in line. While holding down the Alt key, keep pressing Tab until the name of the program you want appears. Release both keys to switch to that program.
- **Ctrl+Esc:** Pops up the Start menu, from which you can start other programs.

F1 — The Panic Button

Stuck? Press F1 to activate PowerPoint Help. With luck, you can find enough information to get you going. Help is *context sensitive,* which means that it tries to figure out what you were doing when you pressed F1 and gives you specific help for that task.

Chapter 29

Ten Things That Didn't Fit Anywhere Else

In This Chapter

- Creating 35mm slides
- Working with several presentations all at once
- Stealing slides from other presentation
- Checking out document properties
- Using passwords
- Organizing your files
- Backing up your files
- Customizing your PowerPoint setup
- Fiddling around with options
- Discovering how to create and use simple macros

Like a good Presbyterian, I like things decent and in order. However, try as I might, I can't always fit everything that's worth knowing about a subject into a rigid framework of chapters and parts. There always seems to be a few tidbits of information that just don't fit neatly into any of the chapters. Rather than just leave that stuff out, I decided to lump them all together in this chapter. Enjoy!

Creating 35mm Slides

If you want to give your presentation using 35mm slides rather than overheads or a computer projector, you'll have to deal with a photo lab (unless, of course, you have your own photo processing equipment.) It isn't cheap (here in California, it costs $7–$10 per slide), but the slides look great. *Really* great. Better than any but the most lavishly expensive computer projectors can achieve.

One way to produce 35mm slides from a PowerPoint presentation is to take the presentation files to a local photo lab with the equipment to create the slides. Call the lab first to find out the cost and to check on any special requirements it may have, such as whether you need to embed TrueType fonts when you save the file and how the lab prefers you to save the file.

To be safe, always embed TrueType fonts.

You can find photo labs that can produce computer output listed in the Yellow Pages under Computer Graphics, or perhaps under Photo Finishing. Call several labs, compare costs, and find out how quickly each can finish the job.

Use the PowerPoint File⇨Save As command to save the presentation to disk. Take two copies of the presentation file — on separate disks — to the photo shop. Nothing is more frustrating than driving across town only to discover that something's wrong with your disk. Or you can always attach your file to an e-mail and send it to the photo shop, if the shop is set up to receive files electronically. Or, if you have a CD burner, put the presentation on a CD.

Carefully proof your slides by using the PowerPoint Slide Show view. Run the spell check. At $10 per slide, you don't want many typos to slip by.

If you can't find a local photo lab or print shop that will print your slides for you, you can use any of several companies that do the job over the Internet. All you do is connect to the company's Web site, upload your PowerPoint presentation and credit card information, and watch for the Federal Express truck.

The price of this service varies depending on how quickly you need the slides. If you can wait a few days, you can have slides made for $2.00 to $5.00 each. For rush deliveries, expect to pay more.

To find online slide production services, go to a search service such as Yahoo and search for "presentation slides."

Editing More Than One Presentation at a Time

Some people like to do just one thing at a time: Start a task, work on it till it's done, and then put away their tools. These same people sort their canned goods by food group and have garages that look like the hardware department at Sears.

Then there are people like me, who work on no fewer than 12 things at a time, would just as soon leave canned goods in the bag arranged just the way the kid at the grocery store tossed them in, and haven't been able to park both cars in the garage since before the kids were born.

Apparently, a few of the latter type work at Microsoft because they decided to enable you to open a whole gaggle of PowerPoint files at a time. Now we're getting somewhere!

To open more than one presentation, just keep using the File➪Open command. PowerPoint places each file you open in its own presentation. This presentation window is normally maximized to fill all the available space within the main PowerPoint window, so you can see only one presentation window at a time. But you can switch between windows by choosing the window you want with the Window command or by pressing Alt+Tab to pop from window to window.

PowerPoint enables you to display the window for each open file in three ways:

- **Cascaded:** The presentation windows are stacked atop one another. This arrangement enables you to see the title bar of each window. To switch to a window other than the one on top, click its title bar or any other portion of the window you can see. This step sucks the window up to the top of the stack. To cause all presentation windows to fall into a cascaded stack, choose the Window➪Cascade command.
- **Tiled:** The presentation windows are arranged side-by-side. This arrangement enables you to see a small portion of each presentation, though the more files you have open, the smaller this portion gets. To arrange all presentation windows in tiled form, use the Window➪Arrange All command.
- **Minimized:** The window shrinks down to a little title bar that is just big enough to show the first part of the presentation's name and the standard window-control buttons. To shrink a presentation window to a minimized window, click the window's minimize button. To restore the window, double-click the icon.

Even though you can open umpteen presentation windows, only one is active at a time. While you work on one presentation, the others lie dormant, praying to the ASCII gods that you won't neglect them forever.

To copy something from one file to another, switch to the first file's window, copy the object to the Clipboard (by using the normal Copy command, Ctrl+C), and then switch to the second file's window and paste (Ctrl+V) away. Or use the Edit menu commands to perform the same task.

Here are a couple of tips for working with multiple windows:

- You can open more than one file with a single pass through the File⇨Open command. Just hold down the Ctrl key while you click each file you want to open or use the Shift key to select a block of files. When you click OK, all the files you selected open, each in its own window.
- Alt+Tab lets you cycle through all the windows you have open on your desktop, whether those windows contain PowerPoint presentations or other documents. To constrain your window hopping to PowerPoint presentations only, use Ctrl+F6 instead of Alt+Tab.
- Some men especially love to use the Alt+Tab or Ctrl+F6 shortcut to flip from one window to the next. They sit there at the computer, beer in hand, flipping incessantly from window to window and hoping to find a football game or a boxing match.
- If you want to shut down a window, use the File⇨Close command, press Ctrl+W, or click the window's close button. If the file displayed in the window contains changes that haven't been saved to disk, PowerPoint asks whether you want to save the file first.

Stealing Slides from Other Presentations

What do you do when you're plodding along in PowerPoint and realize that you want to copy slides from an old presentation into the one you're working on now? You steal the existing slides, that's what you do. No need to reinvent the wheel, as they say.

To steal slides from an existing presentation, you get to use the Slide Stealer — oops, it's actually called the Slide Finder — feature. To use it, follow these steps:

1. **Move to the slide you want the stolen slides to be placed after.**
2. **Conjure up the Insert⇨Slides from Files command.**

   This step displays the Slide Finder dialog box.
3. **Click the Browse button.**

   This brings up an ordinary, run-of-the-mill Open dialog box.
4. **Rummage around until you find the presentation you want to steal. Highlight it and click Open.**

   You return to the Slide Finder dialog box.

5. **Click Display.**

   The file opens and displays the first few slides of the presentation.

6. **Select the slides you want to copy.**

   Click once to select a slide. When you select a slide, a heavy border appears around the slide so you'll know it's selected. You can select more than one slide by simply clicking each slide you want to select. Use the scroll bar that appears beneath the slide images to scroll through all of the slides in the presentation.

   If you click a slide by mistake, click it again to deselect it.

7. **Click Insert to insert the slides you selected.**

   The slides are inserted into the document, but the Slide Finder dialog box remains on the screen.

8. **Repeat Steps 3 through 7 if you want to insert slides from additional presentations.**

9. **Click Close to dismiss the Slide Finder dialog box.**

   You're done.

Here are a few points to ponder as you drift off to sleep tonight, wondering in amazement that PowerPoint lets you plagiarize slides from other people's presentations:

- As the slides are copied into the presentation, they are adjusted to match the master slide layout for the new presentation. Embedded charts and diagrams are even updated to reflect the new color scheme.
- If you want to insert all of the slides from a presentation, you can dispense with Steps 5 through 7. Just click Insert All to copy all the slides from the presentation.
- If you find that you frequently return to a particular presentation to steal its slides, add that presentation to the Slide Finder's list of favorites. To do that, click the Browse button and open the presentation. Then, click the Add to Favorites button. Thereafter, you can click the List of Favorites tab to display your list of favorite presentations.
- Stealing slides is a felony in most states, and if you transmit the presentation across state lines by way of a modem, the feds may get involved — which is good, because it pretty much guarantees that you'll get off scot-free.

Exploring Document Properties

PowerPoint stores summary information, known in Windows lingo as *document properties,* with each PowerPoint presentation file you create. Document properties include the filename and directory, the template assigned to the file, and some information you can type: the presentation's title, subject, author, keywords, and comments.

If you use PowerPoint much of the time and have trouble remembering which file is which, the summary info can help you keep your files sorted. The summary info is also handy if you know that you created a presentation about edible spiders last year but can't remember the filename.

To view or set the document properties for a presentation, follow these steps:

1. **Open the file if it isn't already open.**
2. **Conjure up the File⇨Properties command.**

   The Properties dialog box appears.
3. **Type whatever summary info you want to store along with the file.**

   The Title field in the Summary info dialog box is automatically filled in with whatever you type in the first slide's title placeholder, and the Author field is filled in with your name. (PowerPoint asked for your name when you installed it, remember?)
4. **When you're done, click OK.**
5. **Save the file (Ctrl+S or File⇨Save).**

When you fill out the Summary information, spend a few moments thinking about which keywords you may use to look for the file later on. Choosing descriptive keywords makes the file much easier to find.

Also, explore the other tabs on the Properties dialog box. You find all sorts of interesting information about your presentation there.

If you want to include summary information with every PowerPoint file you create, use the Tools⇨Options command and check the Prompt for file properties option on the Save tab. This causes the Properties dialog box to be displayed whenever you save a new file so you can type the summary information for the file.

Using Passwords to Protect Your Presentations

If you're worried about bad guys getting in to your presentations, either to steal them, snoop for interesting information, look for juicy gossip, or to plant an insult aimed at the boss in the middle of the show, you'll be relieved to know that PowerPoint now lets you protect your presentations with passwords. You can use two types of passwords in PowerPoint: a Read password, which lets only those who know the password open the presentation, and a Modify password, which requires that you must enter a password before saving changes to a presentation.

To password protect a presentation, follow these steps:

1. **Come up with a good password for the presentation.**

   Bad passwords are things like your name, phone number, or guessable words like "Password." The best passwords are random combinations of letters and numerals, such as 58dK33pJK2.

2. **Open the presentation you want to protect.**

3. **Choose the Tools⇨Options command and click the Security tab.**

   The security options appears.

4. **Type the password you want to require when opening the presentation in the Password to Open text box.**

   As you type, your password does not appear on the screen. Instead, asterisks are displayed no matter what you type. This is to keep nosy neighbors from spying on you while you create passwords.

5. **Type the password you want to require when saving the presentation in the Password to Modify text box.**

   Once again, the password is not displayed on the screen as you type.

6. **Click OK.**

7. **When a dialog box appears asking you to confirm a password, retype the password and click OK.**

   This is just a precaution to make sure that you didn't make a mistake when you entered the passwords in Steps 4 and 5 since you can't actually see the passwords as you type them.

8. **Write down the passwords you used so you won't forget.**

   Keep the passwords in a safe place — not on a yellow sticky note attached to your computer's monitor or stuck on your bulletin board.

Whenever you (or anyone else) tries to open or save a password-protected presentation, a dialog box appears asking for the appropriate password. Without the password, PowerPoint refuses to comply.

Organizing Your Files

My first computer had two disk drives; each drive held 360K of data. A year later, I had a gargantuan 10MB hard disk and wondered how I would keep track of two or three hundred files that I would store on the disk. (I never thought I would fill it up, either.) Today I have more than 40,000MB of disk space, with more than 20,000 files. It's a miracle I can find anything.

The key to getting control of the files on your hard disk is organizing them carefully. You must do only two things to organize your files, but you must do them both well: Use filenames you can remember and use folders wisely.

Using filenames that you can remember

One of the best things about Windows is that you have finally been freed of the sadistic eight-character file-naming conventions foisted upon you by the DOS moguls many years ago. With Windows, filenames can be as long as you want or need them to be (within reason), so instead of names like CNEXPO99.PPT, you can give your presentations names like COMPUTER NERD EXPO 99.PPT.

The best advice I can offer about using long filenames is to use them. I'm amazed at how many people are still in the habit of assigning short, cryptic names to their files. Breaking that habit takes some conscious effort. Using long filenames seems strange at first, but trust me: You get used to them.

Here are a few other things to consider when composing file names:

- If your presentation includes notes, add the filename to the bottom of the page on the Notes master. That way, the filename is printed on each notes page, which makes it easier to find later.
- Be consistent about how you name files. If 2001 Arachnid Expo.ppt is the presentation file for Arachnid Expo '01, use 2002 Arachnid Expo.ppt for the next year's Expo.
- If you're going to store a file on the Internet, don't use spaces or other special symbols in the filename.

Using folders wisely

The biggest file-management mistake most beginners make is to dump all their files in the My Documents folder. This technique is the electronic equivalent of storing all your tax records in a shoebox. Sure, all the files are there, but finding anything is next to impossible. Show the shoebox to your accountant on April 14, and you'll be lucky if he or she stops laughing long enough to show you how to file for an extension.

Use folders to impose organization on your files. Don't just dump all your files into one folder. Instead, create a separate folder for each project and dump all the files for each project into its folder. Suppose that you're charged with the task of presenting a market analysis every month. You can create a folder named Market Analysis to store the PowerPoint files for these reports. Then each month's PowerPoint file is named by using the month and year: 2001 January.ppt, 2001 February.ppt, 2001 March.ppt, and so on. (If you're not up to snuff on how folders work, see the sidebar, "Don't read this folder stuff if you can avoid it.")

Here are some tips:

- Every disk has a *root (or top level) directory,* a special folder that should not be used to store files. The root directory is kind of like a fire lane, which should be kept free for emergency vehicles at all times. In short, don't use the C:\ directory to store files.
- There's no reason you can't store files that belong to different application programs together in the same folder. Each file's extension identifies the program that created the file. No need to segregate. Most Office Open dialog boxes filter by type anyway, so when you use the File⇨Open command in Word, you see only Word documents, and when you use File⇨Open in PowerPoint, you see only PowerPoint presentations.
- The My Documents folder is where Windows programs expect to find your documents. If you're going to create additional folders to organize your files, feel free to create those folders in My Documents.
- Don't forget to clean out your folders periodically by deleting files that you no longer need. It also may be interesting to clean out your Recycle Bin — who knows what you have in there!

There is no limit to the number of files you can store in a folder, nor is there a limit to the number of folders you can create.

Backing Up Your Files

When was the last time you changed the oil in your car, took your dog for a walk, or backed up the files on your hard disk? The neglect of any of these three tasks can have disastrous consequences. This isn't the time or place for a stern lecture about the importance of backing up, though, so I'll spare you the soapbox lecture.

One way to back up a file is to use the PowerPoint Save As command to save a copy of the file to a floppy disk.

But the best way to back up your files is to use an Official Backup Program. Fortunately, Windows 95 and higher comes with a fairly decent backup program that can back up your files to diskettes or to a tape drive, if you're lucky enough to have one. You'll find the Windows backup program buried in the Start menu under Programs, Accessories, System Tools. (If you can't find Microsoft Backup in your Start menu, it may not have been installed when you installed Windows 95 or 98. You'll have to rerun the Windows setup program to install Microsoft Backup from your installation CD or diskettes.)

Keep in mind these hints about backing up your files:

- Remember what I said about this not being the time or place for a lecture? I lied. Back up your files every day. You never know when a stray asteroid will strike your city and possibly wipe out all human life and erase your files, too. So don't put it off! Back up today!
- Always have plenty of disks on hand for backups.
- You don't have to back up every file on your hard disk every day. Just back up the files you changed that day. Microsoft Backup has a slick feature called *incremental backup* that does precisely that, and it does it automatically so that you don't even have to think about it.
- If you have more than a few files, you'll quickly grow tired of backing them up to diskettes. Why not invest in an inexpensive 250MB removable disk drive (such as a Zip drive) or a tape drive? You can get either for under $150.
- You'll sleep much better tonight if you back up your files today.

Customizing PowerPoint's Menus and Toolbars

Hiding down near the bottom of PowerPoint's Tools menu is a command called Customize. Lurking within the dialog box that appears when you conjure up this command is the ability to improve PowerPoint's menus and toolbars. For example, if you routinely use a few specific AutoShapes, such as the Smiley Face and Lightning Bolt, you can easily add buttons for those AutoShapes to the Drawing toolbar so you don't have to wind your way through the AutoShapes menu to get to them. Or you can create new Insert⇨Smiley Face and Insert⇨Lightning Bolt commands.

To customize a toolbar or menu, choose the Tools⇨Customize command to bring up the Customize dialog box. (If necessary, click the Commands tab at the top of the Customize dialog box.) From the Commands tab of the Customize dialog box, you can add new buttons or commands to toolbars or menus.

The Commands tab lists all the commands that are available in PowerPoint, sorted into categories such as File, Edit, View, and so on. You may have noticed that these categories correspond to PowerPoint's menus and toolbars. When you select a category in the Category list on the left side of the Customize dialog box, the commands that are available for that category are displayed in the Commands list on the right side of the dialog box.

To create a new button on a toolbar, first select the category from the Category list, then scroll through the Command list until you find the command you want to add. For example, to add a Smiley Face button, first choose AutoShapes in the Category list, then scroll down the Command list to find the Smiley Face command. Once you have found the right command, all you have to do is drag it from the Customize dialog box to the toolbar location where you want the button inserted.

Adding a new menu command is similar. First select the category, then locate the command, and finally drag the command from the Customize dialog box to the menu you want to add the new command to. For example, drag the Smiley Face AutoShape command from the Customize dialog box to the Insert menu to add an Insert⇨Smiley Face command.

To remove a toolbar button or menu command, call up the Tools⇨Customize command. Then, simply drag the button or command you want to remove off of the toolbar or menu in which it currently resides. When you release the mouse button, the toolbar button or menu command vanishes.

When you've made all the customizations you care for, click Close to dismiss the Customize dialog box.

Setting PowerPoint's Options

Like any good Microsoft program, PowerPoint has billions and billions of options you can play with to affect the way PowerPoint works. Most of PowerPoint's options are consolidated into one mega dialog box known as the Options dialog box, which you reach by choosing Tools⇨Options.

To set PowerPoint's options, choose Tools⇨Options, click the tab that contains the option you want to set, and then choose the options you want to use. When you've had enough, click the Close button to dismiss the Options dialog box.

The Options dialog box has seven tabbed sections. The following paragraphs summarize the options that are available from each of these tabs:

- **View:** Options that affect PowerPoint's overall appearance, such as whether to display the task pane when starting up, whether to display a quick menu when you right-click an object, and whether every slide show should automatically end with a black slide.
- **General:** Options that affect PowerPoint's overall operation, such as how many recently opened files to display at the bottom of the File menu, as well as your name and initials.
- **Edit:** Options that affect how PowerPoint's editing features work. For example, you can turn off the smart cut and paste feature or certain new features of PowerPoint 2002, such as advanced animation or multiple masters.
- **Print:** Printing options such as how to handle TrueType fonts.
- **Save:** Options that affect how files are saved, including your default file location and whether automatic recovery information is saved.
- **Security:** Passwords and such.
- **Spelling and Style:** Options that control the spell and style checkers.

Using Macros

Macros are a nifty PowerPoint feature that let you record a sequence of commands and then play them back at any time with the simple click of a mouse. For example, suppose you're working on a presentation and realize that almost every new slide has used the Title and 2-Column Text layout. Wouldn't it be great if there were a button right on a toolbar somewhere that inserted a new slide and automatically applied the Title and 2-Column Text layout? As an added bonus, the button would leave the Slide Layout pane closed — a big improvement over PowerPoint's existing New Slide button, which inserts a new slide and opens the Slide Layout pane so you can apply a layout to the slide.

Macros to the rescue! With a macro, you can record the commands necessary to insert a new slide, open the Slide Layout Pane, assign the Title and 2-Column Text layout, and close the Slide Layout Pane. Then, you can place this macro on a toolbar as a button, so that you can insert a new Title and 2-Column Text slide with a single click.

To create a macro, follow these simple steps:

1. **Open the presentation you want to save the macro in.**
2. **Choose Tools➪Macros➪Record New Macro.**

   The Record Macro dialog box appears.
3. **Type a name for your macro.**

   Anything would be better than Macro1. (The name can't have a space in it, however.)
4. **Click OK.**

   A little Stop Recording toolbar appears to let you know that you are now recording a macro.
5. **Do that thing you do.**

   Do whatever commands are needed to perform the task you want to record in a macro. For example, to create the macro that inserts Title and 2-Column Text slides, follow these steps in sequence:

   • Choose Insert➪New Slide

   • Click the Title and 2-Column Text layout in the Slide Layout Pane.

   • Click the close button (the "X") in the Slide Layout Pane to close the pane.

6. **Click the Stop button in the Stop Recording toolbar (shown in the margin).**

   The macro is finished!

To run the macro, choose the Tools➪Macro➪Macros. This brings up a list of all available macros, from which you can choose a macro to run.

To really get the benefit of macros, you should assign them to toolbars or menus. You can do that via the Tools➪Customize command. In the Command tab of the Customize dialog box, you'll find a category called Macros that lists macros you have created. Just drag the macro you want to use from the Command list to the toolbar or menu on which you want it to live. (For more information, see the section "Customizing PowerPoint's Menus and Toolbars" earlier in this chapter.)

Chapter 30

Ten New Features of PowerPoint 2002

In This Chapter

- The new look of PowerPoint
- New features for formatting slides
- New ways to animate objects
- Features PowerPoint users have been begging for years

If you're an experienced PowerPoint user just upgrading to PowerPoint 2002, you probably turned to this chapter first. It lists the ten most important new features of PowerPoint 2002 for Windows.

A New Look for Normal View

Microsoft has once again revamped the look of PowerPoint's Normal View, which is where you spend 90 percent of your PowerPoint time. Figure 30-1 shows the new look of Normal View.

With the last version of PowerPoint (2000), Microsoft combined several views into Normal View by adding the outline and slide notes to Normal View. In PowerPoint 2000, Normal View was often referred to as Tri-pane View because it consisted of three panes: one to display the slide, one to display the outline, and one to display the notes.

PowerPoint 2002 improves Normal View even more by adding a list of thumbnail slides that lets you navigate through your slides visually, much like you can in Slide Sorter View. In fact, now that PowerPoint has these thumbnails, I hardly ever work in Slide Sorter View anymore.

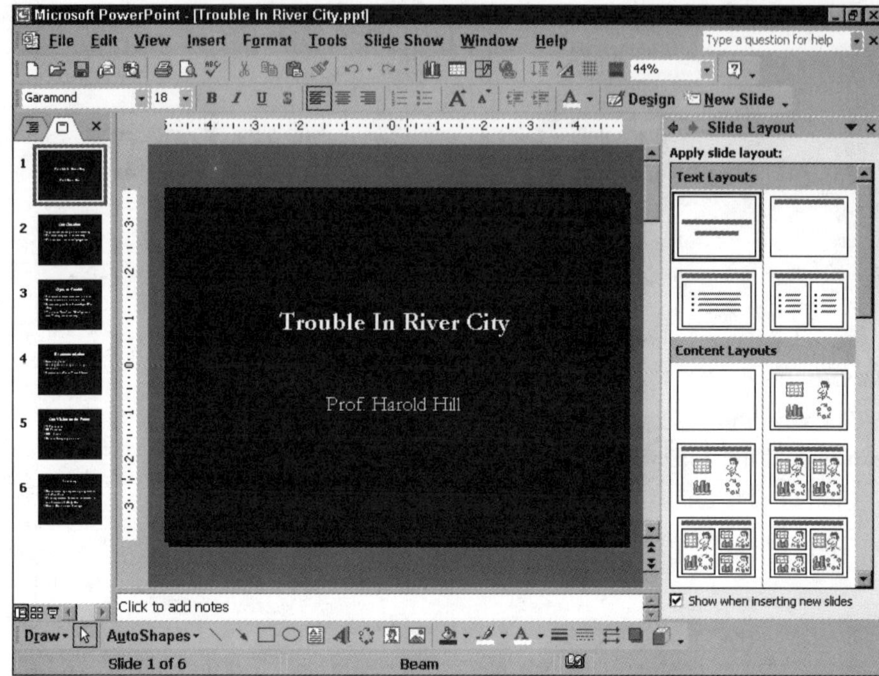

Figure 30-1: The new look of Normal View.

The thumbnails are to the left of the slide, where the Outline Pane used to be. This pane now contains two tabbed sections: Outline and Slides. If you click the Outline tab, the thumbnails are replaced by your presentation's outline. To get the thumbnails back, click the Slides tab.

To accommodate the outline, PowerPoint automatically adjusts the width of the Outline/Slide Pane when you switch between Outline and Slides View. In addition, the tabs contain the words "Outline" and "Slides" when you're viewing the Outline tab, but when you click the Slides tab, the words are replaced by icons.

For more information about working in Normal View, refer to Chapter 1.

The Task Pane

One of the most obvious new features of PowerPoint 2002 is the Task Pane, located to the right of the screen. The Task Pane appears in several incarnations:

- **New Presentation:** Helps you get started by offering several ways to create new presentations or to open existing presentations. In PowerPoint 2000, a dialog box appeared when you started PowerPoint, offering four ways to get started: create a new presentation from the AutoContent Wizard, use a Design Template, create a blank presentation, or open an existing presentation. The New Presentation Pane replaces that dialog box. (See Chapters 1 and 13 for more information.)
- **Clipboard:** Lets you use the new Office Clipboard feature of Office XP. The Office Clipboard collects and organizes information you copy or cut to the clipboard and lets you choose what information you want to insert when you use the Paste command. (See Chapter 2.)
- **Search:** Lets you look for lost files based on keywords or other file properties such as the file name, creation date, and so on. The Search Pane can search for files on your hard disk, in your Outlook folders if you use Outlook, or on the Internet. (See Chapter 2.)
- **Insert Clip Art:** Lets you search for clip art. The Insert Clip Art Pane replaces the old Clip Gallery dialog box from PowerPoint 2000. (See Chapter 10.)
- **Slide Layout:** Lets you apply a layout to your slide. All of the possible PowerPoint slide layouts are displayed in a neat list so you can just click the one you want to use. (See Chapter 2.)
- **Slide Design:** The Slide Design pane is actually three task panes in one. Slide Design – Design Templates lets you pick a Design Template to apply to a slide or an entire presentation. Slide Design – Color Schemes lets you choose a color scheme. And Slide Design – Animation Schemes lets you apply a predefined animation scheme to your slides. (See Chapters 11, 13, and 19.)
- **Custom Animation:** Lets you play with PowerPoint 2002's new animation features. (See Chapter 19.)
- **Slide Transition:** Lets you set up slide transitions. (See Chapter 19.)

The Task Pane pops up on its own when you use certain commands. When you're finished working with the Task Pane, you can close it by clicking its Close button (the little X in the upper-right corner of the Task Pane). It will reappear automatically when you need it.

Multiple Masters

One of the features PowerPoint users have been asking for since the dawn of time has been the ability to have more than one Slide Master in a single presentation. Jump for joy for this long-sought feature is now a part of PowerPoint 2002. PowerPoint now allows you to have as many Slide Masters as you need, so you can create presentations with slides that have several different looks. This is especially useful if you merge slides from two separate presentations and you want the slides to keep their original appearance, or if you want to create a presentation with two or more sections, each of which has its own look.

For the lowdown on working with multiple masters, have a look at Chapter 12.

Animation Schemes

Previous versions of PowerPoint have sported animation effects, such as having drawings or pictures appear by sliding in from the side of the slide or dropping in from the top. But you had to apply those effects manually, one effect at a time. PowerPoint 2002 has a new feature called Animation Schemes, which consists of a set of predefined animation effects that you can apply to slides all at once. Animation Schemes make it easy to create slides that build text one paragraph at a time using consistent entrance effects.

The Animation Schemes that come with PowerPoint 2002 range from subtle effects such as Fade In One by One or Brush on Underline to more exciting effects such as Pinwheel and Bounce.

One of the most asked questions in previous versions of PowerPoint was how to create text that rolls up the screen like credits at the end of a movie. PowerPoint 2002 answered that question by providing an animation scheme called Credits, which does just that.

You can find more information about animation schemes in Chapter 19.

Custom Animation

PowerPoint 2002 adds many new animation effects, all of which you can access through the new Custom Animation Task Pane. The Custom Animation features aren't powerful enough to produce another sequel to Toy Story, but they will let you create effects you could only dream about in previous versions of PowerPoint. Here are a few of the new animation features that PowerPoint 2002 now sports:

- New entrance effects, such as Unfold and Magnify.
- Exit effects, which let you specify how an object leaves the slide.
- Emphasis effects, which let you draw attention to an object by changing its color or size, or causing it to teeter, spin, flicker, blush, or break dance.
- Custom motion paths, which let you choose from a large collection of predefined motion paths or design your own path for your objects to follow.

- Simultaneous animations, which let you have two or more objects moving on the slide at the same time.
- Timing controls and automatic animations which follow one after another.
- Triggers, which let you initiate an animation by clicking another object.

You can read all about custom animation in Chapter 19.

Diagrams

A new Diagram Gallery feature lets you create organization charts and five other new types of diagrams: Cycle Diagrams, Radial Diagrams, Pyramid Diagrams, Venn Diagrams, and Target Diagrams. Figure 30-2 shows the Diagram Gallery dialog box, which includes an icon representing each of these diagram types. For complete information about creating diagrams, refer to Chapter 15.

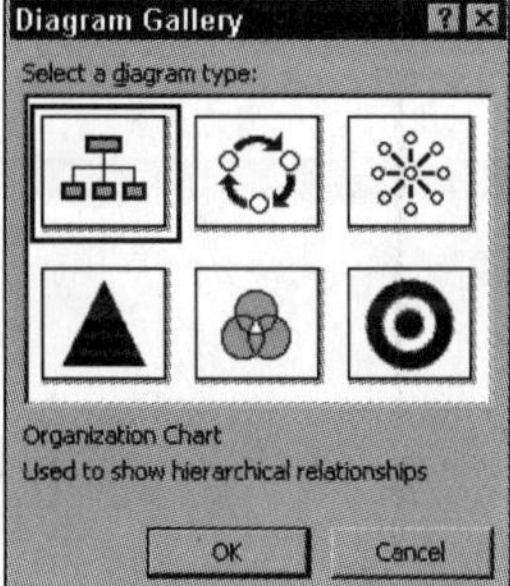

Figure 30-2: The Diagram Gallery dialog box.

Photo Albums

One of the most common types of presentations is a simple collection of scanned photographs. PowerPoint 2002 has a new Photo Album feature that makes it easy to create this type of presentation. Just call up the Insert⇨Picture⇨New Photo Album command to summon the Photo Album dialog box, shown in Figure 30-3.

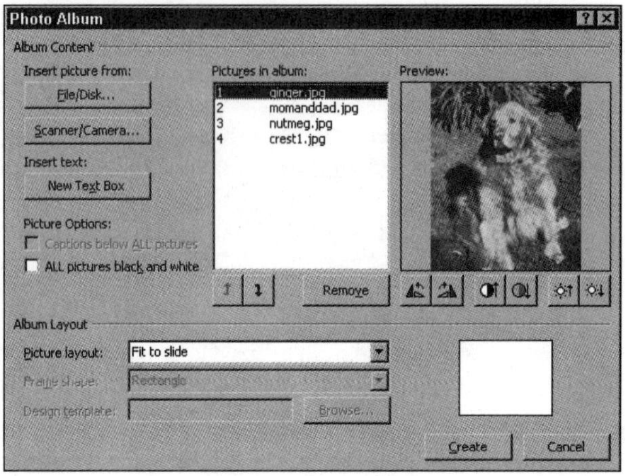

Figure 30-3: Creating a photo album.

You can use the controls on the Photo Album dialog box to locate the pictures you want to include in your photo album and sort them into the right order. You can also choose to place one, two, or four pictures on each slide, a shape for the picture borders, and a Design Template to use. Figure 30-4 shows a finished photo album.

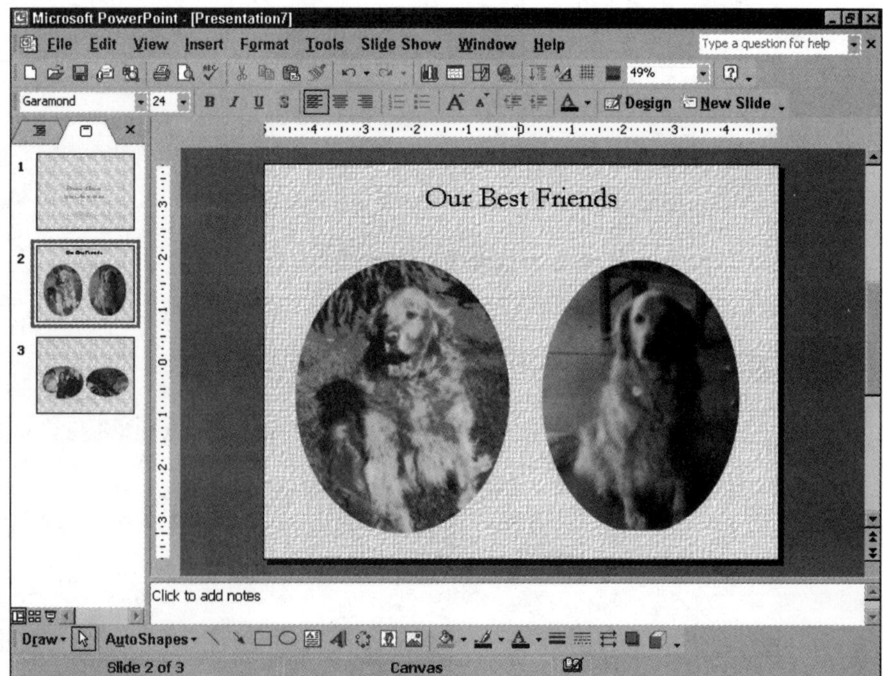

Figure 30-4: A finished photo album.

Comments and Reviewing Features

Word and Excel have had reviewing features for many years, including the ability for other users to post comments throughout a documents or worksheets. PowerPoint 2002 now has those features as well. With PowerPoint's new reviewing features, you can send a presentation to other users for review. The reviewers can make changes to the presentation and add comments. When all of the reviewers return their copies to you, you can combine the changes into a single presentation.

All you need to know about comments and reviewing features can be found in Chapter 23.

Print Preview

All of the other Office programs have had a Print Preview command since before the Depression, but PowerPoint only now gets this basic command. With the new Print Preview command, you can check out the appearance of your printed pages on your screen before committing them to paper. For more information, see Chapter 6.

Speech Recognition

One of the major new features of Office XP is speech recognition, which lets you dictate commands and text into Office programs. With PowerPoint 2002, you can tell the computer "File New" and up will pop the New File dialog box.

Speech recognition is pretty neat when it works — it's kind of like *Star Trek*. And if typing is difficult for you, it can be a real benefit. For most users, however, speech recognition is in the category of "Gee Whiz." It's neat, it's cool, it's fun to show it off to your friends and relatives. But it's not all that useful for actual work.

Index

• Numbers & Symbols •

• A •

• B •

• C •

• E •

• F •

• G •

• H •

• I •

• P •

• R •

• S •

• T •

• U •

• V •

• W •

• Z •

Notes

Notes